Vic: Lambeth to Lambourn

By
Victor Cox

First published by Plowright Press in 2001

British Library Cataloguing in Publication Data
A catalogue record for this book is available from the British Library

ISBN 0 9516960 8 4

PLOWRIGHT PRESS
P O BOX 66
WARWICK CV34 4XE

Orders from Plowright Press £11.95 (plus £1.50 towards p & p UK), through bookshops or Internet bookstores (eg Amazon, BOL)

Printer: Warwick Printing Company Ltd, Warwick

CONTENTS   Page

EDITOR'S FOREWORD

Victor Cox spent many afternoons in 1999 and 2000 setting down his memoirs at the suggestion of his niece, Jill Wohlgemuth. What he has written, sitting at the table by the living room window in his bungalow, illuminates several diverse areas of history: Lambeth, hotel work, the RASC in World War Two and the Berkshire village of Lambourn. It also shares with us the particular experiences of one family and one individual in 20th-century Britain.

The following pages appear largely as Vic wrote them in terms of style and expression although, for reasons of space, some cuts in the text were necessary, as well as often substituting the past for the present tense: he used the present tense because he was back in the scenes which he describes, seeing events as they happened.

My thanks for enthusiastic and patient help go to the following: Ashbury Local History Society, especially Marian Turner; Babcock International Group, especially David Lewis; Berkshire Local History Association, especially Jan Thomas; Berkshire Record Office; British American Tobacco; Birmingham Post and Mail library; Caerphilly Library, especially Mr Williams; Daily Mirror library; Cherry Drummond (Baroness Strange); Guildhall Library; Nova Jones; Lambeth Archives; Betty Lang; Ian Lang; Le Meridien Waldorf London Hotel, especially Olivia Aubry; London Metropolitan Archives; Edie Morley; Museum of London; National Monuments Record; Newbury Central Library; Pembrokeshire Record Office; Joyce and Arthur Rockhill; Royal Army Service Corps & Royal Corps of Transport Association; Royal Logistic Corps Museum; Southwark Local Studies Library; Westminster Archives; Westminster Reference Library; Wiltshire Local History Forum, especially Ivor Slocombe; Paul Wohlgemuth. Finally, I cannot thank enough both Vic Cox and Jill Wohlgemuth for a constantly rewarding and memorable working partnership.

Anne Bott, Warwick, 2001

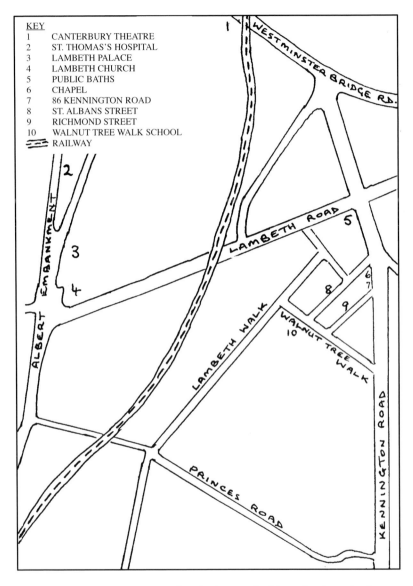

KEY
1   CANTERBURY THEATRE
2   ST. THOMAS'S HOSPITAL
3   LAMBETH PALACE
4   LAMBETH CHURCH
5   PUBLIC BATHS
6   CHAPEL
7   86 KENNINGTON ROAD
8   ST. ALBANS STREET
9   RICHMOND STREET
10   WALNUT TREE WALK SCHOOL
===   RAILWAY

The area around Victor Cox's home in Kennington, before rebuilding in the late 1920s. Map drawn by Jill Wohlgemuth

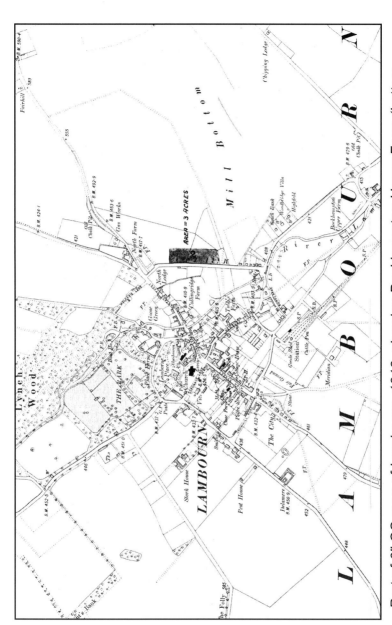

Part of 6" OS map of Lambourn, 1913, showing Bockhampton Upper Farm (bottom right) where Vic Cox and his family lived. Map reproduced courtesy of Berkshire Record Office (reference no. OS 1913 – 6" – XXVNE)

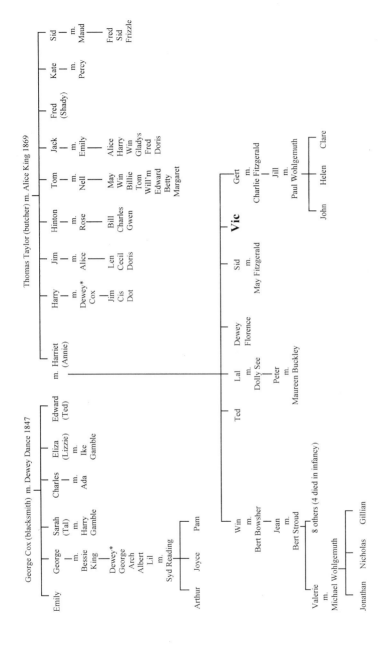

George Cox (blacksmith) m. Dewey Dance 1847

Thomas Taylor (butcher) m. Alice King 1869

Emily

George
m.
Bessie
King

Dewey*
George
Arch
Albert
Lil
m.
Syd Reading

Arthur   Joyce

Sarah
(Tal)
m.
Harry
Gamble

Charles
m.
Ada

Eliza
(Lizzie)
m.
Ike
Gamble

Edward
(Ted)

Pam

m. Harriet
(Annie)

Harry
m.
Dewey*
Cox

Jim
Cis
Dot

Jim
m.
Alice

Len
Cecil
Doris

Hinton
m.
Rose

Bill
Charles
Gwen

Tom
m.
Nell

May
Win
Billie
Tom
Will'm
Edward
Betty
Margaret

Jack
m.
Emily

Alice
Harry
Win
Gladys
Fred
Doris

Fred
(Shady)

Kate
m.
Percy

Sid
m.
Maud

Fred
Sid
Frizzle

Dewey
Florence

Lal
m.
Dolly See

Peter
m.
Maureen Buckley

Sid
m.
May Fitzgerald

Vic

Gert
m.
Charlie Fitzgerald

Jill
m.
Paul Wohlgemuth

John   Helen   Clare

Ted

Win
m.
Bert Bowsher

Jean
m.
Bert Stroud

8 others (4 died in infancy)

Valerie
m.
Michael Wohlgemuth

Jonathan   Nicholas   Gillian

Albert Cox, Dewey F. Cox, Billie Taylor died in infancy
George and Arch Cox, Ted Cox (s. of Annie), Len Taylor, Will'm and Edward Taylor, Charlie Fitzgerald all died in the two World Wars

Vic Cox's family tree, compiled by his niece, Jill Wohlgemuth

1. FIRST DAYS IN KENNINGTON

It was my sister Win who would always tell us about family life at home in the days before I was born, on September 2nd 1909 in the district of Kennington in the London borough of Lambeth.

My father was Edward Cox, known as Ted. His family were blacksmiths and farriers in the borough of Southwark next door, but they came originally from Berkshire: his father was christened in Hungerford, and his grandfather in West Hanney. My mother Harriet, generally known by her second name Annie, was born in Berkshire, in the village of Lambourn nearby, where her father was a butcher. She had come to London as a young girl to be in service, and until she married, she worked for a family in Queen's Gate, near the Royal Albert Hall.

Win was the eldest of our family, and she used to help our mother in running the home. It was a pretty large rented house we were living in, three storeys high with a sub basement, 84 Kennington Road. The front entrance was through the garden and down a few steps to the sub basement, or the few steps up, to the main front door. All our row of houses were still using gas for lighting, as I think with most other houses.

If you go along Kennington Road now, you will see the same type of houses. Unfortunately our row, which had St Albans Street on one side, and Richmond Street on the other side, was pulled down to make way for blocks of flats about the early 1930s.

I was told that up until the time that I was born, it was usual for theatre people who were appearing in London to come to Kennington way for lodgings or short stays, also medical students who came from St Thomas's Hospital, it being a teaching hospital. So, apparently, we had three or four people that came to stay with us. It was only for short stays. One person who had stayed three or four times previously, appearing on the stage in drama plays as Win told me, happened to be staying at the time of my christening.

As the name Victor had already been given to me, she asked if I could have the second name of Allerton as at that time she was playing Lady Allerton in her production. She also became my godmother, but I forget her name. I think she originally came from Newcastle upon Tyne. Another person that used to stay was Jewel Viola, one of the Viola Bros, Acrocomedyists. He sent us a folding pictures card of San Antonio in Texas, it was very interesting. I don't know if that was the part of America he came from.

NIFTY—FAST—CLASSY.

ACROCOMEDYISTS

En-route VIOLA BROS.

JEWEL VIOLA,
Touring European Theatres.

Jewel Viola, who used to stay at Vic Cox's home in Kennington Road

My sister Gert was born in 1912, and so time was beginning to move on. I was still small when we moved next door into 86 Kennington Road. The houses had a front garden, divided by a low wall, with railings in front, and during the move everything was being thrown over the wall, although Mum was still indoors. I was managing to run about all right now, as Mum told me when I was born I was just a weakling, at times they didn't give me a lot of hope.

But after a while, they started to feed me on Virol, a brown sticky malt food supplement in a jar, and it's surprising how one grows up. Of course at that time I didn't really take notice of how many of us were living in the house. I'm just checking up . . . Mum, Dad, Uncle George (Dad's brother), his daughter Lil, who was six months older than Win, my brother Ted, Win, my brothers Lal (Henry) and Sid, me and Gert. And of course Auntie Kate (Mum's sister), that's eleven.

Uncle George was living in St Albans Street when his wife died, so he and Lil decided to live with us. Lil's two brothers, George, the eldest, was married, Arch was a butler in service at St Albans I think with very well known people. Her older sister Dewey had died aged twenty seven in 1908 and her husband, my mother's brother Harry, left London and returned to Lambourn with their three children.

Family group, 1909. Back row (from left): Dad, Win, Ted, Uncle George, Lil. Front row: Sid, Vic on his mother's lap, Granny Taylor with Cis and Dot, two of Uncle Harry's children, and Lal

Both Gert and I were gradually growing up together as all the others were much older than us, and we seemed to have been two on our own. Win was born in 1894, Ted in 1896, Lal in 1898, and Sid in 1902. My health seemed to have been improving although I was told I didn't put on much weight. I often had to be taken to the doctor's for some little thing or the other. Dr Miskin was the doctor, at 156 Kennington Road.

I started school when I was five years old, and the year being 1914, that was the year war broke out. Gert started school a couple of years later. We went to Walnut Tree Walk School, situated at the back to where we were living. We always used St Albans Street to walk to school as it was bigger than Richmond Street, and being open for through traffic, it seemed more open and pleasant.

Richmond Street was non through for traffic, although certain vehicles did use it where necessary, there was a small open builder's yard at the top end where they could turn round. We both seemed to have soon got used to school and got on well with all the other children. As we both began to grow up, we found our playmates in Richmond Street. This was in the bottom half of Richmond Street as we entered from Kennington Road.

The top half, as we called it, was a bit rough, we didn't seem to know much about them. I think there were one or two Irish families lived along there. And of course we had no traffic down the bottom end. My friends went to the same school as me, but Gert's friends went to Lollard Street School. I think we spent all our play time in Richmond Street, except Sundays. Often during our school holidays, there would be a crowd of us from Richmond Street, and

4

with some food slung over our shoulders we would all go over Westminster Bridge to St James's Park, where they had a separate children's playground area with sandpits. This was a very happy but a tiring day, as we were already tired out before we started to return home in the afternoon. And it was quite a long way. Otherwise it was Archbishop's Park, near our church, and that was nearer.

One little incident used to occur often on a Saturday when we were playing around in Richmond Street. The roadway was not very wide, and the houses were all small cottage type with front door which opened into a straight passage leading into the scullery and out of the back door into the yard. Downstairs contained a sitting room and kitchen, upstairs were two bedrooms.

Suddenly there would be a bit of shouting and a lot of scampering about, doors opening and shutting. Then suddenly, it would all go quiet. This all used to take place at the top end of the street, which came out into Walnut Tree Walk. As I began to grow a bit older, one of the other boys told me what it was all about.

It was generally a local man who ran his own bookmaking business, and this was mainly on a Saturday or a big racing day. People would make their bets out on paper with their nom de plume (as they do now) and give it and the money to him where they knew he was hanging around. Also, if anyone was lucky enough to back winners they knew where to contact him to get their winnings. This man's pitch was around the top of Richmond Street. It was surprising to find so many people who would take their bets to him.

Now, in those days, street bookmaking was illegal, and he had a lookout for any police, as that was his great concern. So on race days, it was more or less a game of 'cops and robbers'. In those days a policeman patrolled on foot, compared with today's police who are mainly mobile. Sometimes a policeman would walk round on his beat, then you probably wouldn't see one for two or three days. Their main job was to try to catch the bookie whilst he had all the bets and money on his person. In most cases they knew it was a hopeless task, but sometimes, with more than one policeman, they did manage to appear a bit too near which didn't give the lookout much time to shout. So that's when the bookie had to run.

The police started running to try to get near him or see where he'd gone, anybody else round about seemed to start running, I don't really know what for, plenty of kids were shouting out: "Leave 'im alone!" But he generally had it all worked out. If his way was clear he'd run down Richmond Street, and into one of the houses, as they were all left open for him. If he found the police still hanging about outside, he would climb over the back yard wall into other houses.

Everybody knew who he was, and of course he would make himself clear, until the fuss died down. Mr Flynn, from one of the Irish families that lived up at that end of Richmond Street, would then come out, start playing the bagpipes, and start marching up and down the street with the kids following him. I don't know if he was celebrating or what, but to us, it caused a bit of fun and excitement.

Richmond Street children, 1918 or 1919. Vic is in the back row, fourth from the right; Gert is third from the right, middle row, peeping round the girl in front

3. MUSICAL SUNDAY EVENINGS

I can't say that I remember a lot about those four years of the war, although it was about that time when I would creep upstairs to tinkle on the piano. The main thing I used to look forward to was our Sunday evenings. All the family seemed to be home for tea on Sundays (bread and butter, and cake, after a good lunch with a joint of beef) and that was always a lively affair. We had the sub basement, where we had our food, and more or less lived there.

And then, Sunday evenings during the winter time we would all go up to what we called the music room. This was a front and a back room, which could be opened to make one room. We had a piano there. Win would sit down to play, and of course it would be a musical evening, as Dad was home, the off licence he managed was closed on Sundays. Win would sing, sometimes Lal would sing, and, of course, it was all the rest of us joining in.

Dad liked to have a drink at home (beer mainly but also whisky), the same with the rest of the family, and we would often have visitors call for the Sunday evening. I think, to my mind, the most frequent visitors were Dad's sister Sarah, and her husband. We knew her as Auntie Tal, I suppose that was her nickname. We never found out, as in those days we were always told to keep quiet, and not ask too many questions. She was older than Dad and quite plump.

Her second husband, Uncle Harry, was rather small and with webbed fingers and toes. He had a brother, with the same condition. His name was Isaac, and he was married to another of Dad's sisters Eliza. Their name was Gamble. So it was Uncle Ike and Auntie Lizzie Gamble, and Uncle Harry and Auntie Tal Gamble. They both lived near us, although after a while Uncle Ike and Auntie

Lizzie moved to Camberwell. He had his own taxi, and he would occasionally take a party of us to Lambourn for the day.

We used to like to hear Auntie Kate and Win sing their duet. I forget the name, but it was sung to the melody of 'Alice where art thou?' and I was now able to accompany them on the piano. That always went down well. Then Dad would give us one of his comic songs, he had a variety of songs to choose from. Very often Auntie Tal and Uncle Harry would bring a friend of theirs along, and many times it was somebody in uniform. The uniforms seemed to fascinate me.

One time they suggested they bring their gramophone, to give us a rest on the piano. Of course, in those days we never had radio or anything like that, so the gramophone helped. It also provided music for anybody who had no musical instrument. The gramophone consisted of the main box complete with turntable, and a handle for winding it up to play the record. Then there was the trumpet, which fixed on for the sound to come out.

Auntie Tal and Uncle Harry, about 1912. Auntie Tal's first husband died in 1911

We had three or four other relatives turn up, and so we had a nice little crowd, with a lot of talking and laughing, also a bit of singing, during which Auntie Tal, in one of her comic moods, tried to demonstrate how to smoke a cigarette, but she would puff it out, instead of drawing it in which made everybody laugh all the more.

And so, our visitors started to make a move for home, as it was getting late. Auntie Tal and Uncle Harry would insist on taking the gramophone home, although they must have felt a bit tired, especially after a little drink during the evening. So, he managed to carry the main part under his arm, she carried the trumpet part on one arm and over her shoulder, and some records in a bag in the other hand. They lived on the other side of the road from us.

And so, after seeing them across the road, although there wasn't any traffic about, they went off home looking happy. It was the following afternoon that Auntie Tal called in on her way home from a little job she'd always done, cooking at the flat of Mr Roberts, managing director of Roberts engineering company in Victoria Street. If she called in, Mum always knew she'd got something to say. Well yes, she was quite right. Auntie Tal just wanted to tell us about the little tumble they had last night.

Apparently they had nearly reached home, when Uncle Harry just seemed to nudge against her, I suppose feeling a bit tired and carrying the gramophone he lost his balance a bit. And of course falling against her, they both fell through a gate on to the garden. They never got hurt, as a matter of fact they didn't fall very far, on to the grass. It was picking up the different parts of the gramophone that was the trouble. But she said it wasn't long before they were indoors and the first thing they did was have a drop of whisky.

On Sundays during the summer, providing the weather held, Dad used to enjoy a walk over to Green Park to listen to the band. That meant Gert and me going, with Mum and anybody else who wanted a walk. In many cases Uncle George liked to come with us.

Dad used to have his half day on a Wednesday and quite often with Mum, they would take Gert and myself over to Clapham, mainly to see Uncle Bill and Auntie Jo (Joanna), who was our Grandma Taylor's sister. They were always pleased to see us. For a time Auntie Nell and Uncle Tommy with our cousins Win and May lived on the opposite side of the road from them. Auntie Nell was their daughter and Uncle Tommy was one of Mum's brothers.

During the evening, Dad always liked to take them out for a drink. For us, it meant teaming up with Win and May, and off to the pictures, over the other side of the road. Also, we made other friends there, and I met one of them much later, near Oran in Algeria during the Second World War. He was serving in the forces as a sailor, and I was in the Army.

We used to see quite a lot of Mum's younger brother, our Uncle Sid, and his wife Maud, with our cousins Fred, Sid, and Dot. They were all a bit younger than me, Fred was born in 1913, Sid in 1915, and Dot later. They lived quite near us, and Uncle Sid, who worked at Watney's Brewery, often called in on his way home from work. Auntie Maud would often be round during the day, with Dot in the push chair. I don't know why but we always called Dot 'Frizzle'. Just a nickname I suppose. They would go out shopping with Mum, or otherwise, they would bring anything in if Mum didn't want to go out.

One day we went out, up towards Westminster Bridge, Mum, Gert and me, Fred and Sid, and Auntie Maud, pushing Frizzle in the push chair. Auntie Maud was a bit on the plump side, and inclined to be on the jolly side. We had got quite a good way along the road, when we had to cross rather a wide street. People were looking up into the sky. We couldn't seem to see anything, and as we were only half way over the street, Mum said we'd better go over on to the pavement.

And of course as we hurried, Auntie Maud was still chattering and making us all laugh, she hit the kerb with the push chair. This tipped over with Frizzle strapped in, but Auntie Maud went over as well, on top. We all gathered round, and some other people came to help. Her coat or jacket seemed to have got caught in one of the wheels, so when they were lifting her up, the push chair was still hanging on to her. She was still laughing her head off, and Frizzle just seemed as though nothing had happened. That was the highlight of our day.

One other little thing happened on a Bank Holiday Monday. As Dad was working, Mum and Auntie Maud thought they would take us children to Hampstead Heath to the fair. So we started our journey on the Underground. There were quite a lot of people, and we'd already gone through quite a few stations, when we suddenly came to a standstill in the tunnel. Everything seemed quite still until people started chattering, then suddenly the lights went out.

After a short while one or two small lights went on, that seemed to give us a bit of heart. Then suddenly we heard the crash of another train into the back of ours. With all the noise of the people talking, we couldn't hear the other train. As I was sitting on our mother's lap and Sid was sitting on his mother's lap, we both went on the floor. Afterwards I found a bruise on my cheekbone and Sid had a bruise and a lot of dirt round his eye. Then the guard or whoever he was managed to get through, making his way to the rear of the train.

After quite a while some lights came on, and we started to move very slowly, then we crawled into a station. Everybody started cheering. Quite a lot of people apparently had been thrown on the floor like us, and once on the platform, some were looking to see if they had any injuries. As for us, we went up in the lift, and out into the sunlight. Mum said: "What a relief, and we're going to get a bus and go home." So that was goodbye Hampstead Heath and the fair. I wasn't sorry. Afterwards, I realized how frightened I'd been.

Auntie Maud and Uncle Sid after a while went to Sydenham, where Auntie Maud died, I think in 1942. We never saw the family after the war and when they moved they never notified us.

We started to go to Sunday School, held at Archbishop Temple's School, but mostly we had children's service in Old Lambeth Church nearby, on Lambeth Road, and there we went every Sunday, and Christmas Day. I think we were the only ones of the family that went to church, although Win and Lil were both confirmed. We were never confirmed. I think we should have been.

I began to take an interest in religion, and history, and at school I gained two certificates for religion, and one for history. As I was taught at school, Lambeth is one of the most historical places in London. There is the Lambeth Palace, the official residence of the Archbishop of Canterbury just near our church, and the Royal Palace of the Black Prince, remembered in Black Prince Road. This

Walnut Tree Walk School. Lal is second left, behind the front row

road is situated where Princes Road was, that ran from the bottom of Lambeth Walk into Kennington Road. There was one short turning from St Albans Street which led into the beginning of Lambeth Walk. That was our main market place.

It was a long market, one side lined with stalls from one end to the other, and all kinds of shops on both sides, and it stretched down to the beginning of Princes Road and the beginning of Vauxhall. That was where Mum and most other local people did their week's shopping. And of course we had a small picture house down there. It opened in the evenings, with two performances, first one for the kids, second one for the grown ups and grandads. We used to go, once a week if we could cadge a penny.

There always used to be a few others that went with us, it all helped to make the noise, as there was always plenty of hollering and shouting. Sometimes, before we started to line up, we would go over to the other side to Mrs Kelly's greengrocery stall, and see if we could cadge a carrot to eat in the pictures. Sometimes we were lucky. Mrs Kelly knew us as Mum bought her vegetables from her every Saturday, and of course we always helped Mum with the shopping on Saturdays.

Most of the stall holders knew us as they did most of the other children. And along with others of my age, I think I knew practically every stall holder and the shop people. There were quite a lot of Irish people that lived about there, but we all got on well with each other. Then there was Marcantonio's ice cream parlour, a pretty large place, with small tables like a café. They sold tea and coffee, but it was mostly different types of ice creams and soft drinks.

Further back down our end there was old 'Jack' the Italian, with his ice cream barrow stall in the summer. In winter it would be baked potatoes and hot chestnuts. That was where there seemed to be more fun. With just a few of us, we always finished up at Jack's stall. We used to gather round and have a talk and a laugh with him, and we used to get him to sing 'O Sole Mio', and of course we all joined in, even the stall holders joined in. We never took a liberty with him.

Fridays, Saturdays and Sundays until dinner time were the busiest times for the markets. Lambeth Walk would keep open till about 10 or 11 o'clock in the evening. It was then full of light. Apart from the shops all being lit up, some stalls had electric light fixed up, but a lot had paraffin flares, which helped to make it all look so attractive.

One little thing we were always glad to hear was when the organ grinder came round. Barrel organs were like a piano, except there were no keys showing. It was all closed in, but there was a handle you could turn, and provide the music. It was on two wheels, and provided two shafts, so the grinder could pull it from street to street. Some would have one or two assistants, and they would probably be dressed up, and do some comedy dancing.

This always used to go down well, especially in the market. Of course they would go round with the hat afterwards. I remember another time, although I don't know if it was the same lot, but these were three fellows dressed up as dancing girls. They were really good, as good as professionals, with comedy in between, this delighted the stall holders. And the money was being thrown in.

There was a fair sized building at the beginning of the Walk which was used for young people's recreation in the way of billiards, darts and so forth. This was run by the then Liberal MP for North Lambeth, Mr Frank Briant. He was a very popular man, and he often used to visit us at school.

Towards the latter part of my days at school I had to go on one day each week to Lollard Street School, for carpentry tuition. That meant going through Lambeth Walk, so for a time I think I can say I nearly lived down there. I don't think there will ever be another Lambeth Walk. The main thing was that everybody seemed to know everybody else. It was quite happy and friendly.

5. VISIT TO LEICESTER SQUARE SKIN HOSPITAL

I remember when the maroon went off, to denote the end of the war. That's when the people all came out into the streets singing and dancing, it went on all night long, even the public houses kept open until they'd all sold out.

It was when most of the soldiers had got home from France and other parts of the war zone that I noticed a rash coming out on different parts of my body, and it was very itchy. Of course, Mum noticed it when she bathed me, so it was off to the doctor. Those days, you had to pay the doctor each time you went to see him. I think I must have been a bit expensive, as I was often going backwards and forwards with some little ailment or the other.

Well he gave me a good examination, then made up an ointment to take home and use. It wasn't very successful as although parts of my body seemed to clear up, it was between my fingers and toes which seemed to get worse. The itching wouldn't seem to stop. So, it was back to the doctor. This time he happened to have another doctor with him, so they both examined me. After a discussion they decided to refer me to the skin hospital, at Leicester Square.

That was my first visit to a hospital, that I can remember. And so Mum took me. I had to see a black doctor, and that seemed a bit exciting, as in those days you didn't see any black or coloured doctors about. He took me into a dark room, where he had a spotlight over his table, and he fixed a light on to his forehead. He examined my chest and the back of my shoulders, and then I had to spread my hands out on the table under the spotlight. That finished, he wrote out a prescription and gave it to Mum to give in at the pharmacy department to collect another type of ointment.

Before I'd finished with the ointment, it had cleared my fingers and toes, which were the most infected parts. It seemed a bit strange at the time, as I was the only one of the family that suffered with it. Of course, I had to stay away from school for a time. People were saying it was the troops who brought it over from France.

Well, things were beginning to run normally now, and I was running into my tenth year. I had moved from the infants' school, up into what they called the big school. The classes were nos. 1 to 7 and they all seemed pretty good teachers.

With Loving Greetings.

To My Truest of Pals.
"MY MOTHER."

May the LORD watch for ever between me and thee,
  When we are absent one from the other ;
Are the words that I send with heart full of love,
  To the best of dear pals, MY MOTHER.

For King, Queen and Country we're fighting,
  " Honour and Right " is our watchword true';
Tho' " Might " at first seemed to hold the sway,
  Naught shall conquer the Red, White and Blue.

'Twas some time since that I left my loved home,
  To answer old England's cry ;
The parting was hard, and tho' she tried to be brave,
  There was a tear in my dear mother's eye.

" God bless you " said she, " God bless her," say I,
  For of mothers' no man had a better ;
And while I'm in Camp here, or facing the foe,
  She knows I shall never forget her.

Don't Worry, Dear Mother, my Truest of Pals,
  Tho' at parting your heart may feel sore,
We will all look forward with hearts full of hope
  To true happiness when peace comes once more.

From .... *" Thinking of You."*

One of the postcards that Vic's brother Ted sent to his mother; she was at Lambourn when it was posted from Fovant Camp, Wiltshire, in September 1916. Ted was killed in France four months later aged 19. On the back of the card he wrote in pencil: Dear Mum, Getting on alright. Just having a walk round. Hope you're enjoying yourself. Had a good march today was tired when got back. Has Lal gone home. Love Ted xx

16

Gert and me still played in Richmond Street, especially during the winter time when the skipping took place. When the evenings were beginning to get a bit lighter the mothers would come out with a big proper skipping rope. They would line us all up, boys and girls, and they would turn the rope for us to take our turn. All the time we would be singing the skipping songs.

Then we would often get interrupted by the street sellers. After the war finished, there was quite a lot of unemployment, and money was short if you didn't happen to have a job to go to. So many men like these street sellers had to try to do something of their own to enable them to earn some money.

In this case it was the cats' meat man. He would have his own little home made barrow on wheels, with cats' meat all wrapped in paper or put on skewers and he would be shouting out "Cats' meat!" He would be followed by an army of cats from street to street. Then a man would be selling home made lemonade and other kinds of drinks, then a man or woman would be singing or playing a musical instrument. We used to get quite a bit of entertainment at times.

Opposite to where we were living was a row of shops. One was a tobacco and newspaper shop, with hairdresser's adjoining, belonging to Dan Lipton, the next a second hand shop, then a confectionery shop (Mr and Mrs Harrison and Jackie), chemist (Mr Heeley and brother). Then, what they used to call them, a dining shop, which was for meals, mainly lunch (although it was coffee rooms before), and then the off licence.

I used to go over to Dan Lipton's to get Dad's tobacco and the paper. He was a bit funny with people, could be on the nasty side and upset a lot of people, although I got on with him all right. He used to sit behind the counter all day long till 8 o'clock at night when he closed the shop. I think he was a composer or something like that and he was a great friend of Charlie Chaplin, the comedian (Charlie Chaplin said Kennington Road was where he spent most of his boyhood). In fact I remember seeing Charlie Chaplin, twice, when he came over from America, as he was then beginning to make a name for himself.

He would always visit Dan Lipton in his shop, as I think Dan was one of the people that helped to start him off. As soon as the news got around that Charlie Chaplin was in the shop, you wouldn't be able to see it for the people crowding around. I knew Dan's son Danny and Mrs Lipton. Danny was about my age, although I never used to see a lot of him.

I was now beginning to get friendly with Jackie Harrison. He was a cripple, and had both legs in irons, although he could walk with a stick. He never walked out unless somebody was with him, and then he would prefer to lean on to your shoulder. He used to go to a special school, and the school bus would pick him up in the mornings and bring him back in the afternoons. He liked sport, but of course he couldn't take part in any.

He was about my age, and his mother had a light type of wheelchair that she used when she wanted to take him out, and she asked me if I would I like to take him out sometimes. Of course, I agreed, and took him out at weekends when I didn't have any errands to get. I had to get a bit used to pushing him, as one of his legs was completely in irons, so when he was sitting in the wheelchair, his leg was sticking straight out. You had to be careful that you didn't run into anybody. The other leg he only had in irons to the knee, and so he could bend that leg. Of course he had to wear special boots.

I eventually told the other boys from Richmond Street about taking him out. They then asked me, why couldn't we all take him up to Kennington Park one Saturday, and play cricket. A couple of the boys had home made cricket bats, and they could soon get a ball. I decided to ask his mother first, she agreed as she knew there would be two or three to help to push him along. So then I told him. He 'jumped' for joy.

18

Kennington Road was a nice straight road, until it came to Kennington Park, where the road turned off into Clapham Road with just a little bend towards the end. It had lovely wide pavements and was lined with plane trees on either side with trams running along in the middle, and also buses. One good thing in our favour: in those days, compared with the present day, the traffic was very light. You could take your time in crossing the road, and we had to cross the road to go into the park.

So, the first Saturday available that's what we did. We all took some lunch or something to eat, drinking water we could get in the park. Jackie's mother had given him a bag of sweets, to share with us, so it was quite a crowd that went along. From where we lived it was roughly a mile to the park, but we were used to that. There was plenty of room, so we soon settled down to play some cricket.

Of course, there weren't enough of us to play as a team, so we played individually, to see who could score most runs. One boy was bowler, and one was wicket keeper, as we'd managed to fix up a wicket, and a couple were fielders. We got Jackie out of the wheelchair, and decided he could bat first. We gave him the bat, and he was just itching to start. I stood by, as I said I would run for him, if he hit the ball away. The first two or three balls he missed, as he was just getting into his stride.

But then he managed to slog the ball about, and I had to run to gain a few runs for him. After a few more bowls, he got run out, and then took his place as wicket keeper. After a while, we ate our sandwiches or whatever we'd brought with us and had a rest. Then we had another game, and so played on into the afternoon, when we thought we should soon start to make our way home. I think Jackie had a really good day, and surprised himself how he could use his bat. We had two or three more days like that.

In the Harrisons' shop window, they always had a bill advertising the Canterbury Picture House. This showed films and also stage turns.

The Canterbury up to a few years before was a well known variety theatre, with all well known artistes appearing there, but the films were gradually taking over. Well Jackie's mother asked me if I would like to take him to an early evening show.

They used to get a free ticket for two, I think, once a week for displaying the advert. So I agreed, as that was a bit better than a penny worth in the Lambeth Walk. We went on the bus as it wasn't a great way, and they used to stop right outside the Canterbury. I took him to one or two more shows afterwards, otherwise his mother used to take him.

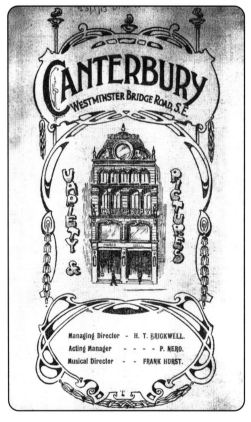

The Canterbury Music Hall, after it had begun staging film as well as variety shows. Reproduced courtesy of Lambeth Archives.

6. PIG KILLING IN LAMBOURN

Gert and myself would often be sent down to Lambourn, I don't know if that was because of our mother's health or not, but we never worried. At one time we both went to school while we were there. We also went for holidays. I used to stay at Grandma's, but Gert used to stay at Auntie Emily's. Still, there were plenty of cousins to mix with down there.

Uncle Fred, the only one of our mother's brothers who was not married, lived with Grandma and he used to do pig killing. Uncle Fred's nickname was Shady. He served in the Army in Egypt and Palestine in the First World War, and when they were short of food, Shady would go out in the night and bring back all kinds of meat and other food, he would go out and kill a sheep perhaps. Even the officers relied on him.

He was very popular in Lambourn, and everybody knew him. In those days, quite a lot of country folk kept a pig, and of course most people relied on Shady when it was time for the pig to be killed. This was not only people who lived in or just around the village. Sometimes it was these isolated farms on the downs, about a three or four mile walk.

I must have been about ten or eleven years old, and I remember the morning, after we'd got up, when Shady said to me: "Get theeself ready, we shall be going pig killing." He told Grandma he was taking me, and she would have the dinner hot for when we got back. It was a beautiful day, and Shady slung his bags with all his butchering knives over his shoulder, and off we went.

I didn't know where we were going until we started to go up

Sheepdrove. After walking quite some way, we left the roadway and walked over the fields until I saw this small farmstead down in the valley. Shady told me: "That's the place we are going to." I was beginning to feel a bit interested as I'd never been over this way before, although at the same time, I was beginning to feel a bit tired. As the weather was getting quite warm, I was also beginning to get quite thirsty.

We eventually reached the farm, a couple of dogs coming to meet us. We met the farmer and his wife and some of his family. The first thing the farmer did was to go into his shed and draw a mug of ale from a barrel which he brought to Shady. I can remember the farmer's wife saying to Shady: "You've brought an assistant today."

Shady, Vic's uncle who served in Egypt in the First World War. His photo is in a frame of stiff brown cardboard, secured by four pins, and there is an oval space in the middle to display the photo. In the frame is a piece of paper on which is printed, in capital letters,
The Allies frame
for your boy at
the front

He said: "Aarh! That's my boy." Anyway she went and brought me out a large bottle of, I think, cherry cider. I just gulped the lot down. That was my first real enjoyment of the day.

Well, now they were starting to get ready for work. The farmer had two younger men there. I don't know if they were his sons or not. Anyway they'd got everything ready: a large heavy wooden stool, plenty of straw. For my introduction to pig killing, I couldn't stand and watch everything, but I must say, I did watch three or four more afterwards, and I began to get quite used to it. The main thing you do hear is the pig squealing.

Then they had to get the pig on to the stool. I don't know if they tied him down or not, and then Shady cut its throat and so drained the blood into a bucket. In some cases, where it was convenient, they would hang a pig upside down by his back legs, and they would cut his throat and bleed him that way.

It's surprising that, as Shady told me, there's nothing wasted in the pig. The blood is used, the trotters, the chitterlings, the head made into brawn, and of course the rest of the meat cut into different joints. Shady was always given some, especially the chitterlings.

He would bring these home to Grandma, and then you would find her sitting in the wood shed which adjoined the cottage and she would be cleaning and washing the chitterlings ready for cooking. Then with other little bits of ingredients she would make faggots. These she would get ready by Saturday when so many people came to buy them, she could never cook enough. Grandma's faggots were famous.

Another time Shady took me into the Lambourn Woods when there was a hunt meeting. He knew exactly where to find John Dack, the keeper of the woods who was waiting for us. He told Shady what he wanted done. After he went off, Shady came back and told me: "The hunt will be moving in from the Market Place very shortly. When you hear or see the hounds, stand up against that tree." It was rather a large tree and he said I would be protected when the hounds started coming in with the riders following. I didn't know where Shady went to, although he wasn't far away. I then heard the bugle sound, and so I thought I'd better make myself safe.

It wasn't long before I could hear the hounds and then they were all around me just trying to pick up a scent, and then the riders were coming down on both sides of me. This went on for quite a little while. And then I heard the sound of the bugle again, the sounds of the hounds and riders seemed to be moving away in the opposite direction to where they had come in, so I presumed they must have picked up a scent and were now moving to the open country.

Fancy dress occasion for a procession in Lambourn, about 1919, for Alexandra Day flag day. Vic and Gert are far right, with Auntie Emily and Uncle Jack's children Harry (left), Winnie (second left), Gladys (front), Alice (third right), and Uncle Harry's daughter Dot. The photo was taken outside Emily and Jack's house

To me, it was very exciting, and I was sorry to see it was over. I don't know if they eventually killed a fox or not. And then we met up with John Dack again. He reminded me of Sherlock Holmes with his deerstalker type of hat and heavy coat with a cape fixed around his shoulders. We went with him to his large house with grounds all around at the bottom of Folly, we had bread and cheese and a drink, and then, for me, it was back to tell the others all about it.

At the end of the summer, mainly the beginning of September, Dad and Mum always went to Lambourn. The reason they took their holiday then was because the Lambourn Flower Show was held at that time. Now Dad was very friendly with Mr Bellinger, the landlord of the Sawyers Arms pub in the High Street, and Mr Bellinger held the licence to run what was called the beer tent at the Flower Show.

Mr Bellinger liked Dad to help him run the beer marquee, Dad understanding the trade. Our Dad really enjoyed it, and always looked forward to this event. The Flower Show was held in what was called the cricket field in the Upper Lambourn Road. It is quite large, and although you can run straight on to the field from the road, it is quite encircled by the Lambourn Woods on one side, and trees all around the rest.

There were always two or three marquees to house the different showpieces besides the beer marquee. There was pony racing with betting, athletics in the afternoon, dog show, besides the flower, fruit and vegetables and different craft shows. Then there would be a fair with roundabouts and swings and the different whatnots. And in the evening, the village band would arrive for dancing on the green. Altogether, providing the weather held, it was a really good day.

When I was young, I always had a tear in my eyes when we came back to London. Each year was the same. Mum would be carrying a great big bunch of flowers, Dad would be carrying the luggage, Gert and me would be carrying the bags of fruit and veg from Grandma's garden.

7. LONDON FACES AND PLACES

Now I was back to town life, and school, all the old faces I hadn't seen for some time, and all the familiar places. I soon seemed to settle down, and realized that I still belonged to London, especially when I saw all my friends again. George Oliver, who we had played with since we were quite small, used to spend all his time round our house, in fact he nearly finished up as one of the family.

One day, I was on my way home from school when I met Harry Kelly down St Albans Street, where he lived, he was talking to Len Wohlgemuth. So I stopped to talk to them. After a while, Harry went indoors so I continued with Len down to his house. As that was the way I used to travel backwards and forwards to school.

St Albans Street, like Richmond Street, was not very long, but the houses were nearly all the same, brick built, and if I remember, a sub basement. But this one where Len lived was different. It was a double fronted house, with entrance door in the middle, and it had a kind of cement facing, not bricks. In fact it was much larger than the other houses. It was once the Walnut Tree pub. After a while, Len and myself gradually got a bit more talkative to each other.

Some time later there was a special event being held one evening at the school. So as I was going, I called for him. He wasn't quite ready, so he called me in to wait for him. That was my first introduction to his family. This was all a bit of a rush, but it wasn't long before he took me in again, and I met properly his Mum and Dad, elder sister Alice, sister Girlie (Anne), brother Jimmy, and younger brothers and sisters, who were then quite small. I think they had a piano there, as that's why we got to talking about music. I always got on well with Len's dad.

He wasn't only interesting to talk to, he was interesting to listen to, he was very intelligent. George and Len remained my pals until the end of their lives and in later years Gert's daughter married one of Len's sons and Win's granddaughter married another.

I was now beginning to make a few strides up at school and had reached the 7th standard. We'd formed a choir at school, and I had been picked, after a test. I remember, on two occasions, along with other schools we sang before the King and Queen. That was then King George V and Queen Mary. The second time, I think they'd been to Greenwich by river. We were all sitting on the steps behind Westminster pier, to await their return. Then we all stood and gave them our 'Song of Praise'.

Being in the upper standards we used to have quite a few outside studies. We went to the Tower of London twice, Westminster Abbey, and quite a number of museums. Often, on Sunday afternoons I would go out on my own, and visit the Tate Gallery to see the different paintings, as you could study them better when you were on your own. Also there was no entrance fee.

The school started an ex 7 standard, which was the top standard. I think there were about five or six of us who qualified, so that's where I finished up. We used to have plenty of football and cricket, and a sports meeting during the summer, which was of course athletics, for both boys and girls. I was very interested in athletics but didn't turn out too well myself.

Also during the summer months we had swimming lessons once a week at the Lambeth Baths. It was quite a large building in Kennington Road where it meets Lambeth Road. It had gentlemen's first class swimming bath, second class swimming bath, ladies' swimming bath, and, for both sexes, first class and second class slipper baths, which otherwise meant, to have a bath. Of course, there was a charge, but that included soap and towel. This was a great help to us, as the majority of houses in those days were not built with bathrooms. And also, we only lived a short walk away. A part of the building was made available for people to take and do their own washing, as a lot of people didn't have the proper means to do a lot of washing, especially if they had a family.

During the winter months the first class swimming pool was closed. This being a large area, the pool was emptied, and a dance floor laid down, with a stage erected at one end. So this was where dances, concerts or meetings were held. The committee of the Lambeth Walk traders used to run two dances during the winter season. One was always a fancy dress and carnival affair. We often went from home, especially on the carnival night.

In the back yard at 86 Kennington Road, about 1920: back row (left to right), Dad, Jim, Lil, Sid, Uncle Hinton; middle row, Auntie Kate, Grandma, Mum, Granny Nunn; seated, Fred Taylor, Gert, Vic

In those days, the majority of well run dances were hosted by an MC (Master of Ceremonies). The first time I remember going, I was attracted by the MC. He was a fine figure of a man, well built, and in full evening dress. After a while, I suddenly realized. Of course, it was the pie and eel man from down the Walk, and he was very popular. Bob Burroughs was his name. He had a pie shop, and that's where you bought the average Londoner's dinner, pie and mash with liquor.

The shop was run by his wife Rose and an assistant, who I think belonged to the family. The reason I say this is because I think his wife was either Italian or Spanish, as she had lovely, completely black hair which was taken up right to the top of her head, and of course it made her look much taller. Her assistant had the same complexion, and especially wearing their white jackets they looked really attractive.

They also had seating arrangements in the shop for customers to sit down to a meal if they wanted to. Of course the other most important items they sold were stewed eels and jellied eels, in cartons.

Bob Burroughs was not idle, he had a stall outside the shop, but on the other side of the road, in the market. On the stall were three or four large metal trays about five or six inches deep, and these contained live eels, all writhing about, if people wanted to cook their own. Bob had a large chopping block with a knife to chop the eels' heads off before weighing them up as needed. He used to look very smart out there in his white jacket with striped apron around him.

So that was the man who first caught my eye on my first visit to the carnival dance standing in the middle of the dance floor in full evening dress. I thought afterwards when I'd got home, there are always two sides to life. And of course being young you began to learn how people like the market traders can soon change their style of life.

8. CHRISTMAS, THEN NEW YEAR AT KEW

After our yearly school exams, we always had our prizegivings, mostly in the way of books. During schooldays I think I won about three books besides the certificates for history and religion. My lowest marks were always for writing. As much as I tried I could never seem to improve.

We never seemed to go to Richmond Street now, all our playmates were growing up like us and we had other things to occupy our minds, although Gert would go round to see her friends Ada and Nellie Swan. And of course I was still friends with George Oliver and Len Wohlgemuth.

Soon after two days' school holiday, that would be half term, we started learning and rehearsing for our Christmas festivities. The infants occupied the ground floor of our school, the boys the first floor and the girls the second floor, which was the top, and so each arranged their own type of festivities.

With the boys, the last day of term was first morning prayers, and then two lessons until mid morning break. After that, it was packing up all our books to put away, also cleaning out and washing inkwells and pens, and a general clean up. And then it would be lunch break, or as we used to call it, dinner break. The afternoon was given over for all classes to assemble in the main hall, when the Headmaster would take charge. His name was Mr Morant, and I found him a very nice man.

In cases like this when we were going to spend the afternoon in the hall, he would always apologize, as we were not supplied with seating of any kind, so we sat on the floor, and the older boys got round the sides. After all it wasn't a very large type of school hall, and we had an average of two hundred boys, so that filled it up. He would always start with a short talk. After that he would call on the different teachers to bring forward any boys from their classes who they thought were talented enough to entertain.

This was the procedure that took place each year. In the case of trying to find talent, some years it was good, other years not so good. This year I remember, there were only about four or five boys who came forward, and they were really good. We had one teacher who belonged to a dramatic society, and who helped boys with any kind of talent after school hours during the run up to Christmas.

One boy sang a comic song. The best of the lot he was. I think the whole boys' school laughed from beginning to end. It was all about a sailor, and the different islands he'd been to. He had a strong voice, and he did all the actions. I think it was the actions that made us laugh. I've never heard the song since.

The Headmaster, who was a good pianist, would accompany anyone who was singing. He also gave one or two piano solos. Then a short carol concert and that was the end of the afternoon, which I think was rather enjoyable. On the way out, each boy was given one apple and one orange.

I remember my last Christmas when I left school. It was arranged for the three prefects to sing a carol on their own, 'We three Kings of Orient are'. The prefects were the three eldest boys from ex 7 class, so that included me. Each verse we sang as a solo, mine was 'Mine is Myrrh, its bitter perfume'. The chorus, we each sang our own part – alto, bass and tenor. It all comes back to me each year I hear that carol sung at Christmas time. I think, if this had been the present day, we would have to have dressed as the Three Kings.

I always used to look forward to Christmas. We always managed to have a Christmas dinner with turkey and Christmas pudding. Mum made the puddings, and for quite a few years, Uncle Jim, her brother who lived at Kew and had been in the butchering trade, would go over to Smithfield Market for our turkey, and theirs, as they had their own Christmas party.

The presents were always kept to be given out after Christmas dinner and then we would go upstairs to the music room. That meant a musical evening, perhaps with one or two friends or relatives calling in, although it was on Boxing Day that most turned up. Our Dad was always a good entertainer, a few years before he had belonged to a minstrel group. Amongst all the friends and relatives who came to our musical evenings, most could sing or entertain in some way. They were always happy evenings, especially Christmas times.

New Year we spent with Uncle Jim and Auntie Alice at Kew, they always held their party on the first weekend after the New Year. So we travelled down on the Saturday evening, Mum and Dad would take Gert and me. We'd catch the train at Waterloo and travel to Kew Bridge, and from there we would walk over to where they lived on Kew Green. Sometimes my brother Lal would be there, as that's where he first met Dolly, whom he married afterwards, the sister of Ethel, who was married to Auntie Alice and Uncle Jim's son Cecil.

Auntie Alice gave a good sit down supper party, that started about midnight, and then it was back upstairs afterwards for more music. They always had a good crowd, mostly everyone we knew. The party would keep going as long as everybody could keep awake.

Auntie Alice would always make some arrangement for older ones to lie down in beds, but the men would go downstairs in the kitchen to play cards or other games and stayed up later. Otherwise it was kip down where you could make yourself comfortable, and make the best of it. Come the morning, after everybody had freshened up, Auntie Alice prepared a breakfast. That party was one of the delights of Christmas time, besides our own parties.

Then of course it was the pantomime season. We always went to see the pantomime at the Kennington Theatre facing Kennington Park. This was a first class theatre that produced good plays at other times, but now it was pantomime. There were always first class artistes appearing, and full orchestra.

When we were younger, Gert and me, we were always taken, often by our sister Win, but later we went by ourselves. Mum or Dad would give us the money to pay for the admission, and a bit extra for some sweets. We went to a matinée. Lined up for the gallery entrance with all the others, mostly children, of course quite a lot with their parents or carers. It was always a good show, and something we looked forward to every year.

Time marches on, and already my sister Win was married, to Bert Bowsher, brother of Tom Bowsher, a farmer in Lambourn. Bert came over from Canada, I don't know if he was with the army, but he never went back. They had a daughter, named Jean. She was born in 1920. When she was big enough to go out in a push chair, that was my next job for a time.

At one time they moved to the Bloomsbury area, I think to a caretaker's job. These were all large types of houses which were used as offices. They had the sub basement part to live in, as was the same with most of the other buildings.

They lived in Didcot in Oxfordshire for a while, and that's where Bert's sister lived, the Morse family. We often went down there to visit Win, and got on well with the Morse boys, Jim, Tom, Geoff and Frank, all about my age, and Les a younger one. They had a sister Jean, who when very young was killed by a car at Bockhampton whilst on holiday at Lambourn, visiting the Bowsher family.

Mr Morse was a very nice man and a strong Methodist preacher. And so when we were down there, when it was Sunday, it would be chapel and not church.

My brother Ted was killed in the 1914-18 war, as were cousin Lil's brothers George and Arch, but I have little recollection of it. Lal and Sid still lived at home. Lil, who worked for the *Sketch* newspaper as a bookfolder*, had become friendly with Syd Reading, a regular soldier in the Duke of Cornwall's Light Infantry and a friend of her brother George.

They were to marry in 1922 after Syd had left the Army and become a bus driver. My dad gave her away as Uncle George refused to do so. He liked Syd but having lost his wife and all his other children, he wouldn't give his remaining child away to anyone.

We seemed to have quite a full house again. Uncle Harry at Lambourn, our mother's brother, died and left three teenage children, my cousins Jim, Cis and Dot. Their mother, Lil's older sister Dewey, had died when they were very young, so then Harry left London and returned to Lambourn, where he had a butcher's shop, and Grandma cared for the children.

When Uncle Harry died in 1920, it was thought better for Dot and Cis to come to us, as Grandma was over seventy by this time; Jim was already living with us and working. Uncle George was of course their grandfather. After settling down with us for a while, it was arranged for Cis to go and stay with Auntie Kate and Percy who now lived at Highbury.

We also had Granny Nunn living with us. She gave a bit of help in

*The *Sketch* published books as well as the newspaper. Several pages were printed on to one large sheet and girls were employed to fold the pages ready for cutting. Lil acted as spokesperson for the others. For example, the room where they worked had a cold damp floor and she persuaded the management to provide duckboards for the girls to stand on. Her nickname was Dick – Vic's dad used to call her a clever dick because she was quick and bright at school. She continued to work as a bookfolder until shortly before Arthur (my brother) was born. – Joyce Rockhill, Lil's daughter, 2000 the housekeeping. I was told her husband was a policeman, but had since died, and they were living in the East End at the time of Jack the Ripper. She had a married son Willy who was deaf and dumb who used to come and visit her occasionally. But what part of the family she came from I never knew. She had been living with us for quite some time, when she had to go into the Lambeth Hospital. I think she had been having some kind of trouble with her nose. She wasn't in there long before she died.

I left school at Christmas time 1923. That's when you start thinking you're grown up. I was fourteen years old.

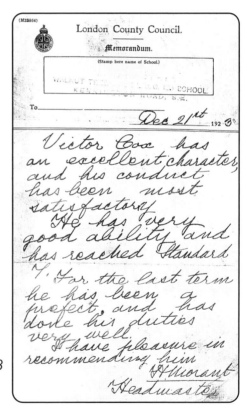

Vic's school leaving report, December 1923

9. A JOB IN KENNINGTON LANE

We had entered the year 1924. I felt as though I was starting a new life, and of course, must look for a job. We had to realize that in those times, there was mass unemployment which had more or less continued since the end of the war. So I visited the labour exchange to sign my name, and was offered a job at a light engineering firm in Kennington Lane, not too far away. After going for an interview, I started on the following Monday.

Meanwhile, my cousin Jim, who lived with us, found a job as a junior at Frascati's restaurant in Oxford Street in the vicinity of Holborn, and told me about it when we went to bed, as he now slept in the same bedroom as me, the small room at the rear in the top part of the house. My eldest brother Lal worked at Faulkner's tobacco factory in Blackfriars Road, my next brother Sid worked in the City.

My friend George Oliver's older brother Ted left school at the same time as me and found a job at one of the noted restaurants off Piccadilly, and George joined him. My friend Len Wohlgemuth left school about the same time as George and secured a job in a ladies' shoe manufacturing firm. I think it was quite a nice little job.

My job seemed quite simple and easy. The building I was in was an extension to the main building which was in Reedworth Street, a short way around the corner from where we lived. I had two or three small light jobs to do, besides having to take a few bundles and specific items round to the main building. I was also tea boy and sweeper up, which wasn't too bad as the building wasn't very large.

It contained, I think, six men, including the foreman, and their different machines. And so, after the first few weeks picking up a weekly wage, I think one begins to feel a bit independent, anyway that's how I began to feel. Meanwhile, Gert had passed a scholarship, and was now at West Square School, which was termed a secondary school. It wasn't very far away.

Before I left Sunday School, my teacher was quite a nice person, her name was Miss Drummond. She shared her sister's flat in a house at 122 Kennington Road, a little way past where we lived, and the lower part of the house was used as club rooms, the Queen Victoria Girls' Club. Win told me that she and Lil used to go there when they were younger. There were also four houses on the opposite side of the road, which the community workers the Lady Margaret Hall Settlement rented.

Miss Drummond always seemed interested in me, as I suppose I seemed to study a bit more than the other boys. She would call at our house to deliver a book or something else interesting for me. Most times I was out when she called, as happened the last time. When I got home, she'd left a box of chocolates for me. After that I didn't see her again. I was told when I asked one of the other church ladies, that she came from a very good Scotch family.

Quite a few years later, it was in the daily papers that the daughter of a well known Scotch family had gained the honour of becoming the first female to hold the post of Chief Marine Engineer. I did make further enquiries and was told it was the same person. I felt quite delighted to think that my Sunday School teacher had attained something unusual for a female.*

One thing we always looked forward to was our Sunday School summer treat, a day out in the country, and it was always an enjoyable day, providing the weather was good, otherwise it was

*Victoria Drummond's life is recorded in *The Remarkable Life of Victoria Drummond Marine Engineer*, by Cherry Drummond, published by The Institute of Marine Engineers, London, 1999. – Editor

postponed. We had a short service at the church first, and although we took sandwiches, a large tea was arranged for us in the afternoon. I've passed through some of these places now where we used to enjoy ourselves, but, I'm afraid, there are no green fields or any greenery, it's all houses now.

One year we also had a good outing from the Band of Hope which we belonged to, quite a little crowd of us. We went to Southend-on-Sea for the day. We all had to meet outside the hall in the morning. There waiting for us were two open wagons with horses, of course there were seats fixed in the wagons for us to sit on.

Vic, about 1925

The wagons and horses were decked up with ribbons. We were beginning to think that it was going to take us a long time to get to Southend in a horse and cart. Afterwards, we found out that they were only to take us to Fenchurch Street Station, where we caught the train to Southend. It was a lovely day, especially being by the sea. A lot of the others had never seen the sea before, they really enjoyed themselves.

Gert and me had already been to Southend. Mum and Dad took us by boat. They were rather large paddle steamers, and they started from Tower Pier. They used to sail down the river and call at Greenwich Pier to pick up any more travellers, and then on to Southend, and Clacton. I think we went on the Royal Sovereign. That was very interesting sailing down the river until you came to the open sea.

It was during one Saturday when I was coming out of the house, I saw somebody over the other side of the road waving. It was Danny Lipton. So I went across to talk to him, as I hadn't seen him for a long time, he was at a boarding school or college somewhere in north London. He told me his mother was back home again, their living quarters lay at the back of the shop. She'd come to see if she could settle things down a bit as the old chap was so awkward with his nasty outbursts.

Danny was hoping she would settle down and be happy, as he had to go back to school. And so, as he was going back into the shop, he said cheerio, and we shook hands. I felt a bit sorry for him. I think it was about three or four months later, when Dad gave me the paper he was reading and pointed to an article. It read: "Yesterday a young man jumped off the Highgate Archway on to the road below, and was killed. His name was Danny Lipton."

I can still remember, for the minute I just felt shivery, and then I thought I wouldn't go over to the shop any more, although I did for a while, just to get Dad's tobacco.

10. TRAIN TO SWANLEY FOR WEEKEND AWAY

Uncle George's and Dad's sister, our Auntie Tal, for quite a number of years had worked for Mr Roberts and his wife who lived in a flat in Victoria Street, the flat being attached to the offices of Roberts engineering company. They also had a country house in Kent, where they used to go at weekends. As they were going away until the following week, they wanted Auntie Tal to go down to look after the house. This she was quite happy to do.

The house was near a small village called Fawkham. As she would be travelling down on the Friday, she wanted Harry, her husband, and Uncle George to go down on the Saturday. She gave them their orders, to go to London Bridge Station, and catch the train to Swanley, and, although there would be food down there, they must bring a joint of meat for themselves. And so, Uncle Harry and Uncle George, being brothers in law and quite used to each other's company, arranged to go down on the Saturday afternoon.

Uncle George told us when he arrived back home on Sunday evening how they got on. They caught the train all right, and the first thing when they came out of the station, was to find a pub. After quenching their thirst and asking their way, they found they had to walk about three miles, Uncle Harry with his webbed feet which made him a slow walker, and Uncle George being an old plodder, and each one taking turns to carry the bag which contained the joint of meat and one or two other things, and weighed a bit heavy.

It was a quiet country road, with a nice grass bank each side, which enabled them to have a sit down once or twice as it was a very sunny day. Uncle George thought it was much farther than three miles. Plodding along in the middle of the road, they were on a slight bend when suddenly, something shot between them scattering Uncle Harry on to one bank and Uncle George on to the other one. It was a man riding a racing bike. He must have had his head quite low down to keep out of the sun's rays and didn't see them until the last minute, when he tried to stop and, travelling a bit fast, he went over the top of the bike between the two weary travellers. Nobody got hurt, but they all received a bit of a shaking, and of course a few arguments with it.

One thing, they did get a bit of help finding their destination. The man knew where the house was, about ten minutes' walk, and so, they all parted on good terms. Auntie Tal was pleased they'd arrived safely, after listening to their experiences. Then she asked why they didn't bring a joint of meat with them. That started another argument. Harry said George had it, and George said Harry had it, so they finally came to the conclusion it must still be on the bank.

After a drink and a rest, they decided to trust their luck, and go back to see if it was still there. Yes, their luck was in. There it was, on the bank, still in the bag with the other things. The rest of the family could really see the funny side of this story. Our Dad laughed about it for a long time after.

My cousin Jim Taylor got himself a new job at the Waldorf Hotel, in the Aldwych. He said he had to look for another job, as Frascati's where he worked was closing down.

I heard from Jim and Tom Morse from Didcot in 1924. They wanted to stay the weekend to visit the Wembley exhibition. They travelled up early on the Saturday morning, and then I took them to Wembley, where we spent all day, returning home in the evening tired out. It was a very wonderful and interesting exhibition called the British Empire Exhibition, each country displaying their own exhibits. You would need to make quite a few visits to be able to say that you'd seen it all. There was a second year, 1925, of the Exhibition, the boys from Didcot came up, and so that was another enjoyable visit.

Uncle George's daughter Lil and her husband Syd Reading still occupied the big room in the top part of the house, doing their bit of cooking on a stove on the landing. Their son Arthur was born in 1924. When he was beginning to grow, he spent nearly all his time downstairs with us, I've always looked on him as another brother.

Sid would often go down to the Brewery Tap, the off licence which Dad managed for quite a number of years, to see if he wanted any help. The Tap belonged to Jenner's Brewery and was situated alongside the main gates of the brewery in the Southwark Bridge Road. It was a family brewery, and they had won one big prize at the Brewers' Exhibition with Jenner's Golden Ale. Dad's brother, Uncle George, also worked at the brewery.

Dad (second left) outside Jenner's off-licence which he managed, 1908

I would go down there one or two evenings a week, and George Oliver would come with me to bring back one or two bottles of ale and stout which we used to drink at supper time. Dad used to have a beer allowance from the brewery, and that's what we brought home. While we were there, we would always have a lemonade drawn straight from the barrel, the taste seemed a lot better than the present day taste of lemonade.

One little thing we now used to enjoy was a fish and chip supper every Friday night. It seemed to have become quite popular. There were fried fish and chip shops around, and Friday was always a busy day until late evening. Often, if I was with Len on a Friday evening, his family would want me to stay for fish and chip supper.

Saturday evenings Len, George and myself would arrange to go out to some form of entertainment, mainly the Holborn Empire, which always held good musical and variety shows of the same standard as the Palladium and other West End theatres. Of course, at that time we never used to pay first class prices, we lined up for the cheaper seats with the hundreds of others.

One thing, when you did line up outside most West End theatres, you got the advantage of seeing two shows, inside and outside. Many of the unemployed men, and women, although it was mostly men, would work on their talent, and in this case would entertain the theatre queues. It was surprising what some could do.

Some sang, some were comical acrobats, some danced, another would play a musical instrument. And that was before we went into the theatre. After the show we'd have a walk round to see all the lights and bustle, and probably find a café to have a snack, before making our way home. Most times an enjoyable evening.

I went to St Mary's Old Lambeth Church on Sunday mornings, but Len went to the Baptist Church in the Lambeth Road. Every year during the summer, there was a religious procession held on a

Sunday which started from the Catholic Cathedral in the Lambeth Road, and walked a circular route, eventually arriving back at the cathedral. It was led by the band, then all the boys and girls dressed in white, then the choirboys and the Bishop surrounded by his ministers, then the rest of the followers, altogether quite a long procession. Everyone was singing 'Ave Maria'. Quite a lot of people used to come out to see it go by. We only had to go across the road as they always went down Brook Street (now Brook Drive).

I still found time to put in a little practice on my piano playing. Up to the time I left school, I used to spend quite a lot of time in Lambourn. Whilst I was there, I visited Auntie Emily, where Gert used to stay. She was a piano teacher, and she had quite a number of pupils. Once, she suggested giving me lessons.

I did attend them, but when Gert and I were about to return to London, she told me that she was to give me up, as she'd been trying to teach me things I already knew. And so, as time went on, it may seem uncanny but providing I put in plenty of practice, music just came into my mind. I just loved listening to music, and it seemed so easy when I touched the piano.

Occasionally, over the weekend, I went to visit Auntie Kate and Percy at Highbury. Percy gave me a violin. It was the first he made, as he used to attend a school where he was taught to make violins. As he played the violin, he said he would give me some lessons.

Percy came from Bristol of a musical family. His father was conductor of the orchestra at one of the theatres there, I think the Empire Theatre, and his sister was a very good pianist. His older brother Frank when he was young was no musician, but joined the Navy. When he came home on leave, feeling the odd one out, he bought himself a gramophone. Their mother was a jolly type of woman, and liked to have a drink.

And so I started learning the violin, and after a while I managed to play quite a few scales, but it interfered with piano practice. When they came to visit us at weekends, Percy would bring his violin, and with my piano playing, we always managed to have a good musical Sunday evening, especially if we had our usual visitors, there would be a few willing offers to get up to sing us a song. I must say that Auntie Kate had quite a repertoire, when she sang 'Sunshine of your smile' it set the evening off.

I still went round to Len's house, when we used to have more music. I liked his sister Alice who was a bit older than me, and his sister Girlie, who was a bit younger. The other two sisters were much younger, I didn't know them so well. I also liked Alice's future husband Bill. He came from Islington, and he played the piano.

I was still plodding on in my job. I liked to have a walk down the Lambeth Walk on a Saturday if I was not going out anywhere. I should probably meet Mum and help to carry some of the shopping home. Saturday was the best day for shopping, although Sunday mornings were quite busy. Quite a few stalls were out and a lot of the small shops were open, although the big shops were closed.

We often had to run down the Walk on a Sunday morning for something we'd forgotten to get. One thing we did have to go for, was the laundry. In those days, collars were often still worn separately on men's shirts, and they were stiff collars, and of course the ordinary working man liked to wear a clean shirt and stiff collar (mostly white) on a Sunday, with a tie.

Quite a lot of people used to take their dirty laundry to the shop on Mondays to be cleaned and ironed, and it was usually ready for collection on Saturday from the old lady who ran the shop, but sometimes not until Sunday morning. Dad and Uncle George always needed a clean collar for Sundays, and so, if the laundry hadn't arrived, it was either Gert or me, being the youngest in the family, to go round on Sunday for it, and very often we had to wait about a bit. Then we missed church.

My brothers and I would often wear shirts with soft collars attached to them and our mother did a lot of that washing at home, or a friend of ours would take two or three of our items if she was going up to the washing area at Lambeth Baths. Mum would give her something, some money, for doing our washing.

Gert left school, and was working.* Cis had a job, and a boyfriend who was Welsh, his name was Brinley Rees. She brought him and his brother over to us at home and introduced us. After a while Dot also found herself a boyfriend, and brought him home to meet us. His name was George Lipscombe and his family ran a gentlemen's tailor business, not a great way from us. They lived on the premises, Dot spent quite a lot of time at their home now.

Uncle Charlie, Dad's brother from Rotherhithe, paid us an occasional visit now that Auntie Ada, his wife, was dead. I suppose he felt a bit lonely at times, although he had two sons, Bert and Vic. I don't know if Bert married or not, but Vic married Lizzie and had a son, Derek, in the 1930s, and they lived at Barnehurst. Dad's eldest sister, Auntie Emily, was the only one of his family that I never met. She lived at Silvertown on the Isle of Dogs with her family, and she seemed to be cut right off from the rest of the family.

The Christmas I was sixteen, we had our Grandma up from Lambourn. I think she enjoyed her Christmas with us. I used to love our Granny Taylor. It was during the January, when she had a stroke, she lay at home for two or three days, then she died. I cried my eyes out. She was taken back to Lambourn to be buried, and most of her family who were now living in London went down to Lambourn for the funeral.

*My mum worked for Woolworth's in Oxford Street. At that time they had a printing department and she printed visiting cards. She told me she got the job because she was good at spelling and was always neatly dressed and polite. They had some titled ladies amongst their customers. Unlike her cousin Lil, she had to leave work when she married, as Woolworth's did not employ married women then. – Jill Wohlgemuth, 2000

12. COMMIS WAITER AT THE WALDORF HOTEL

My cousin Jim Taylor didn't have time to find a girlfriend. He'd been working at the Waldorf Hotel for nearly a couple of years, and he asked me if I would like a job there as a commis (assistant) waiter. He said that the hours would be a bit longer, but the wage would be more than my present one. And as I didn't seem to be making any headway at the engineering company, I accepted his offer. He arranged for an interview with the Manager, or otherwise the Head Waiter, of the Grill Room, where he worked.

That all went well, and so my next job was to see about a uniform, as all in this trade of waiter had to provide our own. This consisted of black short jacket, and black trousers with black dress waistcoat, white stiff collar and shirtfront, black shoes, and white bowtie. Uniforms for the pageboys, hotel porters and those who worked at the main entrances were supplied by the hotel, dark blue, with gold braiding.

And so, with Jim, I went round to Soho, to a small tailor's shop which was run by a Jewish family and was well known by a lot of hotel workers. A young chap about twenty guessed what I'd come for and measured me up. For shirtfront, collars and bowties I had to go elsewhere.

It was mid week, and I didn't start till Monday. I'd already finished up with my old job, and was looking forward for something a bit different. Jim had already told me quite a lot about it. Next day I went to collect my 'togs'. The young fellow told me to call him Marcus, and said the two middle age women working at the back of the shop were his sisters. Anyway, he told me to come upstairs to the fitting room as the trousers and jacket had got to fit quite perfect

The Waldorf Hotel, Aldwych, 1922. 'Zozo' was at the Strand Theatre. Bedford Lemere photo reproduced by permission of the National Monuments Record (English Heritage)

to be able to look smart. Apart from having to make one or two small adjustments, everything fitted quite well. Arriving home, I thought I would try everything on. Yes, I was quite satisfied, and Uncle George thought I was the Prince of Wales!

And so Monday came. The staff entrance being at the rear of the hotel, I reported to the timekeeper and was given a clock number. Then I was taken downstairs to be shown where our lockers were, with washbasins and toilets, and the dining room for staff, that was also for maintenance personnel, and hotel porters and pageboys.

When we reached the bottom of the stairs, we entered into a long passageway, which led to the front of the hotel. Before we started, I noticed the door on my left was open and I was told that was the boiler room. Quite a large area with two of the largest boilers I'd ever seen and mounds of fuel which was shot down from the street above. I was told, that it was nearly always ex sailors that worked in the boiler room.

Then carrying on along the passageway, we passed the engineer and electricians' workshop, next to that the carpenters', and then the painters' shop, and so we came to our locker and changing rooms, with one on either side of the passage. To continue along the passageway would eventually lead you to the wine cellars which were in connection with the front of the hotel. That was beyond our approach.

Then I was taken back upstairs along to the Grill Room to meet the second in charge, M Manceau, who was responsible for all the staff. He was French. The Grill Room Manager whom I previously saw was M Otts, he was Swiss. And so, after my introduction, I was taken to work with a chef waiter whose name was Len Higgins, a young fellow, as most of the others I had seen so far were all on the young side. So far, I'd only seen half of the staff.

The Grill Room was quite large with an extension room added on to one end, which made it run to the whole length of the hotel. It consisted of approximately a hundred tables of various sizes, which were not allowed to be grouped too close together. The staff consisted of fifteen chef waiters with about seventeen or eighteen commis waiters, all about my age. Chef waiters were qualified waiters, the commis waiters were their assistants. Then there were five floor Head Waiters.

As Jim had already told me, the staff were divided into what they called two brigades. Number 1 brigade started in the morning at 9.30 to prepare the tables, a clean cloth on each one. All silverware to be sorted out and polished, the commis waiters dusted and wiped all the chairs which were armchair type, polished glass mirrors and did other little necessities. All this until 11 o'clock, which was their lunch time until 12 o'clock, when they took their stations, as their sideboards were called. Each chef waiter had a sideboard to work on, and keep all his essentials.

As Grill Room lunch started at 12 o'clock, No. 1 brigade must be on duty, and the commis to collect a clean white apron for the day, and then carry on till 3 o'clock when lunch time was on the finish. This was when No. 1 brigade was finished until 6 o'clock, to start for dinner and then carry on until approximately 11 o'clock. That was called the long day.

Number 2 brigade started at 11 o'clock in the morning, to finish laying the tables with glasses and serviettes and menus. At 12 o'clock, they went off for lunch until 12.30 when they must be back on duty, when they carried on until 4 o'clock, taking over responsibility for any customers still at their tables when No. 1 brigade went off duty. Number 2 brigade finished for the day at 9 o'clock in the evening. That was the short day. Each brigade worked one long day and one short day alternately.

The hotel had three main entrances in the front, each one with an attendant. Number one entrance was for the hotel residents, number two for the Restaurant, Palm Court and Ballroom, number three for cold buffet lunches, which were on ground level, and Lounge, American Bar and Grill Room downstairs. At the bottom of a flight of stairs was the small counter for cloaks and umbrellas, just behind was a Gentlemen's cloakroom and a short way away the Ladies' cloakroom. Pat, who I eventually got to know quite well, was in charge of this area, apart from the Ladies'. He was also in charge of the telephone to receive any calls through to the Grill Room.

From here, you passed into the Lounge. As you walked along the Lounge towards the centre you came to three wide steps going down into the Grill Room. The Lounge was like a long balcony with a polished rail along the side. It was complete with small tables each with small lamps and basket chairs and used for cocktails, sherries and liqueurs. Although quite a lot of whisky was drunk.

Behind the steps to the Grill Room was a glass mirrored partition which you walked behind into the American Bar, also another entrance to the service bar, which was used by the waiters. In front of the partition stood the cashier's desk, which was chest high and was where chef waiters cashed their bills, that is to say paid in their customers' money, although there was a cashier's desk in the extension at lunch time. Everywhere was red carpeted except the American Bar which was a stand up bar, used for short drinks, no beers served.

To walk from the Lounge down the steps into the Grill Room the first thing you saw was the cold buffet table consisting of various meat joints on a stand, and when in season a large salmon on a special tray, and other specialities, and various fruits. It was during the summer season when this showed the largest display and was more interesting.

The Head Waiter and second Head Waiter were always at the bottom of the steps to receive customers. All chef waiters with a commis waiter were allocated a sideboard with all necessities and on the average five tables. The five floor Head Waiters were spread out to work with about three waiters each.

When I was shown to my station (sideboard), and my chef waiter Len Higgins, he already had a commis working with him who stayed on and showed me the routine before he left to go into another job. We were in the extension where the ceiling was much higher. The lighting came from chandeliers with lamps on side tables.

To go from the Grill Room to the kitchen you went through two communicating doors (In and Out) used by staff at this end of the room. Staff at the other end, which was the other side of the buffet, were able to go through the opening by the large mirrored partition which hid the grills being cooked. Also in this area was a hotplate where orders for roast joints would be carved, and worktable for the boy who was in charge of the hors d'oeuvre trolleys, of which there were three and had to be kept filled up all the time.

Now it was through two more swing doors into what was called the pantry. This was where all the used crockery, eating utensils, silver and glasses were brought. There were three male workers in the pantry, and they arranged between themselves for one to come in early each day, the main thing being to get the fire alongside the grill ready for lunch time cooking. The fire, which burnt coke, had to be cleaned out, and relit, and banked up. Really an expert's job.

Crockery, eating utensils and glasses were washed here. The crockery was washed and put up to drain. The glasses were kept to one side and us younger ones would have to wash and polish them. They were dipped in soapy water, transferred to warm water, set to drain, and then polished. All used serviettes and any other linen were kept in one area, and it was a commis job every morning to count them and take them up to the ninth floor to the linen room and change them for clean ones.

Now it was up a short flight of stairs into the kitchen. You were in a main gangway which led from the timekeeper's office at the back entrance straight past towards the other end, past the bakery and then coming to where all used silverware was washed and cleaned, the silver dishes put into one big tank, then another, then another.

Finally, there were the kitchen chefs' dressing and changing rooms and toilets. Coming from the rear entrance towards the kitchen, you first came to a large office which was used by the Head and Second Chefs. It was screened by glass windows to keep it from the noise of the kitchen. The two Head Chefs' dressing room was a short distance away.

It was a large kitchen with one large type of hotplate in the middle containing many fires fuelled by coke which were in each side of the hotplate. This enabled the chefs to work each side on their specific job. Kitchen porters cleaned and lit the fires each morning but the chefs kept them going during cooking time. On one side of the kitchen were the women who prepared all the vegetables.

At the far end, and which led off the kitchen into its own area, was the larder. This contained fish, which was kept on ice, cold meats, and all other items which were to be kept cold. There was also a chef, whose job was to make up all the hors d'oeuvres and different sauces. Then the butcher's cold store.

At the front of the kitchen, just a little to our left, we crossed over the gangway to the fairly long hotplate, which contained all the plates being kept hot. Along a metal shelf over the top were stacked all the metal covers to go over Grill Room orders that had been completed and were awaiting collection.

Behind the hotplate stood the kitchen clerk, who received all the orders, and shouted them to the chefs concerned. All orders had to be written on checks issued by the chef waiter, with the table number showing. This enabled the clerk to pin them on to his number board which stood just behind him.

A bit farther along to our right, stood another hotplate which was used for the Restaurant. The stairs to the Restaurant were just opposite. It was upstairs to the Restaurant, downstairs to the Grill Room, the kitchen lying half way between. A little to the left was the salad and cheese room, a bit farther along the still room which issued coffee, tea, and all kinds of milk drinks. Adjoining that were the hand service lifts which were run by two personnel for any food requirements by floor waiters for room service to hotel residents.

The large windows along the back of the kitchen opened at the top to allow some fresh air in, although it was still below ground level, but of course the hoarding along the back stopped a lot of daylight coming in. The hoarding was green, and ran right along the rear of the hotel, and stopped people looking in.

At the time that I started to work at the hotel during the 1920s, Covent Garden Market was still in its original place. Now it's been moved to Battersea. The hotel was situated right on the edge of Covent Garden, and I used to notice very often on Monday mornings representatives of some of the firms from the 'Garden' in the Head Chef's office. His name was M Dupont, he was French.

They would bring specimens of different fruits and vegetables and he would always inspect them, as he was responsible for buying them. It was the same for all the other foods. During my time at the hotel I used to go through the 'Garden' quite a lot on my way to work although that was when they were about to close as they worked all through the night receiving stores from the country and selling them to market traders and other people ready for the day's trading.

The hotel was also surrounded by theatres. We had one on each side. One was called the Strand Theatre, and the other one, the Aldwych Theatre. Then nearby were the Gaiety, Winter Garden, Drury Lane, Lyceum and the Covent Garden Opera House.

The lunch period was always a very busy time. The hotel was right on the edge of the City and other large business offices, also Lincoln's Inn and the Law Courts, with all the lawyers and business people feeling hungry.

Before we started for the meals, which was lunch and dinner, the Head Waiter often, although not every day, wanted to inspect our hands and fingernails for cleanliness, but one soon got used to that as it was a must, that meant looking smart all over.

I found I had another cousin Jim working there. He was Jim Gamble, the son of Auntie Lizzie, one of Dad's sisters. He was a bit older than me, and he'd been working there for quite some time. Another cousin, Sid Taylor, one of Auntie Maud's sons, was to work there later on, and so was my friend George Oliver's brother Ted, he was a first class patissiere who worked in the kitchens.

I was getting to know the routine now. I'd got a good chef waiter to work with, and a good Head Waiter. My chef waiter Len Higgins I had found to be a really nice chap. He lived with his widowed mother, near St Pancras, and was not married. Our Head Waiter was Italian, Reggie, who was always out for a bit of a laugh.

The chef waiters were supplied with three different colour check books, one colour for lunch, one for dinner, and one for drinks. The Head Waiters also carried a check book. Also the waiters carried a bill book on which they made out the bill, and presented it to the customer when asked for. Then they took the bill to be cashed at the cashier's desk and returned the receipt bill and change to the table. Meanwhile, if it was a busy time, such as lunch time, and the waiter was busy with these little side jobs, it was the commis who had to see to customers' needs, especially if they were regular customers. Many luncheon customers were regular clients and we got to know them and all their wants and desires, and they got to know us, and liked to know our names.

The majority of the lunch time trade customers were business people from the City and the newspaper world. And so from Mondays to Fridays it was a lot of running about. The Grill Room being below ground level, it could get a bit warm, especially during the summer weather. Although it was a pretty even temperature.

I was in the same brigade as my cousin Jim Taylor, so we worked the same times each day. Our late night, when we finished about 11 o'clock we went home together. We used to catch a tram on the Embankment which ran straight past our house. The early night, which was 9 o'clock, Jim would go off somewhere, but he always had his own key if he was late getting home.

As for myself, I used to go straight home. By the time I'd finished, gone to my locker, washed and changed into my outdoor clothes, waited for a tram to take me home, it was always gone 10 o'clock when I got in, and that was the early night. Of course there was always somebody up at that time, they never went to bed very early, as Dad never finished work till 10 o'clock.

Saturday was always on the quiet side, unless there was any special occasion in London which would draw people there. On Saturday night the Grill Room closed at 10 o'clock. When the last of the customers had left, the fifteen or so members of the brigade on late duty got their jackets off. During ordinary working times, the carpet cleaners were always used, but Saturday night was when the bass brooms were brought out. These were big, with deep heads made of piassava fibre.

The waiters would top each table with another one and get them moved out of the way, while the commis waiters would take the brooms. The waiters used to see that something was strewn over the carpet to keep the dust down, I don't know what it was. And then as there were always seven or eight commis to do the sweeping they would line up and make a start, working to the middle, and after a few laughs, the job soon got done and the tables put back in place, with their green baize undercloths.

The Lounge was also done, as not many people sat there late evening, most people used the Palm Court upstairs for late drinking or coffee. That was the regular Saturday night performance, ready for Monday. Sunday the Grill Room was closed, so that was our day off.

It came to my turn one morning to do the linen job. As I've already explained, all used linen was put to one side in the pantry, mostly tablecloths and serviettes. These had to be counted accurately, then put into the linen basket, and then with a bit of help, got upstairs, along the gangway to the back where the timekeeper's office was. But we turned to the left where the service lift was which took us up to the ninth floor where the linen room was situated. I soon found it out, and it seemed quite pleasant to see a few young ladies busy working. I think they seemed quite happy to see a fresh face.

As time went by, although I was beginning to get on quite well with my job, I began to realize that one had to give all their time to the hotel. As I had been used to free evenings and seeing different friends for a bit of gossip, I began to feel a bit isolated. Still I thought, I must get adjusted to the new life and give it a trial. I was working with a lot of quite decent fellows, all about my age, and as I was off on Sundays, I should have to make up for lost time then.

George Oliver I didn't see so much, as I was told that he was working nights. I did see Len Wohlgemuth, he said he was getting on all right at work.

Sundays at home carried on the same as usual. In the morning Gert liked to help Mum and study her cooking. Arthur, cousin Lil's son, would be downstairs keeping us company. In the afternoon in summer time, providing the weather was good, our mother with Dad and perhaps Uncle George liked to have their stroll over to the parks, St James's Park and Green Park, and probably listen to the band, and call in somewhere on the way home to have a drink.

My Sundays now were nearly always booked up for something to do, or somewhere to go, although I did like to be home for Sunday dinner.

In the front garden at 86 Kennington Road, late 1920s: standing (left to right), Gert, Sid, Vic, Lal and Win; seated, Dad and Mum

Since my cousin Jim Taylor had been working at the hotel, he'd joined the football team, and in the summer time he liked to keep himself fit. He'd been told that he could keep up training if he went to Battersea Park, where there was a proper running track complete with pavilion containing dressing rooms, showers, and massaging if needed. This was all for a small charge.

Jim asked me if I knew where it was, and I told him I knew it from schooldays. I was also interested in it myself, I said I would take him there as we could get a tram from the Lambeth Baths. Since working in the hotel, I realized I was seeing very little daylight. One alternate day I got a three hour break in the afternoon at 3 o'clock, but it amounted really to about two hours, after washing and changing to go off duty and the same to start again at 6 o'clock.

The other alternate day, we started at 11 o'clock and didn't come out again until 9 o'clock in the evening, unless, whilst on afternoon standby duty, we slipped outside across the road to the Italian café for a cup of tea and a chat. So that's what created my interest in the running track. As I've always had an interest in athletics, I thought a run in the fresh air would help to keep me fit.

And so, this is what we did, and although there were quite a lot of people there, there was still plenty of room, and I really enjoyed it. It was something I kept up for a long time afterwards. I also noted that there was a good boating lake there with two bird islands in the middle.

Quite a lot of boats were out, being Sunday morning I suppose, and I thought when I got a chance I'd go out for a row, especially if I could get a skiff with a sliding seat. Still, that would have to wait. Sundays seemed to fly by, especially if you were fully occupied, and so it didn't seem very long before one was back at work on Monday morning.

One thing I had noticed at work. There were always three or four of the older ones, mainly the chef waiters, who liked to have a gamble. They rigged up some boxes amongst the lockers where we changed, and made a table to lay the cards on, and then it was all go. This was my cousin Jim Taylor's favourite. He was a proper gambler. This often carried on at different times, although with caution, especially on late nights, as they must be careful of the night duty fireman looking in, he could make a report.

I think there was one good thing about my job which I felt satisfied about. I suppose I must be a bit lucky in having a good waiter to work with. Since I'd worked with him, Len Higgins had taught me quite a lot, and things seemed to be going along so much easier. He'd been like another brother.

We had a special customer Mondays to Fridays at 12.30 for lunch. This man was always on his own, and he was also prompt on time. His name was Mr Hill, and he was of the British American Tobacco Company. He was American. He liked to have a Dry Martini cocktail on the table as soon as he sat down, he never liked to be kept waiting. He always used to come down the other end of the room which led from the main reception hall upstairs.

Of course his table was always kept reserved for him, so the next thing was to have his cocktail on the table as soon as he sat down. He wanted it to be really ice cold, otherwise he wouldn't drink it, and got very annoyed. He was a very short and stout man and very smart. And so to keep to his wishes, the main part of our job, I used to go up to the Lounge and stand by the cashier's desk, so that I could look towards the end of the Lounge to the stairway there. I used to wait, until I saw the first signs of a pair of short fat legs, and then I would rush into the service bar and get the girl to make up the cocktail and shake it in ice.

If the girl was quick and not otherwise occupied, I should be down with his cocktail on a silver tray whilst he was just sitting down. Of course where we were working was in the extension room, so that was quite a little way before he reached his table. This went on for two or three years. We had some very good regular customers for lunch time.

I was beginning to understand the menu, it was mainly in French. It was a large menu with quite a variety, mostly a la carte, also with special dishes of the day. Everything was served in silver dishes except grills which were cooked behind the mirrored partition, and served on plates. The portions of food were very plentiful and often customers would not eat the whole amount.

The remains would be kept outside in the hotplate, which was like a large oven, and kept hot in case the customer still felt hungry, otherwise we finished it. As I began to feel established in a first class hotel, I got to study proper manners, and, especially in the Grill Room, table and eating manners.

Back at home Gert had joined a dramatic club with Len Wohlgemuth and one or two of his girlfriends. It was only a short way past our house but on the opposite side. It was run by the Lady Margaret Hall Settlement, as they had about four houses they used. At the rear there was a stage built, so that helped to create some interest.

I was beginning to think of my own interests, the piano and violin. I just didn't have the time to practise on the violin, I could play one or two kinds of tunes, which gave our cat the bellyache. As for the piano, I could play what I wanted to, but I didn't have the time to do a lot more practice. One funny thing, talking about the piano. The front room where the piano was, it was two rooms made into one.

The room had to be divided with a curtain across the middle and the back room made into a bedroom for Mum and Dad, whilst their own bedroom was being altered. Of course the piano was in the other part of the room.

It was well into the night when everybody was fast asleep, when suddenly the piano started playing. Dad said it woke him up and then he woke Mum up, she wanted to know who it was making such noise at that time of night. It went a bit quiet, and they thought they heard someone moving about. Then something got knocked on to the floor which made more noise. Then they heard the scales being played up and down on the piano. So Dad said: "We'll have to get up and find out who it is."

Vic's mother, at the gate of Grandma's cottage, Lambourn (left), and in the front garden at 86 Kennington Road (above)

He picked up the walking stick he kept in the room, and both trooped silently over to peep through the dividing curtain. It was quite a relief, it was only the cat. As there was a door to each room that led out into the passage, Mum said she shut the door to that room when she went to bed, and I suppose the cat was sleeping in there, and afterwards found he was locked in. I don't know why he went on to the piano. Still it caused a bit of a laugh afterwards. I'd never heard of a cat playing the piano.

We did have two dogs at different times, they belonged to my brother Lal. The first one died after a short while, I think he had something wrong with him. The second one, a nice little dog, we called him Rusty, we had him for quite a long time. One day he managed to get out, and then was run over and killed, so Lal wouldn't have any more dogs.

He seemed to be a bit unlucky with pets. At one time, he fixed up a chicken run at the end of our back yard, and then had two or three chickens. He used to go out most evenings, and it was one time when my cousin Jim Taylor happened to be home that he and my brother Sid had a game in the yard with a ball.

The ball got knocked over to the back of the chicken run, and so, to retrieve the ball, one had to climb over the top of the run, and in doing so, it all collapsed. Between them Sid and Jim tried to do their best with it, when Lal got home later on they had to tell him. I don't think he was very pleased as he got rid of the chickens the end of the week.

At work, quite a few customers who drank coffee liked Cona Coffee. This we had to make on our sideboards with a small spirit lamp using methylated spirit. As I'd been at my job for quite a time now, I always did this if Len Higgins was busy or otherwise occupied. And so, during one early evening at dinner, I had to finish making the coffee and blow the lamp out. When I picked the lamp up the flame seemed to spread to my face. For one minute it was all confusion.

A couple of customers jumped up to come to my aid, but the commis who was working next to us rushed up to me and with his serviette covered my face. I felt a bit shaky, but I was told a car was waiting to take me to hospital and the other boy came with me.

I went to Charing Cross Hospital and they examined me. My eyes were all right, but parts of my face needed attention and had to be covered with a kind of mask. I was told to attend hospital every day, and so I was escorted home in the car. Of course it created a bit of panic when I got there, but after explanations everything settled down. After thanking the other boy who kept with me all the time he went back to the hotel in the car to tell them about the situation.

I didn't feel any pain, but I couldn't go back to work until I was discharged by the hospital. I thought at least I could do a bit of practice on the piano. And so I attended hospital each day for about three weeks. During that time, I had a visit from the Head Waiter and second Head Waiter. They spent nearly the whole afternoon at home, and were glad to see I was making good progress.

They said it seemed strange that a thing like that should happen. Cona Coffee had been in use for quite a long time, and always used the same method. Apparently I was the only one ever involved in an accident like that. The solution would be for Cona Coffee to issue a safer type of lamp with their machines.

My cousin Jim Taylor missed all this excitement and bustle, as he had the week off. He wanted a summer season job, and so, he had made an application to a hotel at Cowes, in the Isle of Wight. He was to start in a month's time, and had gone down to make further arrangements. So that would be one less at home. There had been three or four changes in the staff since I'd been there, one was my other cousin Jim Gamble. He had left, but I'd heard no more of him.

After three weeks, the hospital finished peeling off my bits of loose skin on my face, everything was all right and I was now discharged.

15. OPERA SEASON IN THE GENERAL STRIKE

A General Strike was about to start in sympathy with the coal miners. The main trouble would be the transport, trams, buses and trains. As for myself, it was only a short tram ride, so I thought, why not walk. So that's what I did. I went through the market called the New Cut, past Waterloo Station, over Waterloo Bridge and then I was more or less at my destination. But the tram went round the Embankment to Savoy Street, not a lot of difference.

Still I couldn't grumble, as we had another commis, same age as me who lived right near Epping Forest, a much longer journey. His name was Charlie Brown. I think he had a brother or sister, but his mother was a widow. He was a bit worried about getting home at night, as he travelled on the Underground.

It was now back to work after my accident with quite a few smiling faces to greet me. Len Higgins said he had been rather worried as he was concerned for my eyes. It was a very busy lunch period. I thought it would have been the opposite as the strike had started. On my way to work that morning I noticed there were quite a few buses running, being driven by private volunteers. It created big business for the taxis, especially as it was the month of May, then the start of the opera season at Covent Garden.

This was when we prepared for the evening dinner rush. The Waldorf was very convenient in being situated near the Opera House and I can explain why. The season started with German opera, in which the best known to be sung were very long running, and commenced about 4.30 or 5 o'clock in the afternoon. This meant there was a short break for dinner, roughly 6.30 till 7.45 pm. There was always a large audience for these operas, and we saw the same faces every year. It was quite a rush when it meant taxi or car from the Opera House, dinner, toilet and return. It meant the same for the people who went to the Savoy or Cecil hotels. Still it didn't go on for long, about four weeks, and then the Italian opera took over with normal times. This always seemed such a colourful time as everyone was wearing evening dress. Quite a lot of elderly ladies had followed the opera for quite a number of years and still wore the gowns they had had since they were young.

We had a customer that came here twice a year, always at opera time and later on during the year. Her name was Miss Murphy, and she came over from Dublin. I presume she was a business woman, as she never came in to lunch, but she always brought an elderly lady in to dinner with her, an old friend Len Higgins told me.

Anyway if they were going to an opera performance, they would be wearing their evening gowns, Miss Murphy a more modern gown, the elderly lady's much before my time, but still, she looked outstanding. As they liked to know our names, they would always greet us with a smile, and ask if we were keeping well. This helped to make the day go well, as we did occasionally have the odd type of customer who could be awkward, and perhaps temperamental.

During the strike, it meant walking home. On late nights it was a bit late getting home, just after midnight, but it was nice to walk through the cool air. I asked Charlie Brown how he'd been getting on, he said it was different every day, and you just had to trust to luck. He was allowed to leave early every evening whilst the trouble lasted.

The miners from Scotland and the North and the Midlands marched down to London, and it seemed they were getting every support. There seemed to be quite a few more buses running, all being driven by civilian volunteers, with a policeman on board as escort. Lil's husband Syd Reading, who was a bus driver, reported to his garage every day as normal, as the other drivers did, but that was all, they just used to stay at the garage.

16. PAUL ROBESON AT DRURY LANE

The number of theatres close by always helped to keep our evening trade busy. This time it was the other way around. It was early evening when Pat from the cloakroom came down with a phone message from the Theatre Royal, Drury Lane. Of course he gave the message to the Head Waiter who passed it on to Len Higgins. It was for sandwiches, chicken if possible, to be delivered to Mr Paul Robeson at the theatre.

Len made out an order for a double portion of chicken sandwiches for me to take up to the larder for the chef to make up and to get them neatly wrapped for delivery. After bringing them down, when that was completed, Len made out a bill, as he found that Paul Robeson wasn't a resident at the hotel. Then he told me, that I had to take them to the theatre and bring the bill back to be cashed.

And so I took the packet and went out our usual way at the back entrance, across the road just a short way along and I passed the front of the theatre. People were already lining up. I then turned the corner to go quite a distance along to the stage door, I asked the stage doorkeeper for Mr Paul Robeson. He wanted to know the reason. When I told him he went on the phone, and then told me to take the sandwiches to the dressing room. He showed me where to make for.

After I found my way, I knocked at the door. It was opened by the dresser. I said why I was there, then I heard the deep voice call out from inside: "Come in, boy, I could eat a goddam horse!" And so, I gave him the sandwiches, which I hoped would satisfy him before curtain up. And also the bill, which the dresser settled up with me and a bit extra for myself. I thanked them, and went back to work. I was told afterwards Mr Robeson had been delayed, which often happened at the gramophone recording studios which gave him no time for a meal break.

It was a change to hear the American twang, as then the talking pictures had not properly entered the entertainment world and it was only by American tourists or business men you heard the twang.

On another occasion, during the morning when I was on early duty, I was working on the Lounge on my own as it only needed one to clean the tables and put them straight and see that things were in order. I noticed two people coming down the stairs which led from the main part of the building, which was the Reception Hall, Palm Court, Restaurant, and Breakfast Room on the other side of the Restaurant.

They walked into the Lounge, the older man was quite a small man, rather dark with a small moustache, the other was a bit taller, but much younger, not much older than me. I just carried on dusting and they were looking around, when they came over and spoke to me. The older man said he was looking around as he had not been down this part of the hotel before. He spoke good but what I call foreign English.

Towards the end of the week, we always had a small card to put on every table to note the Sunday evening concert that was held in the Palm Court with the orchestra under Signor Mantovani, and noted singers. And so, as he was telling me that he'd been busy up in the music room which was above the Ballroom, I realized who he was.

I said: "Excuse me, sir, but would you be Signor Mantovani?" He smiled and said: "Yes, and this is my son." The son became one of the most noted band leaders of the day.

17. WALKING TOUR OVER EXMOOR

We were going to be allowed a half day off during the week. It would be from 3 o'clock, as, on the whole, the dinner period was much quieter than the lunch rush. It was arranged for the extension room to be closed for dinner, which would allow staff to take their half day. It was a pleasure to be able to go out and have a look around, although it meant being on my own. I didn't like going to the cinema during the summer, unless there was anything special to see.

One thing I did like to do during the summer, and that was something I had promised myself some time ago, I did enjoy boating. I now spent my spare time on the lake in Regent's Park, where it was a lovely lake and a good selection of boats. I managed to get a skiff, which I preferred, and it was really enjoyable. Otherwise, I did find a lot of pleasure in walking my way about London, to find where different places were, and what it looked like.

I still managed to have a little run round on the running track at Battersea Park on a Sunday morning. I did manage to go to church now and again, but there always seemed so much to do on a Sunday. My friend George Oliver called round at home once or twice when he was off work, and it was the same with my friend Len Wohlgemuth but only occasionally, as I was not always there.

I did happen to be quite pally with a young chap at the hotel, he worked in the pantry. He lived with his family near St Thomas's Hospital. I knew him as Alan, and his parents came from a Scandinavian country, but he was born in England. He was a good reader, also a keen cyclist and walker. He told me about a book he'd been reading called *Lorna Doone*. He'd been very interested in it, also the type of country it mentions, and so he asked me if we could both do a walking tour over Exmoor and the 'Doone country'. As I'd already told him I was a lover of the fresh air, I suppose that's why he asked me as he said he didn't feel like going on his own.

At the end of August we started our tour, I had a rucksack which just carried my bare essentials, the same with Alan. We made our way by train and bus to Porlock in Somerset, and that's where we started walking. We made for Dunkery Beacon, and then on to the Lorna Doone country, visiting all the different places named in the book. It proved very interesting. Alan had arranged to make it a four day tour as he had to get back home. As Mum and Dad were spending their holiday at Lambourn, I suggested to Alan that I leave the train at Newbury, whilst he carried on to London.

At Newbury I caught our Lambourn train, just a little tank engine and two carriages on behind, to cover the twelve miles, stopping at seven stations or halts. Apart from signal failure or trouble of any kind it was always dead on time. The journey used to take about thirty five to forty minutes. The train used to start from Lambourn about 8 o'clock in the morning, and the last train arrived there about 8 pm. There were, I think, five trains a day, and one goods train.

Often there would be a racehorse which had to travel to a race meeting. According to how many horses were travelling, there was either the single or double box, and they would be attached to one of the trains when needed. As there were quite a few trainers in and around Lambourn, there would be quite a few horses travelling to the same meeting. Then it meant a train of horseboxes on its own. In those days it was the only method of transport and the only way to get the horses to a station was to walk them.

Mum, Dad and me travelled home on the Sunday. During the early years, there were no Sunday trains on the Lambourn line, but now there was a train about 5 pm to Newbury which then got on to the Didcot line. We didn't have to wait long at Newbury for a London train about 6 pm, which stopped at Reading and then Paddington.

70

18. SINGAPORE WORK OFFER

A friend of the family, Mr Clarke, belonged to the Corps of Commissionaires. I think that was something to do with ex army personnel, they wore a uniform, and he used to be on duty outside branch offices of the water tube boiler makers Babcock and Wilcox in the Kingsway, which turns off just past the Waldorf. I often saw him if I went along that way when I was off duty.

One day he called me to one side. He told me the firm were looking for applicants for office work with the chance of travel, and would I like him to put my name through. I gave it a thought and agreed, to see what happened. A few weeks later, I received a packet of examination papers through the post for me to fill in. I managed to answer all the questions, although some were a bit tricky.

Quite a few weeks after that I received a reply. I had passed my exam except for one item. Could I just improve on my grade for writing, and they would contact me later on. When I was walking along the Kingsway, I told Mr Clarke, he told me that it was for young personnel for their large new office in Singapore.

After dreaming about all these picturesque places abroad, I suddenly changed my mind and thought of all the friends at home. I can still remember how I worried about it. I thought, have I turned the chance of a good job down, as Mr Clarke had told me that the wages were good. But no, I still belonged to London and that was where I'd stay. I intended to stay put at least for the time being, as when I looked around there was still so much unemployment about.

Mr Clarke and his wife and two boys often visited us on a Sunday evening. I thought it very good of him to put my name through.

We began to prepare for Christmas. At home it was the usual, busy buying presents. Our mother always started to make the Christmas puddings early, as she liked to make three or four. As for myself, I had to work Christmas Day. The Grill Room would be open for lunch only, the Restaurant upstairs was being prepared for the Christmas evening dinner. Of course everything up there and in the Palm Court had been decorated. There would be dinner with concert, that is the orchestra which always played there, and noted singers.

We didn't expect a busy lunch, no outside customers, it would be hotel residents, although the majority would pass lunch and wait for dinner. That's how it turned out. The extension room was closed, so as we waited for customers, we sat down and made ourselves comfortable there. M Otts, the Manager, was off duty, so it was the second Head who was in charge.

We just had a few customers, and when the room was finally cleared it was still early. The lights were dimmed and we were told to clear the tables, then to lay a table for the staff on duty. There was a Christmas dinner ready in the kitchen for us. The Head Waiter and the chef waiters did all the serving, with also a few bottles of wine. This turned out quite a surprise. As soon as it was over, we cleared up, the lights were turned out, and we all went our own way.

There was Sunday service transport until 12 o'clock mid day and after that all transport stopped for the rest of the day. I found out afterwards that arrangements were made as best as possible for the staff on duty to be those living nearest to the hotel, although some paid to have the day off, so we only had half the staff on duty. It was about 5 o'clock when we left the hotel. I walked home.

19. BOGNOR BY MOTORBIKE

Time marches on, waiting for the next thing to happen, and something did happen. I was promoted to chef waiter. I was given a station to work and a commis. I had to go up to the control office to get my check books and bill book and then I was all right. I must mention about the control office. This was where all the check slips that had been through the kitchen and service bar were collected to compare with the appropriate bill. If there was any deficiency in the bill, the responsibility lay with the waiter who was involved.

I don't know if all the other large hotels ran on the same system but I'll just explain how we worked. The commis waiters got what you might call a full wage, and the chef waiters just a small one, as well as tips. I think the Head Waiters were the same. The amount we received was according to the tronc system.

Along to the centre of the Grill Room stood a large partition which was all glass mirrored and hid the grill. In front was a large marbled counter which held cold meats and other necessities like Cona Coffee machines. On a small shelf in the middle stood the tronc box. This was about nine or ten inches square, the lid had a lock, and key attached, and a slit on top to put coins in.

A chef waiter cashed the customer's bill at the cashier's desk, he then returned it to the customer's table, together with the receipt bill. It was the regular habit for all customers to leave a tip, they were mostly on the same average, but quite a few were very good. The majority of customers always left the receipt bill along with the tip and the waiter then put his name on the back of the bill, and the amount, wrapped it up with the tip and put it into the tronc box. At the end of each day it was always M Murielle, the third Head Waiter, who checked the tronc box over. M Murielle was Swiss, but I think he'd been in England a long time as he spoke perfect English. As the extension room was now closed for the dinner period he went in there, switched a few chandeliers on and sat at one of the large round tables in a corner. Two or three other waiters who hadn't any customers left would go in with him. They made themselves comfortable, lit up a cigarette and then emptied the tronc box on to the green baize tabletop.

M Murielle had the book, one waiter opened each packet, called out the name and the amount, another stacked the money up to be checked. All this was entered in the book and after the amount had been checked again, it was put into the box which was locked and kept overnight in the cupboard where the cigars and speciality cigarettes were. Next day the box was taken up to the cashier's office.

M Murielle was responsible for working out the weekly wage for everybody, Head Waiters, chef waiters and the commis waiters, everybody in their order. He always had to keep the books in order, for when the tax inspector called to check on our annual wage.

Now I had been upgraded, with my commis by my side I was working on my own. My commis was quite a small lad, a bit younger than me and he came from Gateshead up in the North. He told me about all the unemployed in the North and that was the reason he'd come to London. He said he was fixed up for 'digs' and it all seemed a bit strange to him down here, so I'd just keep an eye on him.

I was still in the extension room, so I knew all the regular luncheon customers that came in there. Once or twice I'd had to go into Soho to see Marcus, the tailor, about a new jacket, and when any alterations were needed. In fact I'd got quite used to Soho. The first time I went to see Marcus, my cousin Jim Taylor had taken me but we didn't see anything of Jim these days. We didn't know if he was still working on the Isle of Wight or where, but we didn't worry.

My older brother Sid used to work in the City, but the firm closed down quite some time ago, and he had been without a job since then, and there didn't seem much hope for the future. He spent quite a bit of time in the evenings down with Dad at the Brewery Tap. Right opposite the Tap were the Queen's Buildings, a block of flats where Mr and Mrs Fitzgerald and family lived and Sid often called over there as he had become friendly with the family.

Mr Fitzgerald who was Irish was a rather tall and well built man, quite pleasant, and Mrs Fitzgerald was on the small side, from a Scotch family, and for quite a time was a Sunday School teacher. Kate was the eldest of the family. She grew up just like her dad, with a bit more fat, but always singing and happy. Cis came next. She suffered from a form of neuralgia in her face and was under hospital treatment from when she was young, but made a great improvement, except her eye. May and Charlie were the youngest and they were the twins.

Kate was an expert needlewoman, and she worked for a private firm who did the court dressmaking and if I think right, she did most needlework for Queen Mary. Cis followed the same type of work. May, she worked in millinery. Charlie and his father worked for Spicer's, the paper makers, in their main office near Ludgate Circus, not far from St Paul's Cathedral. Charlie went there straight from school, he was a clerical worker.

Sometimes Sid brought May to tea on a Sunday and a musical evening. Sometimes on a Friday or Saturday evening Mum would go down to meet Mrs Fitzgerald to have a drink and a chat, and then come home with Dad after he had closed, which was 10 o'clock. And that's when they sometimes brought home fish and chips for supper, as there was a good fish and chip shop near the Brewery Tap, with the name of 'Old Lui's', he was Italian, Luigi.

It's surprising how time seems to pass along so quick when you're not thinking about it. In September 1928 a baby daughter, Joyce, was born to my cousin Lil Reading, so Arthur now had a sister. Alice Wohlgemuth and Bill had a very nice wedding in June 1929, and it meant meeting quite a few fresh faces.

I liked Bill's parents very much, also his brother. Bill and Alice had a flat in Clerkenwell, where Len and I would often go over to see them, either on a Saturday or Sunday morning, and there were also occasional visits to Bill's parents' home in Islington for Sunday tea.

Also, in September that year my brother Lal married Dolly at the church on Kew Green. Dolly lived with her sister Ethel who was married to my cousin Cecil, and they all lived at that time with Cecil's parents, Uncle Jim and Auntie Alice, so that was where the reception was held. We all had quite a pleasant time at the wedding.

It was during the summer 1929 when Len Higgins and a couple of the other waiters each went and bought a motorbike, they had always been interested in motorbikes. This was the time before cars became popular, as they were very few and also expensive. Len and the others made full use of their bikes in the time they had to spare, and gradually became qualified.

And so, some time later on, Len asked me if I would like to go with them on their next Sunday out. I said yes. I told them at home I should be going out for the day, our mother said she didn't mind as long as I was careful. Sunday came, and I had to meet Len and the others, Mario and Antony, at the back of the hotel as they didn't actually know where I lived. I rode pillion on Len's bike. It proved a bit exciting for me as I don't think at that time there were many who rode pillion or come to that who rode motorbikes.

So we started off, and on the way we passed our house, and I thought we were probably going to Epsom or Reigate in Surrey, or somewhere like that. Anyway we carried on through the countryside, most of the time we seemed to be on our own, not much traffic. I was really enjoying it, we just kept at a steady speed.

When I consider motorbikes' speed at the present day, we must have been crawling along. Then I began to smell the sea air. It wasn't long before we were in Bognor in West Sussex. It was a lovely day, and rather quiet there and inclined to be a bit reserved, but otherwise very nice. We stopped on the front, had an ice cream, and after a cigarette and a talk. Antony said he enjoyed the run down, but the scenery wasn't like Italy.

I asked him if he was born in Italy. He said no, he was born in England but his parents were Italian. He went to Italy twice a year with his parents to see relatives. As for Mario, he didn't seem all that interested in scenery, he was more interested in racehorses and race meetings and he liked a gamble. Otherwise he was very comical at times.

And so, after we had a look for a place to eat we had a slow walk round and then back on the beach for another lay about. After a cup of tea, we thought about making for home. We told the other two to go their own way, as I didn't know what part of London they lived in. And so we made a gentle run home. We lost the other two somewhere at Brixton but I got dropped off right outside the house. I asked Len to come in, but he wouldn't stop, and so after I thanked him for an enjoyable day, he rode off. It was just early evening.

After I'd got indoors and they'd asked me where I'd been, I told them Bognor, and they asked if I'd seen the King there. I thought for a minute, and then I realized. The King, after his illness, had been moved some time earlier to a place called Craigwell House, a large house right on the front, and that was where he was spending his convalescence. I'd given no thought to it at the time, but visiting Bognor on later dates, I looked to see where the house was.

About this time there was an outbreak of smallpox. Quite a lot of people contracted the disease including Lil, Joyce, Win, Gert and Jean. Apparently, according to the medical world, this was a mild outbreak, but no chances were taken. All the patients from south

London area were taken to Joyce Green Hospital which was an isolation hospital situated just the other side of Dartford, near the river, and mostly marshland. All the people left at home were living in fear of contracting the disease, as we were. Those that were taken to hospital were kept away for quite a long time, but after they came back they said they were treated well and kept happy. It gradually died down.

Later on in the year I had a holiday at Lambourn, and Len Wohlgemuth came with me. We had quite an enjoyable time. He told me he thought he'd got an aunt that lived in Woolstone in the Vale of the White Horse. One day, we decided to hike over there to try and find her. We went via Upper Lambourn and then turned off on to the downs, and carried on until we came to the bridleway which runs over the top of White Horse Hill.

This is where you get a good view of many miles around. And so, now it was downhill all the way into the Vale of the White Horse. And

Charabanc outings to Lambourn, 1930s, with family and friends (above), and seated behind each other (left) Len, Mr Fitzgerald, Dad

then to find Woolstone. I just can't remember if we were lucky in finding Len's aunt, but it proved a good day's hike. Another day, we borrowed a couple of bicycles and had a good cycle round and then went to Ashdown House, an historic house three or four miles from Lambourn and two from Ashbury.

We had two or three more holidays like that in different years with others of the family, and also my friend George Oliver managed to come one year. We used to stay with Mr and Mrs Moss who were friends of ours and lived in Mill Lane. For two or three years we managed to run a Sunday charabanc trip to Lambourn with enough relatives and friends to fill the charabanc up. Mr Staddon, who kept the Lamb Inn, arranged lunch for us, and that was held in the back garden. They each turned out to be a good trip.

I was reminded of Lambourn at work. During the lunch period I was still working in the extension room. It seemed as though it was divided into two sections because there was a double sideboard in the middle back to back, one facing one way and one the other. That meant three waiters and commis waiters working each side with one Head Waiter each side. I was working with Len Higgins and Paul Munday.

The Head Waiter on the other side was Italian but he spoke natural English. He was rather tall and fair, which doesn't seem Italian. Although he didn't seem all that old, he was married with a wife and grown up daughter. He lived in Covent Garden. I got to know quite a few Italian boys at work, and they all seemed to be the same, you would think they were English when they spoke. It was their parents who came over from Italy years ago and settled in this country. This Head Waiter's name was Marcocelli, all knew him as just Marco. He was very popular with the lunch time customers.

The Chairman of the hotel company was Sir Frederick Eley and when they had a Board meeting in the hotel, Marco always had a table reserved for them. It was the same table each time, and if Sir

Frederick came down on his own or with a friend, he would always use the same table. One day he was lunching with a friend, although I didn't take much notice of them, as the table wasn't on my side, and I was more interested in my own customers. After a while when things were quietening down, and everybody was in the coffee stage and busy talking, Marco came over, and said Sir Frederick wanted to talk to me.

And so Marco took me over. Sir Frederick said his friend was interested in me, as he had told him I was from Lambourn. He said: "This is my trainer, Mr Templeman," and then I understood. Sir Frederick owned racehorses, and they were trained by Freddie Templeman at Lambourn. Freddie wanted to know all about my family name, I said I came from the Taylor family who were butchers in Lambourn. After asking me a few more questions he let me go.

Although I knew Freddie Templeman by sight, I never troubled to see who it was with Sir Frederick. All the time I could just glimpse everybody's eyes on me. When I came away from the table, I said to Marco: "How did Sir Frederick know I came from Lambourn?" He said: "I told him. I thought he might have given you a winner."

I was beginning to get moved around a bit. I moved to two or three different stations in the main Grill Room, and so was getting used to fresh regular customers. One good customer who came to lunch every day was Mr W D Roome. He was a director of the Daily Mirror Group, and, in the 1930s, the general manager. He used to first sit up in the Lounge with an apéritif and talk with business friends, but always came down to lunch at 2.30 when things were beginning to quieten off a bit.

Then he would often like to have a little chat with me or my Head Waiter, who now happened to be M Moran, a dumpy little Frenchman. Often Mr Roome mentioned his yacht which was moored in Poole Harbour, he used it mainly for his holiday and other times during the summer. Altogether he was a very nice man.

20. NEIGHBOURS DANCE TO CHAPEL TUNE

We had a church one house away from us, and it was fairly large, with a grass frontage, and a path leading up to the front steps and main door. It was a Presbyterian church, but after a while, it closed down. It had a railing along the front with the main entrance gate which was locked. And so this stood empty for quite a long while.

Then one day we noticed a small type of man, wearing a bowler hat, looking quite proud of himself, unlocking the gate, and standing there looking up at the old name of the church, marked across the front. After that, he unlocked the main door and went in. A few days later, we noticed him outside with two or three other men, and two or three women carrying ladders and buckets, so we supposed they were going to clean the place up.

A few days later the men came to put a ladder up the front, and paint out the old name. Of course, we couldn't stand and watch them all day, but after a few days, we noticed painted over the entrance door in bold black lettering the name PECULIAR PEOPLE'S CHAPEL. We thought it must be a new religion.

For about a week, the small man we first saw would turn up, just go inside and stand looking up at the name for quite a few minutes and then lock the gate again. Then, on one Sunday following, we saw quite a few people going in, they all seemed to be carrying small bags or bundles with them. The chapel had windows on the side so we could hear everything that was going on.

Every Saturday and Sunday, right into the evening, they used to start off very quiet and then gradually got louder and louder, shouting. And then it was the stamping, and being on a wooden floor, it sounded twice as loud. They always brought their food with them, I think they looked forward to a good knees up every weekend.

Our neighbours next door to the chapel, Mr and Mrs Harris, we got on all right with them although they liked a drink occasionally. It was mostly at weekends when they would go over to the Tankard public house across the road, to meet all their friends. It was during one Saturday afternoon, when they came back after the pub had closed, and I suppose a bit the worse for drink. We'd always found them not disagreeable type of people, and when they were in this state they would sing to each other. They would hold each other's arms.

And so we began to hear a lot of noise and shouting next door, and then it seemed a lot of running about, and then it sounded as if they'd run out into their back yard. The back yards to our houses were rather small, with a wall about five feet high dividing each one. Now their back yard was larger, and towards the end it was all grass that finished up in a mound. So, as we got a bit interested, we went upstairs, as we could see better out of the back windows. There were about three or four of us at home.

Mrs Harris was running round the yard, Mr Harris was trying to catch her. They had a little dog and this was running round as well and barking, and then Mr Harris caught up with Mrs Harris. With a lot more shouting and a wrestling match, they worked over towards the back of the yard on to the grass mound when they both fell over, him on the top, when the dog jumped on top of him. It was just like a circus. And then the chapel started.

After lying on the grass for a bit and getting their breath back, they started to help each other up, and I suppose, hearing the noise from the chapel, they both started to dance. Well we thought that was the limit. It was then Rosie the daughter came out, grabbed each, one at a time, and bundled them into the house. So that ended our afternoon's entertainment, and now calls for a cup of tea.

During these times, there were songs of the day being published. Some were very popular which always started people singing. I think we were beginning to listen to music through the wireless, as radio was called. Anyway there was this song, a comic song and most popular with the youngsters, and one line in the chorus went 'Look at your Grandma, bloomin' ol' haybag'.

Rosie Harris married, her husband was called Bunny, and they had a little boy. Mum told us that she'd been to do some shopping in the Lambeth Walk when she met Rosie, pushing her son along in the push chair. They stopped to have a chat. Rosie's mother happened to come along, and when she saw them, she came over. She first bent down to say: "How's my little grandson?" He shouted to her: "Bloomin' ol' haybag." Rosie shouted to him: "You mustn't call your grandmother a haybag." With that Mum thought she would say cheerio, and let them get on with it.

Our neighbours next door in No. 84, our old house, were quite all right. I think they took over when we moved. They were Mr and Mrs Cuffe. He was an Irishman, a foreman on building and road works. His wife was Norwegian. When he used to come home on Saturday afternoons, and probably Gert or I were about outside when we were younger, he'd always be smiling and looking happy as though he'd had a few drinks, but he would always throw a handful of coppers over to us. They seemed to get on well, and when they went out together, she always wore a lot of jewellery.

She called me Wicky, he called me Micky. She liked me to get her errands, she would often call me: "Wicky, will you get me a bit of milk," or sometimes, "a bit of winegar".

The chapel used to carry on the same, every weekend, and I think it used to be quite full, as I could always see plenty of people going in both Saturdays and Sundays. It went on for quite a long time, then it closed down when the new estate was built. I was told they moved to the East End and joined with another chapel.

Part of Wedgwood House taken at Coronation time, June 1953, by Joyce and Arthur Rockhill. On the top balcony, fourth level, the door to Vic's family's old flat, No. 52, is first left, the fanlight window above it open. Next is the open kitchen window, then the door, of No. 39

21. NEW FLAT ON THE CHINA WALK ESTATE

We had been taking a bit of interest in the building work going on around us at home. London County Council was building a new estate, China Walk Estate. Around the back of the house and including Richmond Street and St Albans Street had all been cleared and already new flats had been built. Just our row in the Kennington Road would be the next for demolition.

Before we left the old house, I had an enjoyable 21st birthday party in September 1930, with quite a few nice presents. Quite a few friends and relatives turned up which helped to make a lot of noise. About this time cousin Dot got married to George Lipscombe which was quite a colourful event. Then in the November my sister Win's husband Bert Bowsher died at the age of thirty nine. They had been living with us at Kennington Road.

Len Wohlgemuth and his family had already moved to their new flat. And now we had notice to move to ours, which was in a block of five storeys called Wedgwood House, and it was No. 52. It was a top flat, on the third and fourth floors, so that meant a few stairs to climb up. After we'd managed to obtain the keys we just had to go and have a look around. It consisted of, entrance, hallway, toilet, kitchen-bathroom, and living room with a bedroom leading off. We also had stairs leading up to three bedrooms.

Syd and Lil Reading, who were still living upstairs with us with their two children Arthur and Joyce, had obtained No. 39 next door, not quite so large as ours, with two bedrooms upstairs. Lil's father, Uncle George, would be coming with us. So it was a busy time ahead. An amusing little thing happened just before we moved. Uncle George, who slept in his own bedroom, was getting himself ready to go out, it must have been on a Saturday. After a while, our Mother and Dad could hear him shouting from upstairs. So Dad went to see what the trouble was. Of course Uncle George was wearing a single neck shirt with a collar stud to connect it with his stiff butterfly type of collar. Somehow, as he grew a beard, the collar stud had got mixed up with his whiskers, right under his chin. So Dad thought he would have a try to help.

First they sat on the bed, and then they stood up. Turned this way and that way, but he couldn't seem to make any headway. Poor Uncle George was walking about with his collar hanging from his whiskers. Dad was getting a bit tired so he thought he would call for help. As it happened, my friend George Oliver was downstairs, as he used to like to come round to talk to my brother Sid, or Dad, on football or racing. Upstairs went George. And so he had a try.

First this way, and then the other way. Dad said at one time they were moving around so much they overbalanced and fell back on to the bed. It took longer for my friend George to get up off the bed he was laughing so much. Finally, they decided to get the scissors and cut the collar stud off from Uncle George's beard. I heard all this after I got home from work. Dad said it was like a pantomime.

We began to settle down into our new flat at Wedgwood House. Of course, it was the eight flights of stairs, eight stairs to a flight, that had to be climbed each time you went out, or came home, especially as Dad was getting a bit older and a bit on the stout side, and also as he worked licensing hours. Out in the morning, home at 3, back again at 6 o'clock, finish at 10, that meant four climbs a day. Otherwise, the advantages we got were electric lighting, a bath, even if it was in the kitchen, and indoor toilet.

Our mother was getting more used to the flat, as at the first I think, she missed the old house, and also looking direct out to the main road. But now, we were a bit back from the road with other flats partly in front of us, which partly blocked our view to the road.

22. LUCK AT EPSOM HELPS FOOTBALL TEAM

I had a new commis, as a couple of waiters were leaving, so they'd got to be replaced. The young chap with me would be working for two or three weeks' trial and then as a chef waiter. He'd been a steward working on the liners sailing between Southampton and New York, so he was still in the same profession. He was the same age as me and quite a smart fellow. He was Scotch, and his name was Bruce Patterson. His parents had recently moved to London from Glasgow, and were living at Clapham. That's probably why he'd turned landlubber for a while.

Now he was working on his own station, and he asked me to go with him to meet his mother and father, so we should go on one of our half days, as he still worked the same times as me. We'd been out together on two or three evenings, so that made a change from being on one's own most of the time. He'd been telling me a lot about New York, and life aboard ship.

Bruce told me his parents were moving to a flat in Earl's Court, and when they had settled down, he would take me over there one evening, and to stay to dinner. It was a top flat, but quite nice with plenty of room. He was a bit disappointed as he had expected his sister to be there. She still worked in Glasgow and apparently, through her work, she was unable to come down, and I think he wanted me to meet her. Still I did have a pleasant evening. In fact I had two or three pleasant evenings there afterwards, and Bruce came to our home two or three Sunday evenings.

When I looked around at work, I realized that nearly all the chef waiters who were running their own stations were commis the same time as me, so it still seemed one big family.

Harry Day, the attendant in the cloakroom and toilet up the stairs to the main reception hall, came to me asking if I would be interested in joining the Sports Club Committee. He had asked me two or three times, but I always said I would consider it. But he would never give up, so this time I agreed. This was mainly to start a football team. And so after he'd managed to scramble a couple more from the hotel staff he formed a committee.

Between us we managed to form a team although they weren't all hotel staff. We had a ground in Finchley, which is in north London, and after a few practice matches Harry wanted to join, I think it was, the Hotel Sunday League. Eventually that's what happened and games were played from 10 o'clock Sunday mornings, and that's how we made our start. We did hold a lot of football kit which was getting a bit old. Players had to provide their own boots.

Harry said the hotel used to play football with a scratch team. He said it consisted of most of those who had now left the hotel (my cousin Jim Taylor played for it), although Marco used to play.

Waldorf football team, early 1930s. Vic is in the trilby (right)

They used to go out to the country somewhere near a pub. And every half time they would all run over to the pub. Finally, they never got home till late afternoon.

We had two or three football matches, so I'd been to see how they played. It was a nice bit of fresh air on a Sunday morning, and then home in time for lunch. We hadn't won yet, but we'd got two or three good players. There was always a first time. A complete new football kit for the whole team – jersey, shorts, and socks – was presented to our Sports Club Committee by the actor Tom Walls who was appearing at the Aldwych Theatre next to the hotel.

As I'd had to take some sandwiches down to him once or twice, he asked how the Sports Club was getting on. He owned one or two racehorses, which were trained at Epsom, and as he had been lucky just lately with a few winners, that was the reason for our presentation. In time our team did quite well for itself. They won quite a few matches, and I was made team manager.

At times we were often in contact with theatrical people. I think the actress Miss Evelyn Laye was the one I had most conversation with. I don't know if she was staying in the hotel, although she wasn't appearing in any show. But the first time she came in it was for dinner, and she was shown to one of my tables. She was always on her own, and always very pleasant. On the first evening, most of the evenings being rather quiet and easygoing, she'd finished dinner, and I was pouring her coffee out.

She told me she would be coming in to dinner for another two weeks, so I said I would keep her table reserved. She told me that she had appeared at the Theatre Royal at Drury Lane a few years ago, and she asked me how long I'd been at the hotel, and from then on it was all talk for the next two weeks. At the end, I think she had told me a lot about her earlier life, and of course she would ask me one or two questions. Altogether, she proved to be a very interesting and delightful customer.

23. TIME FOR A LAUGH AT SPEAKERS' CORNER

During the summer, after I'd finished my early evening shift at work, I would make my way to Speakers' Corner at Hyde Park. If you had time to spare, you could get interested, and get a laugh. There were quite a lot of groups, some small, some large, some political, some religious, some just a lot of nonsense but funny.

Mainly the arguments were over either religion or politics. I've seen two people start an argument between themselves over a certain matter. After a while, if I went back to see how they were getting on, there'd be a large crowd around still carrying on about the same subject, but the two people who started the argument had gone.

Then there was always a Welsh crowd, and an Irish crowd. This was because the majority of these people had come to London to work mostly in service or hotels. This was their meeting place, where they kept in touch with each other. During the evening the Welsh and the Irish formed their own circle and started singing. They both had good singing voices, especially the Welsh. It was a pleasure to stand and listen to them or even join in. The Welsh would sing their own hymns, and the Irish their own Irish songs. One thing, everything was orderly, as police were always on duty.

One Saturday evening I went to a party. It was for the daughter of Marco, one of the Head Waiters. She played the piano, and Marco asked me if I could help with the playing. So, after finishing a late night and with two other waiters, we went off to Marco's. He lived just past the Opera House and it was quite a large flat over a salesroom in Covent Garden Market.

There was quite a large crowd there, mostly young people, friends of Marco's daughter I should imagine. I didn't know her age but she seemed to be in her late teens. There was plenty to eat and drink, and everyone was quite friendly. As the party lasted all night, and it happened to be during the summer, the morning soon got light.

It was then two young lads said they were going to make a move home. And so, after another drink and a song, they straightened themselves up a bit, and wanted to know where the 'horse' was. So most of the crowd including us went downstairs to see them off, and for a bit of fresh air. When they eventually came out, it wasn't a 'horse' but a tandem bike. And that's when the fun started, they just couldn't manage to sit on the bike, let alone ride it.

Anyway, with the crowd outside, there were quite a few willing helpers. This lasted about an hour before, after starting off and falling off again, they reached right to the end of the road, when they seemed to have gained their balance, and on they went. I asked Marco on Monday, how far they had to go, and he said Battersea and it was a good job it was a Sunday morning.

Len Higgins had told me that he was engaged, and now he invited me to the wedding. His future wife lived at Fulham, so that was where the wedding took place, at a register office. The reception was held at the bride's family home with quite a good crowd and plenty of everything. What surprised me was, when I was expecting to make my move home in the late evening Len told me that as they'd been given a small house a short way away, arranged by his wife's family, he'd arranged a bedroom for me to save my journey.

The next morning I enquired about my brother Lal's address as since he and Dolly had been married this was the area where they were living. They knew where it was, about a five or ten minute walk away. So after thanking Len and his wife, and wishing them every happiness, I went on my search.

It didn't take me long before I found the house, and knocked. For a minute I couldn't think who it was who opened the door. Of course, it was Dolly's sister Florrie and her husband Ted Hammond. They were surprised to see me at this time on a Sunday morning. I could then hear Lal's voice at the top of the stairs. Apparently Ted and Florrie had the bottom half of the house, and Lal and Dolly with their young son Peter the top half.

They were surprised where I'd been and where I'd spent the night. It caused a bit of a laugh, as I could have always got a taxi home. When I told them at home, about going back with the bride and bridegroom it caused a laugh, but they were surprised that Lal and Dolly lived so close by.

Dolly, Lal and Peter on the beach at Paignton, Devon, in 1935.
Photo by Remington, Southfield Road, Paignton

One day Harry Day told me that he'd been thinking about arranging a Sunday cricket match, so we should have to talk it over at one of our committee meetings. Another day he told me that there was a small type of drill hall quite near in Drury Lane that was vacant during afternoons, and he thought it would be handy for us to start practising for a small dance band to be used for Sports Club socials.

He'd had this on his mind for a long time. I said to him: "We've managed to find a football team, but musicians?" He said it was all right, because he'd got his own drum kit and I played the piano. I went round one afternoon with him to try the piano. Which was a grand piano. He had got his drum kit round there, and the caretaker kept it locked up for him. It certainly made a bit of a change.

After a few weeks, Harry told me that the young man who worked on the reception desk in the main hall played the saxophone, and was quite willing to help the Sports Club. He already played in a band, when he got time off. He was another what I call English Italian, as he came from an Italian family, but spoke fluently both English and Italian. Another young chap, who worked in the Restaurant, played the trumpet. He happened to be Welsh. The main task was for everyone to get together at the same time.

I don't know why Harry always seemed to come to me for a bit of advice on certain matters as we had two others on the committee, and the Chairman who he knew more than us was Mr Brown, the owner of the Hairdressing and Shaving Salon which was situated on the floor half way between the stairs leading up from the Grill Room and Lounge, to the main hall. Opposite the salon were the toilets where Harry was in charge. The salon always seemed busy with three or four attendants working in there. Harry told me Mr Brown owned more hairdressing salons, I don't know if they were in other hotels or where, but he seemed to spend more of his time in this hotel than anywhere else, as he very often came down with I suppose one of his customers, and sat in the Lounge over a whisky and soda. Still he was not a bad fellow.

We had one or two musical afternoons all together, but our trumpeter was going back to Wales. Still we just carried on, having more practices. Another young fellow started work, and he played the violin, so that made up for the trumpet. His name was Gary, and his parents were Italian but he was born in England. He agreed to have a bit of a practice one or two afternoons a week, as it helped to fill his time. He was married and lived at Streatham, his wife went out to work, so he didn't need to go home in the afternoons.

Gary was lucky in a way, as his parents lived in a flat not far from Charing Cross Hospital, not very far along from the hotel. He asked if I would like to meet them in our break time, I said yes, I'd love to. They were a lovely couple, typically Italian and they made such a fuss of me, they put their arms round me and kissed me. It wasn't afternoon tea they served, it was red wine. Gary then showed me the new gramophone cabinet which he'd just bought his parents.

Of course for those days, it was the latest model, and so, he opened it up to put a record on and we listened to the music from Puccini's opera 'Madame Butterfly'. Before we left, they each had to put their arms around me and kissed me, and said to come again. On the way back, I said to Gary, I didn't think I was worth all that. He said: "They don't often get visitors, but I think you made up for the lot."

Harry Day had managed to arrange a day's cricket outing in Kent, so that meant a Sunday match against the village team. The weather was nice and sunny, and a lovely bit of countryside. We had a full coachload which surprised me, cooks from the kitchen with their wives, girls from the linen room and other parts of the ninth floor, maintenance men, and our own service staff, some with their wives. We managed to field a full team, but I never went over to watch the match. It was alongside the pub with also plenty of green, tables and chairs to sit out. We were provided with a good lunch, and from early evening onwards, we provided our crowd and some of the village people with a bit of singing and dancing.

On the way home, as it was beginning to get dark, some of the crowd were saying, we should have to stop soon, as everyone would want a run out. After a while, the driver found what seemed to be the ideal place for a 'comfort' stop, the area consisted mostly of scrub and bushes, with a few trees.

As I and a few others were first back in the coach, we could see the funny side of it. Just before we stopped we had come round a bend, and traffic now had headlights full on. As different ones were popping up from behind bushes adjusting themselves, the beams from traffic coming round the bend swept right over them. Instead of them coming away, they bobbed down again. So all amongst the bushes it was a case of bobbing up and down.

Sports Club outing from the Waldorf Hotel, 1935. Vic is second left

25. FUTURE BRIDE IN CAMDEN TOWN

My cousin Harry Taylor from Lambourn had been coming to stay with us for one or two weekends. He was a bit younger than me, and after leaving school, he worked with his father, my Uncle Jack, learning his father's trade which was carpentry. However he moved up to live with Auntie Alice and Uncle Jim at Kew, I suppose he now wanted to make progress.

When he came to us, after staying the night he wanted to visit his other relatives, his maternal grandparents, who lived somewhere in Camden Town, but he didn't know his way. As buses that came along the Kennington Road travelled to Camden Town, Len Wohlgemuth, George Oliver and I decided to take him there.

So after arriving at our destination, Harry said that he would look around and find the address himself. With that we said cheerio, and made a slow journey home. From then on he travelled from Kew by himself. I learnt later, through the relatives he located he met his future wife, so that would explain why he wanted to go on his own.

Off to Camden (left to right) Len Wohlgemuth, George Oliver and cousin Harry Taylor

In September 1932 I spent a few days' holiday with Mum and Dad along with Mr Morse and family at Didcot, and while we were there, we received some sad news, sent from home to tell us that Mr Fitzgerald had died. He'd been electrocuted whilst putting out a fire at the offices where he and his son Charlie worked. The news came as quite a shock, as now we knew the family quite well. Mr Fitzgerald was quite a nice man, a strong Catholic. He attended the cathedral in the Lambeth Road every Sunday morning.

My cousin Sid Taylor, who used to live near us, started work at the hotel. The family had moved away from Kennington, and now they lived at Sydenham, near the Crystal Palace.

I had been going to a few musical concerts and recitals, mostly on Sundays. I could never find anyone with my taste to accompany me, so I went on my own. In a way, I enjoyed them all the more, as I seemed to concentrate much better. It was mainly the Albert Hall that I used to visit, as I always found that once you got in there, it was the atmosphere that settled you down before the show started.

Otherwise, it was often the Tate Gallery or the National Gallery I liked to visit to see the paintings. I took my mother and father to the theatre, first to see 'Lilac Time', and then 'The Merry Widow'.

Cousin Lil had a new baby daughter in June 1933, and they named her Pamela, so now they'd have three to worry poor grandfather Jack (Arthur called Uncle George 'Jack', that's where Uncle George got his nickname). Arthur was beginning to grow more, I didn't see much of him now. His Dad had been taking him to the swimming baths. His Dad was a good strong swimmer, so I didn't think it'd be long before Arthur was just the same.

We still had our musical Sunday evenings. That's what our mother always looked forward to, especially if there were any visitors. One thing, the new types of wireless sets, or now they were called radio sets, which were coming on the market, and the new radio shows and music which were being broadcast, all helped to provide a bit more entertainment in the home.

The Brewery Tap now opened on Sunday morning, so our Sunday lunch never commenced till after Dad got home, that was about 3 o'clock in the afternoon.

It was in December 1935 when my brother Sid got married to May Fitzgerald. It was quite a nice wedding. They were married in what I always called our church, which was St Mary's Old Lambeth. They had a nice reception, and managed to secure a flat in Southwark quite near May's home.

Sid and May's wedding in December 1935. On the left are Uncle Jim and cousin Winnie, Uncle Tommy's daughter

It was in January 1936 that the King died, George V. I went to see him lying in state at Westminster Hall. It was a very impressive sight as you first entered the building and then filed past the coffin, a guardsman standing at each corner, with bowed head.

Later in the year there was a lot of talk about the new king and Mrs Simpson, black news was coming from Germany, Oswald Mosley's 'Blackshirts' were still creating a lot more trouble in the East End of London, and on top of it, civil war had broken out in Spain. It was beginning to get a bit worrying. At the end of the year the king gave up the throne as Edward VIII, because of Mrs Simpson, and so it would be the Duke of York who, with his wife Elizabeth, would be crowned King George VI and his wife as Queen at their coronation.

I'd got a new commis with me again. He was only a young lad, and inclined to be a bit shy but that was only natural. He told me his name was Michael. After a few weeks, he seemed to settle down and was getting along quite well. He began to get quite chatty with me when we weren't busy, and he told me he'd only just come to England from Ireland as his brother had bought them a house over here to come and live.

I asked him where it was they now lived, and he said south Harrow. I asked him what his other name was and he said his full name was Michael Doyle. I said to him jokingly: "You've got a name like Jack Doyle the heavyweight boxer." And then he smiled at me and said: "That's my brother."

During one evening, I said to Michael what did he do during the three hour break we had every other day, and he said Pat who worked up in the cloakroom, and happened to be Irish, took him home with him, as he lived in south London, not too far away. Occasionally, Michael said, he liked to go to the cinema, as his home was right on the outskirts of London. After all, three hours is not a lot of time when you know you have to get back to wash and change before going on duty.

We had got to New Year's Eve. I thought we should have a busy time at work. Upstairs was fully booked for the special dinner and usual celebration dance, downstairs in the Grill Room we served the usual theatre dinners, but were to carry on serving suppers, also to arrange for members of the bands to come down for supper break which would be after midnight. So everyone on duty.

The Restaurant and the Breakfast Room beyond it, which were both very large rooms, contained the dining area, the Palm Court and Ballroom were for dancing. Signor Mantovani's orchestra played during the dinner, after which the hotel's dance band, led by Howard Godfrey, took over for the rest of the night.

The early brigade went upstairs from the Grill Room to help in serving dinner, after which, when they had served coffee, they finished. It would only be the wine waiters who carried on. Us, the late duty brigade, carried on in the Grill Room. It was 2 o'clock in the morning when we finally finished. I said to my cousin Sid: "You won't be able to get home to Sydenham now, so you'd better come home with me."

And then I thought of Michael Doyle. I told him: "You won't be able to get home either, as the trains to Harrow will be finished, so we'd all better go home together." I think it cheered him up a bit as he was probably worrying where he was going to spend the night. There were all night trams running, but I knew we should probably have to wait a long time, so we got a taxi.

I did have my own bedroom now, as both my brothers Lal and Sid were married. So Michael was able to sleep in my single bed and cousin Sid with me in the double bed. By the time we woke up next morning my sisters Win and Gert and Win's daughter Jean had already gone to work. And so we had a quiet breakfast with Mum and Dad, as Dad started work at the same time as us, 11 o'clock.

One day, Michael told me his brother was coming in to lunch, and he wanted to sit at one of our tables, so that he could have a little talk with me, to ask how his young brother was getting on. Anyway, he came in during lunch and it was lucky, as we weren't very busy at the time I was able to have quite a chat with him. He told me he used to be in the Irish Guards, and how he came out into the boxing world, and won fights and so was able to bring his family over into a new house.

With that he said he had to go, and asked me to look after his young brother, and he went after his lunch. I told Michael afterwards what he had been telling me, and said that I was only too glad he didn't ask me to have a couple of rounds with him some time, as I would have laid down on the canvas before we'd started.

On the balcony at Wedgwood House, 1930s (left to right), Dad, Win, Lil and Syd Reading, Mum

27. BEST MAN AT TWO WEDDINGS

The coronation of George VI, and Queen Elizabeth, was to be in Westminster Abbey in May 1937. Kate Fitzgerald, elder sister of May and Charlie, was a court dressmaker, and so was busy helping to make the coronation robes. It didn't seem very long before one noticed all the flags and bunting being put up on the route of the procession.

After the coronation, in June my sister Gert married Charlie Fitzgerald at our church, St Mary's Old Lambeth. I was best man. It

Gert and Charlie's wedding: back (left to right), Mrs Fitzgerald, Vic, groom and bride, Dad and Mum. The smaller bridesmaid is cousin Joyce

was a very nice wedding, with a nice reception afterwards. It wasn't long, a month later, before my friend Len Wohlgemuth got married to Irene Mitchell, I was best man again.

My eldest sister Win did a small time job just off Tottenham Court Road, in Gower Street. She went to an elderly gentleman who dealt in different types of art. She didn't cook at all, but looked after his flat, which he shared.

She also went to another flat a short distance away. They were a couple, I think Jewish, but she got on very well with them. She just helped to look after their flat, they did their own cooking. His name was Joe Kaye, he was a violinist and played in one of the West End hotel dance bands, I think he was in the Savoy Orpheans once, and later he formed his own dance band. Win always got home in the late afternoon.

Joe Kaye, who formed his own dance band. The photo is inscribed: To "Flossie" Good wishes J Kaye. 'Flossie' was the Kayes' nickname for Win

Later in the year Bruce, who had been my commis waiter, told me his father had been offered the job in Scotland he'd been waiting a long time for, so they'd be moving back soon. Bruce had decided to go to Southampton to sign on to go back to sea. He wanted to know if I would go and sign up with him. I said rowing on the lake was enough for me. Also Michael Doyle was going to leave. He said his brother had obtained another job for him nearer home.

The Grill Room now opened on Sundays for dinner, so that meant going on duty at 5pm. Both brigades worked alternate Sundays.

On my early nights when I finished work, instead of going straight home I would go into one of the small news theatres. The programme lasted just over the hour. It showed mainly news with perhaps one or two short comedies or cartoons. I always managed to go once a week to one of these cinemas as there were quite a lot in the West End.

Each week I went, I could see the different advances the Nazis had made and some of the atrocities, especially with Jewish people. It began to set people wondering. I had also heard that a lot of refugee children had been brought over from the Spanish civil war, and a lot had been installed at Baydon Hole at Baydon, that's one of the villages next to Lambourn.

I received a letter from Bruce in New York. He said he hoped to see me again, he was at present on the Aquitania, the Cunard liner. A few days before, Pat from the cloakroom came down one afternoon to tell me there was somebody waiting to see me. It was Michael. He was pleased to see both Pat and me.

Coming to England he had felt a bit strange, and when he came to us he began to feel a bit more settled and independent. He said that as he had to come into town to do some shopping, his parents told him to call in to thank both Pat and me for helping him along. So I wished him all the luck and got back to my job.

News still seemed to be getting worse from Germany, also from Spain and Russia, and Italy. All the talk you heard from people now was wondering where we were going to end up next.

A son had been born to Len and Rene Wohlgemuth in January 1938, his name being Paul, and my sister Gert had a baby daughter in December, 1938, so that made a good Christmas present. They named her Jill. Len and Rene had another son born to them in March 1939, his name being Michael.

Bruce Patterson (centre), Vic's commis waiter at one time, after returning to sea as a steward on Cunard liners. This photo, taken with two fellow workers, was sent from New York

28. ESCAPE FROM IRA BOMB AT THE ALDWYCH

One Saturday evening in June 1939 I think I had a narrow escape. When I left off work at night to come home, from the back of the hotel I walked down the Aldwych along to the Strand to go down to the Embankment to catch my tram. Along the Aldwych I had to pass the building which used to contain the *Morning Post* newspaper. This now contained shops and offices and a branch of Lloyds Bank. Along where I used to pass were all rather high windows, with a grid railing across the bottom, not very high, as I suppose it was to stop rubbish being thrown on to the sills.

So, as I was leaving work this Saturday night after 11 o'clock, I had to rush back downstairs again, to get something I'd left in my locker. On coming out of the back of the hotel, I thought I heard a bang. I just carried on until I got down to pass the old *Morning Post* building. There were crowds of people grouped around one small area, as people were still coming out of the theatres at the time. The police were still arriving. I thought I might as well poke my nose in to find the cause of the trouble.

When I got closer I could see one of the windows broken out, with the grid rails. The police were examining all around, and just then, the ambulance arrived. Three or four people were helped in, but I didn't know their injuries. Anyway, as it now seemed to have died down, and it was getting late, I carried on home. The news in the papers was then all about IRA bombs in London. Four bank buildings were badly damaged, one of these was Lloyds in the Aldwych. I then realized, if I didn't have to run back to my locker, I could easily have been one of those people who caught the blast.

I had noticed at work that we'd been getting quite a few Jewish people who had evidently escaped out of Germany and were now staying at the hotel. They came down to lunch and dinner each day, and you could tell by their broken English, where they were from. I don't know if it was the same in the other hotels but I imagine it was. They were just trying to flee into this country or America.

I received another promotion. As the waiter in charge of the Lounge had left, the job had been handed over to me. So I finished with the Grill Room. The Lounge served apéritifs, and cocktails and drinks of that type. I had a young assistant with me and I was in complete charge, and I didn't work Sundays. Also Len Higgins had been promoted to a Head Waiter.

And now the bad news was that Britain had declared war on Germany. And so we'd just got to carry on, and wait to see what happened next.

I heard from Lambourn that one of my favourite cousins May Taylor was getting married to Steve Gulyas, a nice young chap who worked in the racing stables. I thought they'd be happy. A month later I was told that a baby daughter had been born to Win's daughter Jean who married Bert Stroud earlier in the year. They named her Valerie.

It was just a little later on that my father's eldest brother, our Uncle George, died. He was in his eighties, it couldn't have happened at a better time as people were being advised, where possible, to move away from London because of expected bombing, also children were being evacuated. My cousin Lil's daughters Joyce and Pam were evacuated with Walnut Tree Walk School to Exeter, and her son Arthur was also evacuated to Devon, to Starcross and Newton Abbot.

My father was past seventy and I was beginning to get a bit worried for both my mother and father as they were both getting older, also for my eldest sister Win, who still went out to work, as I now began

West Grove
Swanboro
near Lewes Sussex 6 Dec 1939

My dear friend Teddie Cox
            It was nice of you to
write me. Your news is indeed
sad, and I think you will believe
me when I tell you how deeply
sorry I am that this has happened
As perhaps you can guess I have
suffered more disappointments
& horrible treatment in these
last two years than all the
rest of my long life. Perhaps
the less I express myself about
Messrs G & W. the better but I must
add I never met any one like
them & did not know such
men existed I only wish I
could assist you but am going
through a dreadful time myself

A letter that Vic's father's former employer, Harold Jenner, wrote in response to the news of Mr Cox's dismissal after the takeover of Jenner's Brewery and closure of the Brewery Tap. Harold Jenner went on to thank Mr Cox 'for all the many faithful years you have so loyally served my father and myself'

108

to feel responsible for them, as I lived at home and was not married. My eldest brother Lal who worked for Faulkner's, the tobacco people, had been informed that the firm were closing the factory and offices in London, and were moving to Liverpool, merging with Ogdens there. All staff and employees had been offered a move with the firm if they wished. Lal had accepted, as this was his living and pension, also he was now past the military age of call up.

And now Jenner's Brewery, who my father had worked for for the past fifty years, had been taken over. The Brewery Tap which he managed had been closed down and he had been told to resign. With no pension or thank you. It was just a matter of finish and go. My brother Sid, who used to help him quite a lot at the Brewery Tap, made it his business to go and see all the people concerned in the takeover to negotiate with them and to tell them his father, after all these years, should have a better retirement. But it was of no avail.

I think my father felt a bit upset about it all, and began to get quite depressed about it. But I realized that he wouldn't have been able to carry on at his age, and things getting worse, if we started to get any bombing which was expected at any time.

The call up in the age groups was beginning to work quite fast, and I thought, although I was now thirty years of age, it wouldn't be very long before it got to me. And so I wrote to Uncle Tommy and Auntie Nell at Lambourn, also Shady, and asked them if there was any accommodation or whatever in the village for my mother and father and sister Win. I explained what the position was like in London.

There were blackouts at night. No lights to be shown, and of course everybody living under tension. I was quite busy at work, especially during the evenings. Residents from the hotel would come down to sit in the Lounge knowing we were underground and drink all the evening, as they wouldn't trust upstairs in the Palm Court, with a glass roof. Of course I worked late every night. I would send the young lad, my assistant, off earlier.

We had had air raid warnings, but nothing had happened so far. At home we went downstairs to people we knew on the ground floor until the all clear, and then it was back upstairs to bed, still half dressed in case we got another warning. This happened for quite a long time, so many people made the habit of going to the air raid shelter every night to sleep until the morning.

It was during one Saturday afternoon I was home for my break from work, and was getting ready to go back, it now getting on for 6 o'clock. When I went out on to the balcony, I could see quite a long way over the rooftops. It was then I could see all the smoke in the sky, it was a bombing raid over the ports Gravesend and Tilbury, with I think quite a lot of damage.

I managed to call round to Len and Rene Wohlgemuth and their family as they now lived in a basement flat in Monkton Street which was not very far away from us. Len was on duty most of the time as he belonged to the Balloon Squad which he'd joined early on, which now came under the RAF. I stayed with Rene a bit to ask how she was getting on, and the two baby boys. She seemed pretty comfortable, but I didn't know about the raids we were beginning to get. I expected the children would be evacuated.

I heard from Lambourn, and between Shady and Uncle Tommy they had managed to secure a house for us. It was an old farmhouse which belonged to the farmer Eddie Bracey, which was in Bockhampton Road just outside the village. It was rather a large house, which was all the better. I made arrangements for Mother and Father to go down to stay in Lambourn, until I could arrange for the furniture to be sent. It meant waiting a bit as the removal people were so busy, moving people's homes out into the country.

The old gentleman who Win looked after had gone away into the country but the other couple she went to she carried on with her little job there for the time being. She got on very well with them, and they treated her very well. They always liked to be a bit jolly, and

110

they'd now nicknamed her 'Flossie'. Mrs Kaye was always buying new clothing, and clothing she discarded she gave to Win, which was still as good as new. Win had told Mr Kaye that she had a brother who was very fond of music, and played the piano, and often she'd brought home bundles of music for me from him.

One evening when I was on the tram going back to work, I happened to notice as we were going over Westminster Bridge all the people looking over to the river. I noticed small craft from all the different parts of the river, even from as far as Oxford, with their owners answering the appeal to help bring the troops back off the beaches of Dunkirk.

I told Win I thought it would be better if she arranged to finish her job and go down to Lambourn as she knew she could always stay with Tom Bowsher, her brother in law, and his wife and family at their farm. For one thing, it wouldn't be long before I got my call up papers. And if we started getting more raids, and I happened to be at work, I shouldn't be able to get home during the night. When she'd moved, I should then begin to feel a bit more satisfied.

It wasn't long before she was ready. She gave her job up, she said they were sorry to see her go, then packed her things, and finally made her move to Beale's Farm. She shared Tom's eldest daughter Edie's bedroom at one time and our dad slept on the landing. I said I would see to the furniture and pay any outstanding bills.

Things were looking pretty bad. The Nazis had occupied France, Holland and Belgium, Denmark and Norway, so it was only this small country left to look after ourselves, excepting poor little Malta in the Mediterranean, they were still holding out.

The night bombing raids were increasing not only in London, but also in many other towns and cities. They were now beginning to get quite heavy with much damage and large amounts of casualties. With these heavy raids happening nearly every night, I could never get home, I just stayed on, and finally managed to kip down somewhere in the Grill Room until the morning, when I washed and changed to go out, and see what had been happening.

I would often slip along to the Lyons' Corner House to have some breakfast, never knowing if it had been blown away or not. And then I made my way home, to see if that was still there, as I felt a bit worried with the flat still full of furniture.

One morning, after a heavy night's raid, as I got near I saw the dairy and flats which adjoined our part of the estate had been hit, with quite a fair amount of damage. That's when my heart seemed to jump into my mouth. I didn't know if there were any casualties, as there were men still clearing the rubble, but I seemed half afraid to go on any further to see what else I should find. Anyway, everything was all right.

My sister Gert with her daughter Jill had a shelter, in the garden, which they shared with the people who lived in the other flats in the house at Brixton. Gert's husband Charlie most nights had to stay on at Spicer's where he worked to do fire watching. My brother Sid always went with him, most businesses arranged their own staff to do fire watching.

It was all war news in the daily papers. Mostly pictures of all the damage. Pictures of the King and Queen inspecting all the rubble and talking to different people. Winston Churchill, who was now Prime Minister, walking about with a face like a bulldog, as much as to say: "Come over to this country and I'll eat yer!"

They came to move our furniture, that I was thankful for. I next sent my new address to the War Office and then I notified them at the hotel that I would be leaving as I was expecting my call up papers. And so, after making sure I'd left everything OK, and with a rather sad goodbye, I left Kennington. Arriving in Lambourn, I noticed the remains of the family were comfortably installed in our new home, nice and warm, as it was now getting toward December. There was no bathroom and the toilet was at the end of the garden. There was no gas, and no electricity connected, as was the same with many other houses about there. Anyway, oil lamps were better than air raids, and they did manage to get a quiet night. I told Gert if things got too bad, she could always go down to our new family home, as there was plenty of room.

I thanked both Uncle Tommy and Shady for what they'd done to help us. Shady said: "Aarh I'll always do it for my 'ol' boy'."

In December I received my call up papers to report at Stoughton Barracks, Guildford in Surrey, just before Christmas. Uncle Percy had brought Auntie Kate down to stay with us, as they were now living in Perivale in their own house, but within the bombing area. So of course Auntie Kate, being our mother's sister, and suffering with crippling rheumatoid arthritis, was glad to come somewhere peaceful, her childhood village. Uncle Percy would go back to look after their house and carry on work. He was now running his own small car, so that made it a bit easier.

Now my time had arrived to report to barracks. I was thinking how to get to Guildford from Lambourn, but Uncle Percy came down to take me in the car. And so, with another sad cheerio, I left home for another life.

Uncle Percy, possibly about 1920.

Vic, a member of the Queen's Royal Regiment, (above) and (left) at Stoughton Barracks, Guildford, Surrey. Standing next to Vic (left) is Charlie Dear and seated in front of Charlie Dear is the 'coloured boy' Vic was pally with who was killed later in the war

Booking in at the Stoughton guardroom, I was told that as my change of address had been delayed in the post, my call up papers had been delayed for a month, so automatically I was AWOL. After things got sorted out, I was taken to collect my kit and then taken to my billet, which was empty, as all the rest were out. When they returned, I met the sergeant and two corporals who were in charge of the billet and all the rest who I soon got to know.

I was shown to my bed, I changed into my uniform, fitted my cap badge on, and so the last thing was my boots. That being the lot, I now belonged to the Queen's Royal Regiment. I was then given a few instructions by the corporals and the rest I learnt off the other lads.

After a week I was getting used to it. Parades, weapon drill, route marches, the lot. Sunday mornings we marched to church in the village of Stoughton, after church we were then dismissed for the rest of the day. We would make our way back to barracks, where dinner was always at 12 o'clock, then there was tea and supper in their order. There was also a NAAFI canteen open.

As this was a regiment that accepted all the new recruits from south London, some of the lads told me of their first blunder. On their first Sunday, after they were dismissed, they thought they would catch a bus to Guildford Station and get a day rail ticket to London and go home. Fast trains to Waterloo only took just over half an hour. And so that's what they did, only to arrive at Waterloo to find the military police waiting at the platform gates to inspect their passes.

As they had no passes, it was about turn, and back to Guildford. I was very pally with a coloured boy. We often went into Guildford in our off duty time.

We started doing a lot of route marching in the evenings and at night with full pack and rifle. Once, during the day, when we were getting near the barracks my ankle suddenly gave way, and I started to limp. The sergeant gave a halt and inspected my ankle and thought it seemed to be swelling, as wearing boots you had a job to tell. He told me to carry on back to the billet, and marched the others on. Later he came in to see my ankle, it had swollen, so he told me to report to the Medical Officer tomorrow.

I couldn't understand why my ankle should give way. I thought back, and remembered our class leaving school in a hurry to go to a school football match. Coming out to go down the stone steps, somebody in the first lot fell and the rest of us went over on top. I think I received a sprain as afterwards I was home for about a week, but since then I'd forgotten about it. I saw the MO, he examined it, but never said anything. And so, after a restful day I just carried on.

We completed our several weeks of strict training, and were expecting our next move. I then found I was transferred to the Royal Army Service Corps and the day came when we had to pack our kit bags, all our own kit and possessions, and board transport which took us to the station. I found that not all our company was on this move, the same with the other companies. We were all formed into different groups, according to the army units we were destined for.

Charlie Dear hung on to me like a toffee apple. He was a typical Cockney, and he came from near the Elephant and Castle. When I had told him I was from near the Lambeth Walk, a big smile beamed in his face and he shook my hand. He said when he wrote to his wife, as he'd only just been married, he'd tell her he'd met a chap from their part of London, and so was not with a lot of strangers.

We were friends for most of the war. We were not told where we were going, we changed trains at Reading and it was nearly dark when we had to change again, which I could just see was Cardiff. It was now properly dark, and we moved off. We could hear gunfire, and bombs dropping. I realized it must be an attack on Cardiff docks, then I thought it must be Barry docks as well.

We eventually got to our destination where transport was waiting for us, and the docks seemed to be just behind us. After a roll call by the sergeant to make sure we were all there, we moved off, but not very far. We then had to alight with all our kit, and stand in line at ease. We stood there until the all clear, which had been a long time coming, and we were all getting a bit hungry.

We were told to pick up our kit bags and rifles, and cross over to the other side, where we could just discern shops and other buildings, and were then taken through one building into a large hall with plenty of light and there we plonked down for a while. The sergeant was given information at the desk after which he took us to our sleeping quarters and a dining room where we got our meal.

Next day, after a roll call, it seemed a matter of hanging about until we all got sorted out. We were on Barry Island, and could see all around. No 4 RASC Mobilisation Centre was at Barry and the whole of the sea front with all the shops and other buildings had been taken over by the Army so that was where the sleeping quarters and other necessities had been arranged for the time being.

This was where we stayed for about the next three weeks and where we were posted to 59 DID (Detail Issue Depot) RASC, a unit which was responsible for issuing stores to our forces.

There were quite a few other companies that had arrived from different training barracks. One morning we received orders to assemble outside, and await further orders. It was then a sergeant brought another batch to join us to complete our full unit. As our usual sergeant had returned to Guildford, we had a new sergeant and corporal and were about to move to Caerphilly, the other side of Cardiff. We had another unit join with us, 60 DID RASC, and were now settled in Caerphilly. We were billeted in a place called Plymouth Hall, in Pentrebane Street, which was above Woolworth's, alongside an indoor market. Our sleeping quarters were contained in two very large rooms, our unit allocated to one room and the other unit in the other. And this was where we'd all got to get together and get to know each other.

After reveille we had to march for about a mile outside the town to what used to be a Territorial Army centre, but was now under full army control. This was where we should spend most of our days and have our main meal, we had breakfast and supper at Plymouth Hall. It was next day at the centre that both units had to parade for our Commanding Officers to take over. Our CO was Captain Miller.

One day, after we'd had dinner, we were marched back to our sleeping quarters and told to stay by our beds. After a short while we were called to attention, and the CO walked in. He told us to stand easy, and then interviewed each one in turn to know our names, and all about us.

Caerphilly was quite a nice little town and we met some nice people. We used to get a shower at miners' baths. We also found a nice little café we always visited during our spare time. The lady who kept it seemed quite a nice person, and she told us she was a very great friend of Ivor Novello's mother and she watched him grow up from a young boy.

Quite often after our dinner we were allowed the rest of the day to ourselves and so we made our way back to Plymouth Hall. Each time the air raid siren sounded, one member from each unit must go on the flat roof to do fire watch duty until the all clear. We were situated quite near the castle, and we often used to walk in the grounds. I found out there was a piano in the other unit's room, so one day I went in for a tinkle, which brought a cheer from the few

118

lads that were still there. It was a nice piano, quite a pleasure to play on. The same evening, a lad from the other unit came in to ask if it was me who played the piano. He told me he was a bit of a singer, and could we arrange to just have a little try out with the piano, perhaps when it was a bit quiet. That I agreed.

It was a couple of days later, when most of the unit was out, that he came in for me, and there, he was lucky, as I was just going out myself. I was only too glad to see how it went. He told me a few of the songs he liked singing, some I knew, one or two I didn't, but I said I should soon get to know them.

And so, we started on some songs, and my word, what a lovely voice he had, a rather soft type of tenor voice. We went from one song to another when we began to hear quite a lot of clapping from outside. We looked out of the two large windows that were wide open, and outside at the back was a crowd of girls, who worked at Woolworth's, listening to the singing.

He told me he was from Yorkshire, and his father was in the last war. His father was also a good singer and he belonged to the British Legion, and they used to hold quite a lot of concerts. His father was beginning to lose his voice, and so his son had taken his place at their concerts. I said, that's all finished now, but your time will come. In any case we used to give the boys an enjoyable sing song, as well as the Woolworth girls. I remembered he had told me he was 'a bit of a singer'; I thought he was more than a bit.

It was one morning when we had marched up to the TA centre, where we now had lectures before dinner time, our Captain, who had a small office there, sent for me. I thought, what next? I went in, and then he said: "I just want to ask you something, but you are under no obligation. I want you to be my batman." After hurried thought, I decided: "Yes, Sir." With that he gave me a smile. He then gave me the address where he was staying, which was not far away from where we slept, and told me what time he wanted to be woken with a cup of tea. All the rest of the duties I could find out later on. Charlie Dear said to me later he'd asked three or four of the other fellows, but they turned him down. I suppose they couldn't make their own beds.

Next morning, I found the house, quite a nice large house, and I went to the side door, as I had been told. I rang the bell, when the maid opened the door, with quite a beaming smile. I asked if this was where Captain Miller was staying. She said: "Yes. I've made the tea, and one for yourself." She showed me where the Captain's room was, and so I took him his tea up. I had to wake him and asked if there was anything else he wanted. I noticed he had a very nice self contained room.

He told me to come back later on to straighten his bed and the room, that was all. I then went downstairs, where the young housemaid was waiting, to tell me tomorrow morning walk straight in, and she'd have the tea ready. She told me her bosses were just a married couple, but were business people. I got back to Plymouth Hall, where they'd saved my breakfast.

As we were not a great way from Cardiff, there was quite a good train service there from Caerphilly. We found out from the sergeant that only two or three at a time could go, if they had a pass, which they had to apply for. I said to Charlie, my Elephant and Castle mate, what about going in to Cardiff one evening. With that, he was in his element.

One thing I'd noticed about Charlie. He would be busy every evening writing letters. It took him three or four evenings to write a letter to his new wife, and then one to his own family, and then he started another one to his wife. He was missing home, so I thought it would cheer him up a bit if we went out for a change.

After about a week, we managed to get a pass, and so caught a train to Cardiff. One thing about Charlie, he wasn't a drinker, perhaps just a taste, and that was all. We did get stopped by the military police once, but everything was in order, and so we had a good look around. The evenings started to get dark about 7 o'clock, and we didn't want to get lost in Cardiff when it got pitch dark. Our pass was valid until 11 o'clock, and after a walk towards the station, we weren't worried except we were both feeling tired and hungry.

It was now properly dark and the air raid warning started. I said to Charlie: "I was just thinking of fish and chips, but we won't find any shops now." Everything had to be kept dark in the blackout, and we wouldn't know a fish shop from a pub. But we didn't know how lucky we were. Just as we got a little further along the road, two or three people ran out through a door although no light showed as there was a dark curtain behind it. They seemed to have a paper packet of some kind in their hand, and they ran off as fast as they could.

Charlie said to me: "I can smell fried fish." As I opened the door I could smell fried fish. I went behind the curtain, and shouted out to the man behind the counter to find out if he was still open. He said, yes, come in and sit down. I shouted out to Charlie, come in and make yourself at home. Finally, sitting there on our own after enjoying a good supper we made sure about our train time and the man told us where to make for the station, about five minutes' walk.

We started off. The all clear went, and the man had told us the shop would be filled up then. We had noticed that these air raid alerts were not only for Cardiff docks, but the planes were also making for the factories in the Midlands.

I had two periods of leave whilst we were in Caerphilly, one of seven days in late April and one of a few days in early June. I just met with one snag on my first journey home. When I arrived at Newbury Station, the last Lambourn train had gone, and as there was no bus service in those days, I looked about to see if there were any chances of a pick up, without avail. It was dark, I started to walk. I'd walked quite a long way when I thought I heard the sound of a car.

I couldn't see any lights, but eventually a small farm truck drew up. The driver said he was sorry that he was only going for a short distance to another farm, but if I jumped in that would be a help. I thanked him for every little bit of help, and eventually finished my journey on foot. I reached Upper Bockhampton Farm, as that was the name of our new home, feeling tired but glad.

I had a bit of trouble to create some attention as everything was quiet. After throwing quite a few small stones up at a bedroom window, I heard a bit of talking, then saw some candles being lit. I called out, after which it was all activity. They made me a hot drink, which I was very glad of, and after a lot of talking I told them to get back to bed, as I could finish up in the armchair. But no, they had a bed ready for me. So I just flopped in, and all was quiet again.

In the morning, as Auntie Kate was still staying with us, I helped to carry her downstairs, as she needed to be carried up or downstairs, and of course it was then all talking again. I was glad to see they were all now settled in the new home. Uncle Tommy, working on the post round, called in every morning for a cup of tea and something to eat, and Shady called sometimes, so they got one or two visitors.

They were getting used to lamplight, and it did help to warm the place up. We had plenty of space downstairs and also plenty of bedroom space upstairs, including one small bedroom in the attic.

During my next leave I told them about the musical concerts I and the other lad had been giving. I said we didn't bargain for an outside audience, but it used to go down well. And I told them, the other lad wasn't Welsh.

One of the Yorkshire tenor's songs, which Vic hears every year played at the Remembrance Day Parade at the Cenotaph	Oft, in the stilly night, Ere Slumber's chain has bound me, Fond Memory brings the light Of other days around me. Thomas Moore

30. ARCTIC GEAR FOR ICELAND POSTING

We began to receive new equipment. It was a white kit bag, and winter clothes. As a matter of fact it was Arctic gear, especially what was called the trople coat, which was a lined coat, waterproofed, and which was quite a job to roll up to put in the kit bag. It needed two to finish the job. We had a strong idea where we would be going. Our CO returned from leave, and so I knew I should have to wake him in the morning.

Next day, I never had time to open the side door at the CO's accommodation, the housemaid stood there, to tell me she had my cup of tea ready and how pleased she was to see me as she thought I'd left. I thought she'd be disappointed when I had to tell her that we should be moving soon. Over tea she told me her name, which was a proper Welsh name, and which I've now forgotten, and she wanted to know my name, after which I said I'd better get on with my job, before she started to pour me out some more tea.

After one or two more weeks, we had orders to get ready to move. We weren't told where we were going, but had time to say goodbye to a lot of people we had got to know. Before we left our two units had to go into the grounds of the castle to have our photograph taken. The poor little housemaid had tears in her eyes, so I gave her a kiss and rushed back to breakfast as that was the last morning. Kit bags had to be labelled with name and number to be put on the trucks which would come to collect us.

It was then I found out that the other unit were not travelling with us. So I rushed into the other room to find my pal with the musical voice. He was looking a bit sad that he should now miss all those musical moments. I told him not to worry, as he'd got a lot more to come.

And with that, we shook hands and said cheerio. I think I left him with a tear in his eye. I often wonder if he survived the war.

We were loaded on to trucks and taken on to Cardiff station. We were told to make sure we had our drinking mugs handy on our haversacks, as we'd need them on the train. It was early evening before our train shunted in. We had been lucky earlier on, as the Salvation Army came to the station and we had a drink from them.

We had plenty of room on the train, and of course Charlie hung on to me. We noticed we were still travelling through Wales. All the others seemed to be quiet, and looking a bit sombre. I wondered if they were thinking the same as me and trying to look at the last bit of British countryside, while it was still a bit light. With that it was gradually dozing until the corporal came along to tell us to take our mugs up to the end of the corridor if we wanted a drink.

After a bit of a restless night, the sun was shining and we seemed

This photo of 59 DID and 60 DID was taken in the grounds of Caerphilly Castle on 19 June 1941 by F W Gatehouse, Caerphilly. Vic is second right in the row below the back row

to be moving slowly along. I was told afterwards that we were just passing the outskirts of Glasgow. We had tea and a breakfast before we finally arrived at Greenock. There we had to collect our kit, and get ready to leave the train. We then moved over along on to the jetty, where we saw a large ship moored, waiting for us.

We were told to move up the gangplank and shown to our bunks. After settling ourselves down, we were told to go up on deck where we were issued with lifejackets and shown how to wear them, and then shown the lifeboat stations. After that we went back to our bunks, our CO calling me back to show me where he was sleeping, so that if possible, I could take him tea in the morning.

It was during the evening that we set sail, and after a while I went up on deck to have a look around. It was a lovely evening and a really beautiful view, we were sailing along the Clyde towards the open sea. I suddenly realized it was June 20th, the day before the longest day which was also my sister Gert's birthday. I thought, if I could only have shown her this beautiful view, it would have been as good as a birthday present.

Next morning, after a cold wash and shave, we collected our breakfast. For our food during the voyage, we had to go to the galley with our mugs and mess tins to collect what was on the 'menu' and then back to our bunks to finish it. I managed to take our CO a mug of tea, although when I started it was a full mug, when I finally got to his bunk it was less than half a mug. I told him it wasn't worth it, as he was situated in quite a different area of the ship to where we were, and there was a mess room for officers.

It took us about three or four days to reach Iceland, as that was where we were making for. Each day we had to go on deck with all the other troops who were aboard for lifeboat drill. We had an escort destroyer with us, until we reached Reykjavik, which was the main port of Iceland, and where we landed. We had to wait for transport. After being picked up, we travelled for about six or seven miles to a place called Allafoss. There was what looked like a red roofed farmhouse with a couple of smaller red roofed houses, then there were two large glasshouses where they grew tomatoes. These, and I presumed the houses, were heated from the hot springs close by.

We moved a bit further on where the ground was more open until we reached two large Nissen sheds, where we off loaded. Further over the open ground we could see tents, our sleeping quarters. The unit we were taking over from was a bit farther over, and they used to come down to talk to us, and tell us what life had been like during the year they'd been there. Ablutions and toilets were already there, also a marquee for cooking and meals.

The two Nissen sheds, and one or two smaller ones, were stocked with all kinds of food, which we were now responsible for receiving and issuing to the main British forces still on the island. Each man was responsible for so many different types of food, stocktaking took place at the end of every week. Meanwhile, we'd had to make sure the white polar bear (which indicated our assignment to Iceland) was sewn on the shoulders of our jackets correctly.

We knew now that the Germans had 'occupied'* this country until after the outbreak of war, then the Canadians were there and now we'd taken over. Each day was a busy day, especially if it was receiving stores of different kinds of food, some of which were quite heavy and then had to be stacked properly. Issuing to units was usually once a week.

We were settling down to this kind of life, and getting used to seeing the midnight sun and it keeping light for the rest of the night. The air was quite clear, and the temperature was average during the summer time. Our CO was stationed in the officers' quarters in

*Pre-war the Germans took a great interest in Iceland and brought many advantages. Germany built houses for her and constructed their only tarmacadam road – 9 miles of it! – Wyndham Davies, *Icelandic Diary 1944-45,* unpublished manuscript, p. 8. – Editor

Reykjavik, so I didn't have to worry about him for a while, although he knew he still owed me the batman money for our Caerphilly stay. His name being Captain Miller, the boys all called him 'Dusty', milling being a dusty job. He came from Perth, in Scotland.

We often had a run down to Reykjavik when our truck was available and we had permission. We found it quite a nice town, with some quite nice buildings. One café we enjoyed, and the food and pastries were really tip top. The girls who were waitresses in the cafés were really nice looking, and all blondes. There were no language problems, as they were all taught English. Altogether, they seemed to be a very well behaved type of girl, as I later found were most of the Icelandic people, and everywhere was clean.

Often during the evenings we would stroll down to the hot springs. I think the local people used these for bathing but we weren't allowed to use them. Otherwise it was quite lonely out there, as we never saw anybody about apart from our own lads.

One of the essential trades people we had to have in the unit, besides carpenter, butcher, cook and driver, was barber. And so when we wanted our hair cut, we relied on Jack Hutchins. He was a well built fellow with blond hair, and before we went out to Iceland, he was given a few lessons on hairdressing. Jack was really popular, and he would keep us in fits of laughter. He made us a seat out of a couple of boxes, and that was where we would spend evenings out in the open. Sometimes he would burst out into song.

One thing all of us looked forward to, and that was when our mail arrived. I heard from home. They told me that they had a full household, as so many of our relatives liked to go down to Lambourn when possible to avoid the air raids, and the bombing. Auntie Alice and her daughter stayed for a while, but had returned home to Kew where Auntie Alice had since died. May and Charlie's sister Kate was living there, doing dressmaking and needlework for different people in the village. She and her mother went to

Lambourn after their flat in Queen's Buildings in Southwark was destroyed in bombing which killed Mrs Fitzgerald's brother.

Mrs Fitzgerald had died in Sandleford Hospital at Newbury not long before I went to Stoughton Barracks. Cis went to live with Sid and May at Clapham. My sister Win's daughter Jean was also living at Upper Bockhampton with her little girls Valerie and Barbara.

Vic's family, with relatives seeking wartime refuge, and others from Lambourn. Standing at the back (left to right): Sid, Florrie Hammond's husband Ted (with cigarette), Audrey Bowsher held by her mother Nellie (Win's sister-in-law), Vic's Mum, Cecil's wife Ethel, possibly Ethel's mother, Lal, Kate Fitzgerald and her sister Cis. In front (left to right): Jean, Valerie, Florrie, May, Dolly and her son Peter, Win (behind Peter), Gert, Jill, and Doreen Bowsher, another of Nellie's daughters

31. REYKJAVIK EVENING ENDS IN ACCIDENT

After a while, we didn't seem to have so many units to issue to, I suppose they must have been gradually leaving, but I had noticed there were quite a few American personnel about in the town. More arrived. We had a few encamped quite near to us, and they soon made our acquaintance. They were quite friendly with us, especially Jack, as now they knew there was a barber on the site, they were round every evening. All we saw was Jack standing behind his barber's chair, with a great big fat cigar in his mouth. This went on for quite a few weeks, I think Jack must have done well out of them.

On the way back from Reykjavik one nice light evening, we must have come upon a bad piece of road, which caused the lorry to swerve. The roads not being very wide, the lorry went down the slight bank, and then overturned. I was sitting at one end, and George Bonham on the other side. We both jumped out before the lorry hit the ground. All the others were in the front part, so they fell on to each other.

After sorting ourselves out, nobody seemed to be hurt, except my arm hurt a bit. We went round to the driver's cab to see if they wanted help. The sergeant was in the front with the driver. As the lorry was lying on its left side, the sergeant was pinned underneath the driver who was unconscious and would have to be lifted out before the sergeant could move, as he said he was all right. Jack, our barber, then said: "Leave it to me, I've had to do this before."

And so, being a pretty strong fellow he jumped on the top of the wagon and got to work. I looked around. We were completely on our own, not a sight or sound of anything or anybody, just wild and lonely country. After a struggle and the sweat pouring down his face

Jack pulled the driver up and out of the cab as he was now coming round and was more help. He was soon quite himself, so everyone set about getting the wagon righted and up on the road. This was done as easy as pie, and we made our move for camp.

Since our little turn over, my arm had been aching, and I noticed George Bonham's eye was beginning to get really puffed up. I didn't have a very good night, so next day I mentioned my arm to the sergeant. He told me take Pte Bonham along the road to the American camp to see if their medical clinic was there yet. And so George with his lovely black eye, and me with my aching arm, went to see what the American camp was like.

It was quite a fair walk, but we finally reached it. After enquiring of the guard, he said their medic section had not arrived but he told us where to find a couple of medics who might be able to help. After a search round, we found one. He said as they hadn't received any medical equipment yet, he couldn't do much, but he looked at my arm. After feeling along it, he said: "I think you have a broken bone there, but the x ray will show."

We thanked him, and returned. The sergeant said he would inform our military hospital, it was just outside Reykjavik. Next day, the Red Cross van came up and after packing my essentials I was in and off. As they had two ex patients to return to their units, it was a little while before we arrived at the hospital. There I was handed over to one of the medic staff.

I noticed another patient being taken for a walk in the grounds by two nurses. I then noticed him again, and someone told me that his name was Esmond Knight, he was an actor. He was in the Royal Navy, and had been on the Prince of Wales which was damaged in the action with Germany's battleship Bismarck when our battlecruiser Hood went down. Unfortunately, he lost his sight as a result. After the war I went to the cinema one day, and recognized him in a film, and later I saw him in other films, and on television.

After I'd had my x ray, I was taken into a ward, and told to get into bed. It wasn't long before they wheeled me off to the 'theatre', where I was lifted on to the table, and stuck the needle into me after which I knew no more until I started to come round and found they were just on the finish of plastering my arm, which was put into a sling. I didn't have a bad night, as my arm felt a bit more secure.

First thing in the morning the MO made his rounds. He seemed a very jolly type of chap. It was quite a long time before he got round to my bed, as he was talking quite a lot to everyone, even sparring up to some of them, and making them laugh. He asked me how my arm was and said next time don't hit anyone so hard. During the day a sergeant nurse came round to check my number, name, rank and unit, and told me to be ready for returning to camp tomorrow.

The trouble was that it happened to be my right arm, and I wouldn't be able to write letters for a few weeks. George Bonham offered to do any writing for me and as he was a reliable type of chap I accepted. One thing, I didn't have to worry about Dusty, staying as he was in the officers' quarters in Reykjavik. The staff sergeant was in charge at our camp.

The lorry went down to pick Dusty up if he needed to come up. As we didn't have much work to do, we filled in with map reading and rifle drill with target practice. Of course I was counted out of the drill and practice, until the hospital sent for me to take the plaster off, and I was soon back to carry on as normal.

We had been getting our mail pretty well. One of the other fellows who came from Stoughton Barracks with us used to correspond with another fellow who was transferred to a regiment which then went out to join the Eighth Army. He sent a letter, which had taken nearly six months to arrive, wanting to know if he was still in the same unit as me. If so, would he inform me that the coloured chap who I used to go into Guildford with had been killed. I felt really sorry, as he was quite a nice fellow.

We used to visit the American camp quite a lot, we got on very well with them. It was surprising to find how well equipped they were now. They had all modern things, like electric shavers, while we used razors and water, and had to make do with cold water.

As we were soon expected to move Dusty had to show the American OC the area we covered, and the little things we had to do. And so they arranged for Dusty to sleep at their camp for two or three days. The officers' sleeping tent was actually a marquee, which gave them plenty of room, being only a few officers, with camp beds, and a small cupboard and stool alongside every bed. Also they had portable showers and toilets quite close to the marquee.

Before he went up, Dusty told me the day he would be returning. I was to go up that morning to see if he wanted me to bring anything back, and what time to send his driver up. Many of our officers didn't trouble about batmen, the Americans didn't have them. They had an orderly that went in and tidied everything.

When I called in on that morning, the first chap to greet me was the fellow that walked about on watch duty. He gave me a grin and told me it had been Barnum's Circus all night. When I went in, half of them were still fast asleep. A couple were sitting up in bed giving themselves a shave with their portable electric razors. When I got to Dusty's bed, he was fast asleep, but tied to the bed from top to bottom with a lot of electric flex.

One of the officers who was already awake came over to help me to unwind him. He woke up and I asked if he was all right after a hectic night. He was beginning to get up, and told me to tell his driver to call in an hour's time. And so I left, having a good laugh. When I got back to our camp and told everyone, that created a bigger laugh.

32. CONTINUOUS DARKNESS AND SNOW

It was getting towards autumn time. One thing that took our eye when we were returning from town early one evening, and that was, I suppose it was farmers, and two or three policemen driving a large flock of sheep from the mountain area, down to the low ground where we were, ready for the winter. The policemen were blowing their whistles, I didn't notice if they had any dogs.

There seemed to be quite a bit of grass around, although it was inclined to be a bit volcanic. We used to get some good shooting practice amongst the rocks at times, and also a few manoeuvres over the wild country.

We had to start to clear the stores left in the two big sheds, which were being moved to a different site. Then it was us moving away. After saying cheerio to our American friends, we moved a bit farther inland, where another unit had been, and this time into Nissen huts, complete with a home made type of wooden beds. Then of course we had to collect our double sleeping bags, and blankets, and our kit bags containing our winter gear.

There was a brick building which was the cookhouse and another building which seemed to be an officers' mess as there was an officer still there. A short way away from the cookhouse were a couple more small Nissen huts, one which was shared by our CO, Dusty, and another officer. Two lads were working in the cookhouse in the mornings so it was easy for me to get Dusty's tea.

It was now the days were beginning to get shorter and we were beginning to wear our overcoats. Our winter underwear, shirts and denim overalls we had to mark and put in their own bundle which we also marked. They were then sent each week to the unit who saw to the laundry. I think they were from the Royal Engineers. But this was when the fun started. When the clean washing came back, and we opened our bundles, we had to find who'd received half of ours and who half of ours belonged to. We would often see 'Titch' (our cook Taffy) standing on his bed trying on denim trousers, with the bottoms trailing the floor, and someone else who'd received Titch's trousers, with them ending just below his knees.

It didn't seem to matter how much we marked our laundry, it always seemed to come off or be torn off in the wash. The officers had to see to their own washing. Dusty asked me to search around for somebody to do his. I went out one day and after walking over rough country and looking towards the hill and mountain regions, I could just see a house, which I made for, and knocked on the door. A middle aged woman came to the door, and she looked a bit frightened. And then a man came to the door, they each looked frightened.

I felt a bit sorry for them, the only thing I could do was to give them a smile. I tried to speak to them, when I found they could understand some English, and they seemed a bit relieved. I tried to explain to them about the washing, and where I was stationed, and I would pay them in krona, their currency. They seemed to understand and seemed a bit happier after that.

We began to get continuous darkness and snow as winter progressed. It seemed to get colder still, especially when we had to travel about. We had a coke fuel heater in the middle of our Nissen hut, and we kept it alight all night. It was during these nights that we saw what we called in England and Scotland the Northern Lights, the Aurora Borealis. These were beams of coloured light, which seemed to be weaving into each other, and they just kept moving. A most interesting sight.

And of course apart from the snow, it was the terrific winds, they'd probably be up to a hundred miles an hour. Our forage caps were no good in the winter, we then wore our woollen hats. We were issued with snow goggles which were a great help against snow blindness.

One morning I went to take Dusty his tea. He was now on his own as the other officer had left. There were two Nissen huts close together, and he was sleeping in the farthest one. I then started with his mug of really hot tea, and not too far to walk from the cookhouse, but there was a terrible wind out. As I went to pass from the first Nissen to Dusty's, it was just as though it was a wind tunnel.

I saw Dusty's tea blown out of his mug, and it was just like a ball, and the wind took it along until I lost sight of it. When I finally managed to get his tea to his hut, woke him up, stoked his fire up, I told him his first mug of tea had 'gone with the wind', and I don't know if he was still dreaming, as he said: "I liked that film."

One thing I never looked forward to, and I don't think I was the only one, was our weekly shower. We used to have to go to a Royal Engineers' camp some little way away, as they built shower facilities at their camps for the use of other units. As our unit had a four ton wagon, it only needed two trips to take our lot there and back. It was quite roomy inside, enough for about four of us under one shower, and there were two showers. The trouble was it would start off hot, and then go warm and then felt like ice. And so, it used to be in and out as fast as you could.

As it was getting near Christmas time we were issued with our own special Christmas cards to send to our families and friends. We managed to get our Christmas mail in time, and they would send lots of bits extra from home. I told them as everything was now rationed to keep chocolate and tobacco as we got our own rations.

Otherwise all units and RAF were on full duty as normal over Christmas. I still took Dusty's washing to the same house, as they'd got used to me. I had the truck to take me in this weather. What roads there were, were all made well up, with a small ditch each side for the snow to run off. In our daily travels I had noticed one or two small churches with small steeples. I don't think there were many places inland with any people, I think it was around the coastal areas where the main population was.

FORCES
IN
ICELAND

The 1941 Christmas card issued to the forces in Iceland to send home: the front of the card (left) and the inside (below)

CHRISTMAS GREETINGS
AND
THE BEST OF GOOD LUCK
FOR 1942

from

The Northern Lights

33. VOYAGE TO GOUROCK FOR SPRING LEAVE

After our trial through the winter, we looked forward to the spring of 1942. The days were beginning to get lighter, and the snow was beginning to go, we could see where we were now. There was still plenty of snow on the mountains further inland but I suppose it would go in time. It'd be a bit of a relief to get rid of all this winter gear, as it felt like a ton load, although the boots were not that heavy to wear. We'd been into town, there were quite a few more Americans about.

We had a pleasant surprise. We were told we should be be getting leave, one half of the unit first and the other half to follow. I'd been notified my leave would be in the first half. It would be three weeks excluding the travel. Charlie was happy, as he was going the same time as me. I said to him, I wonder if you'll find the Elephant and Castle still there after all the bombing.

He said: "For goodness sake don't worry me any more. I worry every night I go to bed." He used to look worried at times. I think he worried a lot about his wife in the bombing, also his own family, as I think they were getting on.

The time came. We loaded up on the transport which took us down to the dock at Reykjavik, there were quite a lot more troops waiting to go aboard. We had a pretty good voyage, and arrived this time in Gourock during the early morning. We were anchored out in mid stream so it was the ferry which would take us off, and then take us to the landing stage.

The troops who formed part of the crew came round to see that we'd left the area around our bunks all clean and tidy, and then we made our way on to the deck, where it was all bustle. We did have our breakfast down below, which helped to make up for one day and night which were quite rough and we had empty stomachs for a couple of days.

The ferry was alongside, ready to take the first consignment off. Then the OC of the ship announced everyone with passes marked for Scotland would be the first to leave, northern England, Midlands, and Wales in the afternoon, London and southern England in the evening. And so the Scottish clan began to move, officers, sergeants and all ranks. Dusty, being from Scotland, came up to me with a large bundle and told me to throw it to him when he got on to the ferry, as he couldn't carry all his load.

I picked up the bundle, told Charlie to look after my lot and followed Dusty over to the crowd going down the gangplank. I think this was a pretty big ship, as the ferry looked a long way down. I couldn't see Dusty, so I managed to get near the sergeant who was checking them down and gave the bundle to him, and told him it belonged to an officer waiting below. With that he took the bundle, shouted down: "Look out!" and down it went.

When I got back to Charlie, he said: "He had a cheek, didn't he? Why didn't you try and throw him down as well?" I said: "It's all right, Charlie. We've got a long time to wait yet before we leave. It won't surprise me if they get on to us London lot to help to clean up the ship while we're waiting." This they did. They kept giving us little jobs to do, but still it helped to pass the time away. It was early evening before we finally moved.

We were both now beginning to feel tired, and it was nice to walk on dry land. We then made our way to the railway station where we found the transport officer, and he told us the London train was leaving at 23.00 hours. I said to Charlie, that's 11 o'clock. The officer told us there was a NAAFI quite near with a rest room. So that's where we made for, just to get those rucksacks off our shoulders.

Two nice Scotch lasses took our rucksacks off and we were both gasping for a cup of tea. The girls told us to leave our gear there, as they would look after it. After a cup of tea and something to eat, we still had a long time to wait, so I said: "Let's have a walk out."

We hadn't got very far before we saw a cinema, so Charlie said, let's go in. It did help to pass the time away, although later on, I began to feel a bit uneasy, as once I found Charlie fast asleep, and I was feeling sleepy myself. So it was up and out and back to the NAAFI where we collected our gear and had a cup of tea and then waited for our train. There were quite a lot of other fellows still around waiting.

And so now it was just the matter of getting home. I woke up two or three times during the night, but soon we were beginning to enter St Pancras Station. After that it was Paddington, Reading, and Newbury and then the Lambourn train. I finally reached home in the early afternoon. Then it was all talk, talk, talk, but it was nice to be home, and to see everyone.

I was a bit busy doing a few odd jobs, as it was an old farmhouse and there was only Dad to do things. Otherwise I visited all my relatives in the village, also Shady, now living in a little old cottage on his own. When I walked in, he jumped up, with a big smile on his face, and when he came over to greet me, he had tears in his eyes.

We used to sit and talk, and he wanted to know if the Army fed us all right. He would then tell me all the tales of his own army experiences in the last war when he was in Egypt and Palestine. I knew the tales were true, as my cousin Cecil was with him, and two or three men who still lived in Lambourn had said Shady would go out in the night and bring back food.

Of course everyone wanted to know what Iceland was like, and if I'd seen any polar bears out there, as I wore one on each shoulder. And so, after an enjoyable three weeks, my time was up. It wasn't a very happy cheerio with a few tears. Lil Reading, my cousin, had enquired about my departure time from St Pancras, as she said she would come and see me off. There were quite a lot of servicemen about and a few sailors. I said to Lil I'd report to the transport officer first to make sure of the platform. After that, we just waited for the train to pull in.

Lil told me how her husband Syd and son Arthur managed during the air raids whilst she was away on a visit to the two girls who were then still in Devon after being evacuated. They stayed in their flat on the two top floors at Wedgwood House, Syd sitting in the armchair smoking a cigarette, listening to Arthur playing the piano.

Whilst I was in Iceland, Lil had been on one of her visits, when she had to suddenly return to London, as Syd had been taken into hospital with a lung haemorrhage. She brought the girls with her, and then took them to Lambourn. They went to school there.

Jill in the back garden at Upper Bockhampton, with the shed-cum-privy in the background

One thing I noticed since my leave. All the time I was home, I had a head cold. Since I'd been back in Iceland, it had completely gone. After a few more weeks, we moved into Reykjavik where we were stationed in a rather large building which was still in the course of construction, but of course all work had stopped for the time being. We were able to make ourselves quite comfortable. We'd been told we'd be going back to England soon.

And now we were ready to move. We'd been in Iceland nearly eleven months. Charlie was as happy as a sandboy, as a matter of fact, we all were. We had two naval ships escorting us and it was when we were getting towards Scotland that we had an aerial alert. We were ordered to stand by on the top deck but under cover.

All the guns were now firing from all the ships, and we could see the splashes as the bombs dropped into the sea. One or two dropped quite near, but we were lucky. We carried on until we began to see land. First it was quite a number of rocks sticking out from the sea, and then it was land, Scotland. After quite a long while we found we were sailing up the River Clyde. Although it was Scotland, we still said we were home.

We travelled through the night on a train, and morning found us in Cardiff once again, where transport took us to Barry. Afterwards we moved just a short way on to St Athan but we weren't there long before we moved a short way back to Porthkerry which was now ready for us. There was a large house with one or two other small buildings around. We were able to utilize all the rooms in the house, and the outbuildings. Our cook did all our food. There was a small church quite near. It was mentioned that we hadn't attended church for a year. And so, getting to our first Sunday, the sergeant asked who wanted to go to church. I was surprised at the number who volunteered. Apart from three or four, the whole unit put their hands up. During our time there we were found lots of small jobs to do just to keep us busy. We often used to walk into Barry and along the sea front, and we did have two weeks' disembarkation leave.

And so then we were on our way to Norfolk, to a small station called East Dereham. It was a lovely summer day, and when we left the train the air seemed so fresh and clear. Transport was waiting and we soon found ourselves at a place called Lexham Hall. It was more like a mansion than a large house, but I was told afterwards all those type of mansions are called halls in Suffolk or Norfolk. We turned off the road through the gates on to the estate, along a straight drive which was well over a quarter of a mile long, and which was lined with walnut trees.

We then went through some smaller gates which opened out to the front of the house. Woodland was all the way round it. On the left were three small buildings like stables or garages, on the right just by the gate was a small Nissen hut which was the guardroom. A bit farther in, right to the edge of the woods were two more Nissen huts, which were our sleeping quarters.

Much of the building was occupied by young children, we never saw them but we could often hear them. Quite a proportion of the house came under the military, and Dusty had his bedroom there. When I entered the house it was at the rear and this was when I could view the estate at the back, a lovely large stretch of green and then bordered all around with woodland.

There were just about a dozen military personnel left from the previous unit until we took over. The lads told us all about the place, what to do and where to go. There were a few RAF bases around the area, so there were often dances or shows of some kind taking place.

142

We had to do guard duty every night at the gate opening out to the main driveway. Otherwise we didn't have any special jobs to do, it seemed as though we were just waiting for active service. Guard duties were from 10 pm to 6 am for three guards, and a corporal or sergeant as guard commander. We had parade each morning, and after that awaited orders for the rest of the day. Our meals we had in one of the small buildings on the other side of the house.

Our staff sergeant thought perhaps a few of us who were not on guard duty could find our way down to the local pub whilst the evening was light. This we arranged with about half a dozen of us. It was a small pub called the Chequers which was in the village of East Lexham, which contained only a small row of houses. The only way we could visit the pub was through the wood, which bordered our Nissen huts, it was part of the estate and quite thick in parts.

There were quite a few small paths that led off in different directions, so you had to beware, and keep to the straight path. Eventually you came out into open meadow which contained quite a few cattle. It was a fair size meadow, but we soon crossed over to the gate, climbed over and then it was a short way to the left to the pub.

We went in the one door, it was all red brick floor, with a small room on the right with four or five elderly men, I should imagine they were farmhands. On the left was a larger room with a large round table in the middle with chairs all around. This room we went into, when a chap came in to take our orders, and then his wife came in to help. They told us this was where all the soldiers came who stayed at the big house. They were very pleasant, they liked to come in to chat to us. Altogether, it was a pleasant evening. They told us they were not open every day, as beer was rationed.

We managed to find our way back through the wood all right as it wasn't properly dark, and we all walked in single file. When we got back, Charlie was sitting on his bed still writing letters, the others were either writing or reading.

35. ON DUTY AT BIRKENHEAD DOCKS

We were getting used to Lexham Hall and the surrounding countryside. If we turned right when we went out of the main gate, that was the road which took us to the village of Litcham, about a mile away. This was a larger village than East Lexham, with quite a few shops, and one or two bus services to different places. There was a bus that ran to King's Lynn on a Saturday, so we had a trip in a couple of times. Quite a busy little place.

One Sunday, we had a church parade, that made a change. It was for some special occasion and took place at the church at Litcham. There was another company of soldiers who came for the parade and we marched from the hall to the church led by the pipes of the Seaforth Highlanders. After church transport was waiting to take them back to their base, we made our own way back to the hall.

I'd done my turn of guard duty several times. To me the worst two periods were from 12 till 2 and 2 till 4. Otherwise we were in the guardhouse. The first thing was, when you took over from the old guard, you were all tension. You were looking straight along the main drive. Sometimes the night being clear, you could see the main gates, sometimes you couldn't. Sometimes you thought you could see something moving about, sometimes you didn't.

My first two or three duties were rather quiet. The next was a bit more lively. My turn was 12 o'clock till 2. We were in a straight line with the city of Norwich, and it was not a great way away. This night, it suffered an air raid. I could first hear the noise of the planes, and then bombs dropping.

By looking towards Norwich I could see all the different reflections and then I could hear some dog fight taking place, as it was the RAF planes that went up, there being all the airfields around us. Sometimes the noise of the planes seemed to come quite close. Quite often they tried to bomb the airfields, it was something we got used to.

The couple in the pub (their names were Mr and Mrs Grimes) told us that only a short time ago, I suppose it was after a dog fight, two German parachutists had landed at different times – one right on the estate, the other in open country. The one that landed on the estate found his way out from the bottom end and gave himself up to the police, as the other one did. Their planes were both found a few miles away.

We went down to the pub about three times a week. We didn't drink a lot, but it occupied the evening and Mr and Mrs Grimes liked to see us and have a chat. They told us they used to do fire duty when there was any activity in the area, but not now, as I suppose the Home Guard did it.

One evening, as we were leaving, Mr and Mrs Grimes called me back. They then asked me if I would like to go to supper one or two evenings, when they weren't open. And so I agreed and thanked them, and ran and caught up with the others. I often wondered why it was just me they invited. I felt a bit awkward with the other lads, as I had to tell them, but those other evenings, apart from guard duty, there was always a run to one of the nearest airfields where there was a NAAFI or something on, so they took it in good part.

Mr and Mrs Grimes always seemed so pleased to see me, I think just to have some company. Of course they liked to ask me a few questions and where I came from. Mrs Grimes told me she originally was from London, but came to Norfolk when she was small and later on married Mr Grimes. She said they never had children, so I think they were beginning to feel a bit lonely. So after another pleasant evening, which seemed to have lasted a bit longer than usual, I said: "I'll have to say goodnight," thanking them for an enjoyable supper (they always provided a good supper) and so made my way. It had got dark. I got over the gate to cross the meadow to reach the wood, the sky must have been heavily clouded, as it seemed to be extra dark. Crossing the meadow the first thing to happen was, I fell over a cow lying down.

Of course I was stretched over the top of the cow, and the cow was moving and trying to get up. That sent my legs up in the air and me over on to the grass. I got up and then had to find the entrance into the wood. By then, the sky seemed to have cleared a bit, and the next thing was to keep to the right path, there was no lingering, just get out of the wood as soon as possible.

I managed to get along quite well when suddenly I felt as though somebody had knocked my forage cap off. I just happened to have the thought of stray parachutists on my mind, and so I ran as best I could keeping to the path. After what seemed a long time I reached the end of the wood.

There were only about half a dozen lads in the billet sitting on their beds reading when I walked in, a bit out of breath. They wanted to know the trouble. When I told them, they did have a laugh about it, but for me it meant getting up a bit earlier in the morning to look for my cap, as I couldn't go on parade without it on. Just off the path, a small branch sticking out from the side of a tree about my height had caught it. Good job it didn't rain during the night.

This was how we got on during a lovely summer, including just over a week's leave at the start of September, and now it was beginning to change into autumn. We had one or two walnuts off the trees that lined the drive, but they needed to stay a bit longer. We were getting into October and we had further orders to move, this time up to Birkenhead.

This meant another lot of goodbyes to the friends we'd made, although we only made a few there, as East Lexham only had a few houses, but they were all good friends, especially Mr and Mrs Grimes. I think they now looked upon me as an adopted son, and I kept in touch with them for the rest of their lives. All our lads who used to visit the Chequers came down on the last night, with the friends we knew, which made quite a party. And then it was the goodbyes, a lot of noise and cheerios. I think this was the best send off we had, from all the different places we camped.

I had previously given Mr and Mrs Grimes my name, number, and unit, as they had asked me for them. And so I said cheerio to them, they were both wiping tears in their eyes, and put a small parcel into my hands. I gave them a quick hug and thanked them, and as it was now quite dark, I ran to catch the others up.

And so it was up next morning, firstly opening the parcel kindly given to me last night, as I was then too tired to open it. It contained a pair of socks, handkerchiefs and a scarf. I really appreciated that, as all those things were now on ration. I would write to thank them again, when I next got settled. Now I must start packing my gear, help to clean the billet out and wait for the transport, which wasn't long coming. Then it was goodbye Lexham Hall.

We were taken to Thetford, where we picked up our train for Liverpool. We arrived at Lime Street Station, where transport took us off through the Mersey Tunnel into Birkenhead, and then on to a place called Bidston. This was a proper military area with sleeping quarters and food and everything, also guarded as this was where we would leave our gear and we should be at the docks each day.

There were just a few of us detailed to different docks where ships were being loaded for military use. Our main job was to watch out for leaking petrol cans before they were stacked for loading, as we would then take them, and report the number to be emptied. Otherwise the dockers did the work. Of course, there were canteens on the docks which opened for morning break, dinner time and afternoon break. And so when the dockers went, we followed suit. It was nearly a couple of miles from Bidston down to the docks, but a small lorry went down that way every morning at the time we started out. It was open, and when the driver saw us he would slow up and we would all make a run and jump on. The lorry never went to the docks, he would slow up at the nearest point for us to jump off. Otherwise we had to walk.

I had a bit of a surprise one day. When Dusty came round visiting us on the docks, he asked me if I could call at the house he was staying in with his wife just to give them a bit of a musical evening on the piano. Well of course I agreed, he gave me his address.

And so I went along. I soon found the house, I was introduced to his wife, quite nice. They had a drink, they offered me one, and altogether, after a chat and I played, I think they enjoyed their evening. I was wondering, if his wife had come down from Scotland like him, as she didn't sound Scotch in her speech. Of course, I had to tell all the other lads about it when I got back to the billet. Charlie said to me: "You had a cheek to go and meet his wife."

Charlie never came out much on our off duty times, but I did have another good pal that I went out with. His name was Geoff Brooksbank, he was another Yorkshireman, like my singing chum in Caerphilly, and his home was at Guiseley on the borders of Leeds. Geoff was a quiet type of chap, but had much the same ideas as me. He did all the clerical work and he was quite popular with the other lads. When we needed passes to go over to Liverpool he would make them out for Dusty to sign. We were all right in Birkenhead, but needed a pass to go anywhere further.

It was better for us if we wanted to look around Liverpool, to go over during daylight, as otherwise everywhere was in darkness and you had to know your way around. And it was always a wise thing to make sure we had our pass, as the military police were always waiting at the exits of all rail underground, and ferries.

Geoff and I would often go over to Liverpool on the underground, and we gradually got to know our way around. We were told to make our way up towards the cathedral where we would find a NAAFI and amusements for service men and women. The place seemed rather spacious with different rooms leading off for billiards, darts, table tennis, also a music room.

This room was a bit smaller, but contained quite a modern gramophone with a large stock of records, mainly classical. It also contained quite a number of easy chairs, and a notice over the door, 'Silence is requested'. Geoff said, we'll go in and sit down. This we did, as there were about half a dozen servicemen sitting in there listening to records. I asked Geoff if he liked classical music. He said very much, but he liked other music as well. Like me. And so we spent quite a pleasant time there.

Another time a crowd of us went to a concert at St George's Hall. It was given by one of the symphony orchestras, with one or two artistes. It was given for all service men and women, and so we got our tickets through our unit. I don't know about the others, but both Geoff and I enjoyed it. A couple of times our unit was invited out by members of a club in Birkenhead. They had nice club rooms and gave us a concert with full refreshments. It was really enjoyable.

One of the first things I did when I arrived was to write to my brother Lal who was living in Liverpool with his wife and son. They lived at West Derby and it was a tram ride from the centre of Liverpool, and the tram ran straight past their road. I visited them, and they were pleased to see me. Their son Peter was growing up, must be about thirteen years old. They'd got a nice little house and garden front and back, with roses in both, so it was nice to know they were settled, as Lal had not been very happy about leaving London. I made a few visits.

36. DEATH AT UPPER BOCKHAMPTON FARM

At the beginning of December I travelled home, Dad hadn't been too well lately. I reached Lambourn in the afternoon. Dad was in bed, and in rather a bad way, I went straight upstairs to see him. His breathing was bad, and his eyes were half closed, but when he saw me he seemed to rally a bit. He tried to mumble something and put his hand out to shake my hand, but it was very feeble.

And so I sat up with him for quite a long time, he just slept most of the time. I said I would sit up with him during the night, but this they wouldn't let me do. I did sit up till late to give the others a bit of a break, then I went to bed. It was in the morning when they brought me a cup of tea that I was told Dad had died during the night.

I don't think he really enjoyed his retirement. He was comfortable at Bockhampton Farm, he always loved Lambourn; but I think the first thing was the manner of his retirement from Jenner's Brewery. That was his main job through his whole life. He was just given a plain dismissal, with not even a word of thank you. I think this hurt him.

Secondly, it was having to leave the old house in Kennington Road, where he always looked forward to his Sunday musical evenings. All this put together, I think that's where his life ended. He had a nice funeral, with a large family gathering. I was glad I was able to be at home for the occasion. My sister Gert and little Jill had moved down home from Brixton. I'd been a bit worried about them after their flat was damaged by bombing. Gert said they'd now given the flat up.

It was nearing Christmas, and Lal asked me if I was off duty over the holiday. He said he would like me to come over, and if I had a friend to bring, all the better. The whole unit would be off duty

December 25th and 26th, so that gave us two days' leave. Charlie wanted to stay at the billet and take it easy, and so I asked Geoff if he would like to spend the Christmas at my brother's. He was quite pleased with the invitation, and so I was pleased I had someone to go with me. We managed to go over on the Christmas Eve, as the next day there wasn't any transport running, it being Christmas Day. We had a very enjoyable Christmas, quite enough to eat and drink and a lot of talking. We stayed until the Boxing Day.

We carried on just the same, working on different docks according to where ships were being loaded for war supplies. It was about the end of January when we received orders to move. I took the chance to make a quick visit to my brother's and it was next day we started to pack our gear. All that completed, it was the next day when transport arrived to take us to the railway station. After a journey south, we found ourselves in Woking in Surrey.

We were taken to a new housing estate with good types of houses that had never been used, as I imagined they'd been taken over by the War Department. Between us, we used about three or four houses. One was used for the office, where the detail sheet was hung up for the day's duties.

The main thing now was to check all our gear, boots, clothing, battledress, to see everything was in order, and then it was for some of us to pay visits to the dentist, which included me, for teeth inspection. I had to make three visits. While we are on the subject of teeth, I must mention one little story. There were two or three of the lads that came from London that included Charlie. As London was only a short distance by fast train, they were lucky, as they could get a day pass and go home. This is what Charlie did one day.

It was during the evening time, when the few of us in our room were sitting on our beds talking or reading. I must mention it was now the beginning of February and at that time Woking was a quiet place. And so we had no reason to go out in the evenings unless we were invited as it was too dark. I was just thinking about Charlie coming back in the dark, when in he walked. He looked a bit unkempt and dirty, and his mouth seemed different. I said: "What's happened? You don't look like Charlie."

He just looked at me and the others who came over, and said: "I don't feel like Charlie either. I fell out of the train. It had stopped at the station, but I was the only one to get off. As it was so dark, and no lights shining, I got out the wrong side and went on to the track. The people in the compartment pulled the cord and along came the guard and a couple of porters. One porter jumped down to see if I was all right. The others must have alerted the signalbox as they had to beware of the current, the track having an electric rail."

He said he was all right, but a bit shaken. His big worry was, his false teeth. He had a full set, and it was the top set which had come out through the jolt when he touched the ground. The porter had his torch with him, and he was really lucky as the teeth were right by the porter's feet, but they had broken in half. After leaving his name and number with the guard in case of any injuries or trouble, the train moved off.

Charlie had to report to the dentist we'd been using, to take his broken teeth in. I went with him as I'd been there, and it was rather a long way. The next day, I went with Charlie to pick up his choppers, as he called them, as I wanted to call in a couple of shops. Afterwards he came out, beaming all over his face. I said: "You look like the other Charlie now."

Just about that time we had a new intake. He was only a young fellow in his twenties, and looked a bit lost as he dumped his gear on the floor. The room was rather large and there were four of us sleeping on the floor, so there was room for another one. Charlie and me helped him to unpack and go along where the stores were kept to collect his mattress and blankets. After he'd got settled we found some chairs to sit on and asked all about him. Charlie was anxious to know where he came from. He said London, so Charlie seemed a bit happier, I don't know why, as I got on well with all the other lads wherever they came from. Anyway he said his name was Reg Anderson, and he'd got married just before his call up. He'd been working for one of the newspapers in Fleet Street. He'd been transferred from the driving school to this unit, as the Captain would need a driver when we went overseas.

Reg got quite used to us, as he did with all the other lads, otherwise it was a case of having to. We were just the one unit, and like one family, if one was in trouble, we all gathered round.

When the evenings began to get a bit lighter, it gave us a chance to get out for a bit more exercise. Occasionally we went into the town, three or four of us. Also, the people from the church which was nearby would invite us to a little 'do' in their hall, which we always enjoyed. I liked to try and write home as often as I could, although I wasn't allowed to give them much news.

I liked to know how my two schoolday pals George Oliver and Len Wohlgemuth were getting on. I knew Len was with the RAF but they told me George was in the Tank Corps and had managed to make a couple of visits to Lambourn. One visit was when he was stationed in the North of England, and he was starting his leave, thumbing a lift. It wasn't very long before a car drew up, the driver being an RAF officer. He asked George how far he was going, and of course George told him Lambourn.

The officer looked at him and asked his name and then told George he was a lucky chap, as he was going to his home at Lambourn. "So I hope your luck stays." And so George jumped in and off they went. They told me they were surprised when George walked in. It was one of the sons of a local farmer he came with. That made a bit of interesting news, besides news of all the different relatives that kept coming down to keep clear of the bombing in London. I suppose you couldn't blame them.

We had now been told Cpl Brooksbank would issue new shoulder flashes to each individual. It was the crusader's cross, a white shield with a red cross, the sign of the First Army. They were to be sewn on the top of each arm. This meant doing a bit of our own sewing, to some of the chaps a near impossible job, but some were expert. As the job had to be thorough, it meant one helping the other.

Otherwise this was much easier than when we had to wear the polar bears as some were issued with the wrong pairs, which meant, after being sewn on, that one bear was chasing the other. Each side should have been facing forward.

Then we were told we would be moving. We were taken to Clapham Junction and into a large kind of hall where we had a meal, quite a large number of troops were already there, all wearing the same arm flash. It was late afternoon when we boarded a train, and what a long train it was. It was getting towards early evening when we moved off. Later on, and of course we all carried our mugs handy, hot tea was brought round, and then it was dozing and waking up, dozing off again, until it began to get light.

Then we were moving slowly along the outskirts of Glasgow and the River Clyde. We finally came to a halt, and so, as the compartment was pretty full, we had to get out on to the platform before we could sort our gear out. That meant full back pack, gas mask, side pack, steel helmet, rifle and kit bag. And of course they all had to be fitted on and worn before we could form up ready to move. Our unit then followed the others to board a large ship called the City of Durban. It was February 25th 1943.

We used to do exercises every day on deck, the same as all the other companies, in the early morning. One morning we noticed we were heading towards the Mediterranean, then we could see the rising sun right behind the Rock of Gibraltar, it was really a remarkable view.

As we were well into the Med, that's when we had our first submarine alert. Of course we were all on lifeboat stations, whilst the escort ships started depth charging. It put all the ship's company on the alert, but it passed, and so we made our way to Algiers, as that was our destination. That's where the trouble really started. We were told afterwards that enemy planes waited for troop convoys to approach Algiers, and while they were docking, would attack.

Our ship managed to dock alongside a rather long jetty behind another ship which was off loading. There were some naval ships in the dock firing back at the enemy planes. Our own escort ships, although they were a bit farther out, were also firing. We had been standing on the alert for two hours with all our packs on, wearing our helmets, carrying rifle and kit bag, awaiting the order to off load.

It was when the ship finished docking that we received the order to move at full pelt along the jetty until we reached cover. Ships on either side of the jetty were firing away. I didn't hear anything being hit as we were too busy running, and dragging our kit bags, as we couldn't run very fast and carry our kit bag. Finally, we managed to reach cover, and amongst all the confusion, sort ourselves out and find the others of the unit. I don't think there were any injuries of any kind. Eventually we loaded on to transport. It was March 9th.

Moving through the city of Algiers, it seemed a bit strange to see the women wearing white with their faces half covered, and the Arab men and boys walking about. It was all quiet, as they only bombed the docks when convoys arrived. We then arrived at our destination where we were shown through a kind of a tunnel and out into the open where we came to an infants' school. We were taken inside and shown to large rooms, which I suppose were classrooms, and stacks of camp beds. We were shown the ablutions, only cold water, and the toilets which were low down, on the ground, so that meant a bit of manoeuvring.

It was quite a relief that we could off load the heavy packs we'd been carrying for about the last five hours. We were told to lock the place up as we'd dumped our kit down, and then shown to a large building next door which seemed like a type of warehouse. Remains of the last unit were still working there waiting to hand over to us. This building also had sleeping accommodation for the sergeants and our cook Taffy, as it had a kitchen.

Our responsibility was to supply all remaining units, in or about Algiers, with food and other necessities, which were stored in this building. There were only a few units, as everything was being moved east along with the fighting forces. We still had quite a fair amount of stores left in the building. Certain items in the way of beer, spirits or cigarettes and tobacco would be issued to naval ships who had probably run short of their own supplies. We had quite a lot of fruit in the store, especially oranges.

Vic and Taffy, the cook

Dusty gave me my orders for the morning. I was to be outside the building by 7 o'clock, when an officer would drive up in a small van to pick me up. I was out on time, no tea as Taffy hadn't made any yet, so it was a glass of water. The van drew up on time and I jumped in the back. It was then back to the docks, the part where the fish were landed and sorted and laid out ready for sale.

I jumped out and the officer came round and introduced himself, and told me what to do. He went round to buy certain types and amounts of fish, and told the porter to bring them over to me standing by the van. All the different types of fish were in their own trays. When the officer had finished, he came over to inspect them and showed me where to stack them in the van, leaving me room to travel in the back. This being a private van driven by an Algerian he travelled with the driver.

He then left me there with the driver while he went off to the office. I was to find he was often gone for quite some considerable time while he sorted out who was going to get what. Finally he came back and told me that we had to visit four field hospitals to deliver the fish. That's what we did. This was my job each morning while we were in Algiers. Tomorrow, it would be 6.30 when they picked me up and that would be the regular time. I didn't know if the officer belonged to the Medical Corps or our corps but he seemed to know just what kind of fish to get.

It was about 12 o'clock when I got back to our store, and then I helped out with the others during the afternoon. We had a light lunch about mid day, and our main meal in the early evening. Having to start out early every morning, and Taffy not getting up early enough to get any tea made, I just made do, as I now managed to take some fruit with me which was enough until I got back.

It was beginning to get a bit warm. We did get a laugh sometimes when we had to visit the toilets. It was when you walked in and found three or four already there stooped right on the ground like the children, laughing at themselves. There were two or three toilets for adults which I presumed were for teachers, but they were the same except larger places to put their feet.

We hadn't made contact with the Americans yet, as they landed at Casablanca in Morocco, and so were making their advance further south in Algeria, to reach Tunis. The First Army landed at Oran and Algiers and were making their advance to Tunis via the Atlas Mountains range. We did manage to get a bit of off duty and whilst we were there we liked to make a hurried look around Algiers.

There were always lots of sailors and servicemen about, although it was mainly French Algerians and Arabs. They'd always got stalls laid out with souvenirs and whatnots they wanted you to buy, and they'd keep following you all over the place. One time we came to rather a busy little market, all Arabs, showing their wares and trinkets and asking fabulous prices. They'd get as much as they could out of you. Of course we always liked to pick up a souvenir if we thought it was worth it.

I mention 'we' all the time as it was always about half a dozen of us. We kept looking around, and then came to rather a large type of stall, in a kind of circle with a couple of Arabs in the middle doing the selling. It was mainly pictures, as probably they'd painted a lot of their own. They all seemed the type of Arabic background, and not much variation. Also the frames were cheap, and I didn't think the paintings were on canvas, it seemed like a paper backing to me.

We happened to be next to a couple of young sailors busy looking at these pictures. I think this Arab thought he had a good customer here, and so he pounced on one of them, and started bargaining with him. They always started well at the top, and he managed to say in broken English: "Sailor, very good, hundred pounds, very good." The sailor said: "Keep it." I said to our others, it's not worth a pound.

The Arab then picked up the painting, and still said: "Very good, sailor," and kept pushing it against him. Next thing the sailor picked it up and hit the Arab on the head with it. As I thought it was only a kind of paper, and his head went right through. There he was, standing with the painting lying over his shoulders. The two sailors moved off, doubled over with laughter, and we moved off as well full of laughter.

We now had our orders to move, and we had to be at the racecourse in Algiers. That was where they had the pony and trotting races. It was beginning to get very warm, and it was a 'must' to make sure our water bottles were kept filled, that was an order. We had been provided with berets, instead of the forage caps, but we were still wearing battledress, we couldn't expect anything else while we were on the move.

At the racecourse a fleet of three ton lorries were waiting, I think about fifty, all loaded with ammunition. There were already other units from other corps who were loading on to the lorries. We were ordered two or three on each lorry, in the rear along with the ammunition. Our sergeants would be travelling behind with all our heavy kit in our own lorries. And so after an officer came along to inspect each vehicle, it was then we were off.

We avoided a lot of the mountain range, and I must say the road was very good. We had despatch riders trailing up and down to see that the convoy was kept in order, as we may have stretched out for two or three kilometres. The main thing was we had to be prepared for aircraft attack. We did have a quick halt on the way, I didn't know the reason, but we went on until the evening. We'd travelled just over one hundred and fifty kilometres.

We managed to get back to our two lorries right at the rear of the convoy to get our meal which was being prepared. We had a water wagon with the convoy which refilled all our water bottles and tea urns which our own lorries carried. We were told that we would leave the convoy, and travel on our own lorries tomorrow on a different route. And so we returned to seal up the lorry we'd been travelling in all day, as Arabs were always about, night and day.

It was a hot night, and we all kipped down where we could. I, with some of the others, slept underneath our lorries with our rucksacks for a pillow and lying on top of our rifles and any valuables.

Postcard of Algiers, a souvenir of Vic's stay in the city

Although we did hear the despatch riders, who were up and down during the night on guard duty, I slept very well as it had been a tiring day. We were halted near a large house with quite a few outbuildings.

As I awoke and crawled out from underneath the lorry, I looked up to the top of the house and saw a great big bird sitting on the roof. I was told it was a stork, it was the first time I'd seen one. I think the house belonged to a French Algerian, as it seemed like a farm of some kind or a vineyard. Anyway our sergeant went to see if they could provide us with water for washing. They had a spring so that helped us out. It was all right to drink so we filled up while we could.

Taffy, our cook, was able to make us some tea, and so we had a breakfast. The convoy was now ready to start off and leave us. We'd been told we had to wait for our Captain Dusty Miller, who would follow along. It was about mid day when he arrived. He had been provided with a small service vehicle with Reg as his driver. After his talk with the sergeants, we were off again.

On our way we overtook an Arab walking along with a large load, I couldn't see if it was wood or hay or grasses, but it seemed huge. I wondered what was carrying it. After we had moved a bit farther along, looking back, it was a donkey carrying that load. We could just see his head and his feet, otherwise he seemed completely covered.

We travelled away from the mountain region, and over the weekend we stayed at a small town called Constantine in a large kind of building with different rooms. The Americans must have been quite near as the American padre came over to give us a short service on the Sunday. He also brought with him a small organ or harmonium as he told us afterwards that our officer had informed him that there was somebody in the unit who could play. As that meant me, well, I was only too pleased to help out, and it went off quite well, with three hymns.

39. SOUK EL ARBA, NEAR THE FIGHTING

Quite a long way on we came to a place called Souk el Arba, which we had to take over. We were not a great way behind the fighting, and we'd got to fix up an issue depot. We were near the Americans, as both armies were gradually closing up to meet the Eighth Army at Tunis, although the enemy still seemed to be holding on well.

It felt a change to get down on our feet. There were three or four small buildings and a few tents left by the previous unit. We had latrines and washing facilities left by previous units and so were not too badly off. Dusty had his own tent for sleeping, so I didn't have much to do for him, just to fold up any loose clothes. There was nothing much on the bed during this heat, and we had no time for anything like pyjamas.

We were not too far from the village, mostly kinds of Arab dwellings. We had a wadi running along near us, a kind of river bed, but it was already dried up. We did have a few different units stationed round about, such as the Ordnance Corps petrol unit, REME (Royal Electrical and Mechanical Engineers) workshops, and Royal Engineers, so we were not actually isolated.

That first day we had to get busy to arrange everything, ready for storage, sleeping, cooking and feeding, and office and field telephone. It was tomorrow that one of our sergeants, with two or three of us, went with our lorries to the rail head a few kilometres away to open a sealed truck. The sergeant had the key and cutters, and they had to check all the contents which they then off loaded on to our lorries for us to stack in our store. We had two lorries, one coming, one going, and it meant a few journeys before the truck got emptied.

Dusty had given our staff sergeant a list of what we should expect, and it was up to us to stack each type of food in its own area or marquee ready for issue. The majority of food was for hot climates. Bread would be possible only by army bakers, otherwise it was biscuits. Fruit and vegetables would be obtained locally. I must say, mostly during summer time, fruit was always plentiful. It was towards evening time when the last lorry came back, and after off loading, we were ready for a wash and our evening meal. It had been a sweating day.

One good thing, along with our intake of supplies came our KDs (khaki drills, or summer wear): two shirts, one pair of shorts, one pair of long trousers to be worn every evening, overalls to be worn for dirty jobs. We now had a Medical Officer who visited us every so often for an inspection and each day we had to take our anti malaria tablet. We were all urgently looking forward to some mail, as it had been a long time since we received our last lot. Charlie was getting quite worried.

We got ourselves straight, and we started issuing two days later. We were responsible for a large area, and it would be the representative (quartermaster or sergeant) with their transport and helpers who would be collecting. Most of the things that I should be dealing with I'd stored in one tent, and I'd managed to fix a table up, of sorts, just outside, the same as most of the other lads were doing.

Quite a lot of the unit representatives were from well up towards the forward lines, some collecting for a large number, some for a small number, and each representative must first apply at the office situated in one of the buildings. Geoff and the staff sergeant worked in the office, and just divided off to the rear was Dusty's office. After they had reported to the staff sergeant, they passed on to Geoff, who made out their list in order of collection as we were arranged outside.

Altogether this saved a lot of time, as some representatives had to come from quite a distance. I was on the last for issues as apart from some speciality types of food, and surgical supplies, I also had cigarettes and tobacco, or sweets and chocolate. It was the QMs who had to distribute these out in their own units as it had to be one or the other. As they were rationed, we were allowed cigarettes and tobacco, or sweets and chocolate, whichever we preferred. The next thing was the air mail letters, one letter allowed for each person in each unit or company.

That was a bit of a job, especially if it happened to be a large amount. These I had to count out with the unit representative, as he was responsible for taking back the right number. I had a good helper if he happened to be handy. That was Reg, Dusty's driver, as usually on these days Dusty was busy in his office, so Reg was hanging about, and he always came over to where I was working. The first time I was issuing air mails and counting them, I think it was about two hundred. He stood watching me for a few minutes and said: "Let me do it, I can help you," so I handed them to him.

And he just picked a packet up, held them with his thumb and fingers and spread them out like you would with a pack of cards and that's the way he counted. Of course I should have remembered, he was working for the general newspapers when he got his call up, and he said he was doing that kind of job nearly every day. After that he taught me how to do it.

We had a large number of units call on our first day, and the last units went late afternoon, and so it was getting on towards early evening when we were able to wash and have a meal. It seemed a lot better now we were wearing our KDs, but it was still hot. Hotter inside the tent than out in the sun. Next day it was checking remaining stock and making room for our next delivery. During the day I had to call in the office, and noticed our carpenter Geordie's good job in making a small separate office for Dusty. Another day we had a truck to off load at the rail head, so it was my turn, with another, to do the off loading with our sergeant Steve Madden.

It was quite some distance. When we arrived there, we were held up by the gates across the through line which I suppose was the line from Tunis to Algiers. Our truck was over the other side in the sidings. There was an American lorry already waiting, the driver who was a black sergeant standing by his lorry.

After waiting for quite some time, we could hear the sound of a train. It wasn't long before the train came along very slowly, and it was full of prisoners, I think mostly Italians, and they were all crowded at the windows shouting for 'aqua'. It was a long train, I suppose bound for Algiers. And so we managed to reach our truck.

Another day we were told that an ENSA party would be putting on a show near the village. Apparently there was a large type of shed there which had been taken over by the military, and so this was where they entertained. There were three or four of us that went on this particular evening, plus quite a few from some of the different units round about. We were about half way through when 'BANG'. It sounded like a bomb, then another one.

One of the officials who ran the ENSA party came on to the platform to tell us: "Sorry, there's an air raid on. If you want to leave, do so, we will carry on." And so, between us few, we thought we'd better go, as our depot was the nearest to the village. However, when we got back, there was no damage. They said it was a couple of enemy planes who had sneaked over to get rid of their bombs. We found afterwards a bomb had dropped into the wadi, not very far away.

On another day, which was an issuing day, I was attending to one unit, when one of the chaps who was collecting said to me: "How are you getting on then?" When I looked up to study him, I recognized him as one of the maintenance men who worked at the Waldorf Hotel when I was there. And another day it was Ernie Rockhill, he was sitting behind me at a film show. His family lived in the flats at Wedgwood House along on the same balcony as my family, so we knew them well.

40. WE ENTER TUNIS

The battle for Tunis had been going on for some time, and a final advance was being made by combined French, British, Indian and American troops. And so we had to push forward. We moved quite a long way to a place called Béja, and the lorries we were travelling in were all open at the back. That was a really hot journey. All we could see were lorries in front, lorries following behind, all loaded with troops.

Arriving at Béja we off loaded, and all troops were set to clear up any military stores or ammunition left lying around before we moved any further. We managed some food and drink before we kipped down on the ground for the night. Early morning it was everybody up, something quick to eat and drink, drink was the main thing, up on to the lorries, and then off. We were making for a place called Medjez el Bab, about a sixty kilometre drive. It was a small kind of village or town, and I think a rail head.

When we arrived, there were quite a lot of other troops. There was quite a lot of movement and we heard a lot of cracking, we realized it was a lot of loose ammunition left lying about. Some of this had been exploding which started fires to quite a few buildings, of course everything being tinder dry it didn't take long to flare up. The town major, the officer in charge of the town, and other officers were running about giving out different orders, and the only water supply was what was being brought in by the water wagons.

As we had no hoses or pumps, it was everyone to the bucket. Different places seemed to keep bursting out into flame. One large shed by the rail sidings was burning on one corner of the roof, there were troops on the roof with pickaxes trying to cut away the flames.

The only thing to do was to line up at the water wagon until there was a full bucket and then run to the fire you were working on. One little incident created a laugh. The town major suddenly came running along where we were working, one of the chaps who was carrying a bucket of water happened to notice that the back of the major's KD shorts and shirt was smoking, and would soon burst into flames. With that he shouted out: "Sir, your behind is on fire" (he never said 'behind' but we'll leave it at that), and threw the bucket of water at him.

I don't know if this was the result of the enemy, as it was only a few days ago they still occupied this area. What with the heat of the day and the different fires, we were just wringing with sweat. We'd been all day doing this job, now things seemed to be dying down. I began to start looking round for some of our own unit, as most of the day I'd been mixed up with fellows from different units.

We were there for a few days helping to clear up live ammunition, and also hearing the news that the Allies had entered Tunis, and the enemy retreated to Sicily. Then Dusty said we were to move on. We were now on our own, and travelling northwards, as we should eventually reach Tunis from the northern sector. As the ground was beginning to get a bit hilly and rocky it was slow going. After some little while it seemed that we would be travelling on to lower and more level ground.

We could now hear the noise of ammunition and bombs exploding. With that, Dusty stopped his vehicle and got out to look around. Of course us following, we had to stop for the sake of jumping down on the ground for a change. He studied his map along with the staff sergeant and decided the noise was coming from an ammunition dump, where he could see a lot of smoke. It seemed to be a large dump as it was scattering exploding ammunition for quite a long way around although I didn't think our route would be too near it.

As we were getting on to lower ground, we stopped again. Dusty got out, and came back to tell us that over to our left was what looked like a farmhouse standing alone. He said: "We'll go over to find out if anybody is living there and if they are all right." It took us quite a while before we were able to reach it, and Dusty went to the door.

We could see the door open, and it looked like a man and his wife there; Dusty was trying to explain to them. They seemed a bit worried and frightened, the same as in Iceland when I knocked at the house with Dusty's washing. These people living in lonely houses or farms didn't know what was going to happen next, and they got frightened. Anyway, Dusty had an idea, and came over to our lorry I was standing in and called me down. He knew I'd worked in the hotel business, and asked me if I understood French.

Well, I said, a few words, so I might be able to help you. I went over with him, and did the proper thing. I shook hands and announced ourselves with "Bonjour, Madame," "Bonjour, Monsieur," and with my limited knowledge of French I was able to make them understand. I think they were French Tunisians. Anyway they seemed happier, and invited us all in, Dusty seemed quite happy as I told him. I must say, my knowledge of French has now left me.

I think it was three teenage daughters they had and it seemed quite a large house although a single storey, there still seemed plenty of room in there with us lot. There was a piano and all the boys were telling me to give them a tune. They seemed to have a good stock of everything, as the man was getting out bottles of drinks and the wife and daughters were busy getting out different eats. Meanwhile we could still hear the ammunition dump exploding like merry.

I don't think they came in the direct line of fire when the enemy was in retreat, but they said they were very frightened. Then the man brought drinks round, and with that, Dusty shouted to me to play the 'Marseillaise', the French national anthem. With Jack and Geordie kneeling pressing the pedals up and down I could get the piano to play, and so, it was everybody with a glass held up in their hand. I

168

played, and everybody sang with full gusto, the chorus being sung two or three times. Jack and Geordie were only too glad to get up, the sweat was pouring down their faces with pumping those pedals.

The man came over to thank me and shook my hand, also to Jack and Geordie, and I could see tears in his eyes. Then it was Madame and the daughters bringing all the pieces of food round. So far this turned out to be quite a happy day. As it was now getting well into the late afternoon, Dusty said we must move on. And so, after saying a cheerful goodbye we moved off and looked out for a place to kip down for the night. Next day we should reach Tunis.

Entering Tunis from the north end we came through Carthage. There we caught a glimpse of the Mediterranean. It was just a perfect blue. We had to wait a while, as Dusty had to locate the residence of the British Consul. As it was vacant it meant a return for him a bit later. So we went through Tunis.

All the shops were open and some were being repaired through the damage which had been done. The busiest places were the drinking bars and the hairdressers, packed with troops. The water we used for washing was salty, it was treated sea water. This always made our hair feel sticky, so this was a chance to get a shampoo and a trim.

We moved just outside Tunis where we were shown a small building for our sleeping quarters and other necessities. The Eighth Army and other units were following the enemy over to Sicily, so the others left here were just awaiting orders. We'd managed to get some beds and we might be issued with mosquito nets. Taffy fixed up a cookhouse. Dusty had been to the British Consul, as he told Geordie, our carpenter, to report to the Consul with his tools, as they had one or two jobs which needed attention.

After a look round, Geordie found he would be working there for quite a few days, so he arranged for our lorry to take him and bring him back. Otherwise, the unit had been kept quite busy with lots of different orders and things to fetch or deliver. Of course, at this time of the year, summer, the afternoons were very quiet and the shops closed as it was siesta time when people rested until the evening when they opened again for business.

After a few weeks we managed to get some mail which had probably been chasing us. I had my usual letters and small parcel from home, and also another parcel, from Norfolk. This was from the couple at the pub at Lexham. They sent handkerchiefs, soap, a small scarf and socks with sweets and chocolate. For a time I didn't know what to think, I felt so choked.

One evening a few of us walked into Tunis to look around, and we were allowed to go into the Bey of Tunis' palace, the Bey being the hereditary ruler of Tunis, but there was none now. In one large room, it was a lovely room, I think all marble, along the side of one wall it seemed like a huge fireplace with a long marble shelf along the top. On this were six marvellous clocks. The guide told us they

The Bey of Tunis' palace

were all gold, and were a present from Queen Victoria. We saw quite a lot of Tunis and found it quite pleasant.

One day we had to go on the lorry, three or four of us, down to near Sousse to fetch something back. We noticed on the way one huge pile of destroyed and broken aircraft, quite high like a mountain, also broken down tanks.

After some time we had to move back from Tunis to a quieter place. This was two kinds of buildings, single storey with different rooms, and probably had been used by previous units as the rear part was all open and there were the remains of a cookhouse. We managed to arrange our beds in different rooms. With five or six in our room, of course we had to have Charlie and Reg. And that's where we spent the rest of our time whilst stationed at Tunis.

Geordie had finished all his jobs at the British Consulate, and he had been given a nice wireless set and quite a few other things by the Consul's wife. Of course he couldn't use the wireless yet, as for one thing there was no broadcasting here.

The days were beginning to get a bit cooler, although we had got a bit used to the hot sunshine and were quite dark skinned. We should soon be going into October and we had heard there were signs of a move very shortly.

It was late in the afternoon when we were ready for a wash and change into evening KDs before our meal when our mail was handed in, although Charlie and a couple of others were still out on a job. I collected my mail, and Reg collected his, and then we went into our bedroom. Always we couldn't seem to open and read our mail quick enough. And then starting to read my news, it was just as though I was standing, being held tight and unable to move.

It was bad news. Poor Charlie, my sister Gert's husband, had been killed, in Sicily. I just stood there, staring out of the window, and not moving. Then Reg happened to look up from his letter, and noticed me. With that he came over and held my shoulders, and asked me if I was all right. I began to feel more myself and told him my bad news. I felt very sad, and was thinking of all at home, especially Gert and her little daughter Jill.

Reg found a box I could sit on, as the beds were too low on the ground to sit on. He wanted to get me a drink, but I said, leave it till meal time. After I told Reg it was my brother in law, and it happened in Sicily, he said: "And it's only a stone's throw from here."

After I'd washed and changed and had a meal, I felt quite normal, although I still felt sad, I still had the feelings of home. Most of the lads had heard of my bad news and came over to offer their condolences.

Gert's husband Charlie's grave in Catania military cemetery, Sicily. He was killed in August 1943

After a couple more weeks we had our orders to move, and a bit of a surprise. We'd got to go back, and eventually make for Oran in Algeria, although we should be calling at two or three places on the way for jobs to be done. It had been mentioned that there was the likelihood of an Allied landing being made in southern France, but that had been squashed now.

It seemed that we should be heading toward the coastal area which was a bit mountainous and rocky. We were still wearing our KDs and most other units were wearing their battledress which was their winter clothes. After travelling over some rough country we came to a place where we had some jobs which had to be done and where our other gear was waiting for us.

After a couple of days, we moved on, more to the south. We were making our way back along the flat country where we had to make one or two more stops. At one place where we were going to spend the night, there were some Americans with three or four lorries. Taffy managed our food and drink, as it was essential that we carried our food with us when travelling.

After we'd finished, some of the Americans came over to talk to us. They were all quite young fellows and said they'd never been away from America before. They wanted to know if we were British as they never knew what the British were like. Just then a lorry drew up with a piano on board. I suppose it was a piano they'd got from somewhere and of course they'd brought some girls or women friends from the village, mostly French Algerians.

One or two wanted to get up to sing, and it proved quite a musical evening. I had been talking to a young American, mostly about music. When they finally finished up, and started to make for their camp, he darted off for a few minutes, and then came back with a roll of music and a label with his name and address in America for me to visit him after the war. The bundle of song sheets his sister had sent him were for me.

Next morning, Dusty had fresh orders for us. Sgt Madden and four others, including me, would be moving off to a petrol dump which had to be cleared, Lieut Philips was in charge there. Dusty and the others would be going on to another job. We should eventually connect up with them at Algiers. And so off we went in our lorry, we knew we would be near a rail depot and so carried on. It was about mid day when we reached our destination.

Lieut Philips we remembered from when our unit was first made up although for a time he went with 60 DID, then joined us for a time in Algiers. This was a large flat area, mainly sandy soil, which contained forty-gallon drums of mostly different types of petrol. These were stacked in groups in a circle. Connecting up with these stacks was a small gauge rail track which ran over towards where the main line had been laid and where our Nissen huts were.

For our type of gauge rail, we had three long low flat trucks that could be connected to each other and then a small diesel engine, which we had to drive to take the drums over to be loaded on to the main railway trucks. And eventually the main locomotives steamed over to connect up, and then steamed over on to the main line. All this, so Lieut Philips told us, was laid down by the Military Railway Engineers. We could see that a lot of drums had gone already.

Lieut Philips used one Nissen hut, we used one, and the other was for eating and other necessities. We'd have to see to our own cooking, water we got outside. Also, we had electric light fitted up, so that made it a bit easier. Lieut Philips told us there was a gang of Arabs who came in each day to do all the loading and lifting. They had a good foreman and would be there tomorrow. He said driving the diesel engine was quite easy, but it must be used only by us.

We were responsible for the loading as apart from the diesel, there was ordinary petrol and aircraft petrol. And then to complete it all the labels for the railway trucks had to be made out into quantities and information according to metric reading which was different to British reading, and so it had to be the French railway system. This we had to sit and work out in the evenings.

The gang arrived with their chief. He was only young, but rather tall for an Arab, and he did manage to speak English. Most of the drums from the very far end had been cleared, so we arranged the low trucks to be loaded taking note of what the drums contained, as we tried to load the same type of fuel together. We'd checked all the drums and found they'd been stacked together in their right order so that made an easy start.

We'd managed to drive the little diesel engine and there was a rail truck shunted in. Lieut Philips showed us how it needed loading. We'd spoken to the gang leader, I think he was called Assinde, but he already knew it was one gang to load the truck in the field, and one gang to load on to the rail truck, which was a bit harder, as it was higher to lift the drums.

Besides Assinde, we had to keep an eye on these Arabs, as they didn't trouble too much, and did like to sit down and rest every time you weren't looking. It used to take up a lot of our time chasing after them as they would be inclined to wander off, or sit down.

And so we had a busy first day, and that was how we went through the next three or four weeks. Although we were now into October the sun was still quite warm, all we needed was our underwear underneath our overalls. Assinde brought us in a lot of fruit, we used to have melon every evening with our meal and other types of fruit. He seemed a real nice chap.

And of course it would always get dark at the same time, so apart from perhaps letter writing in the evening Lieut Philips came in with us, and had a game at cards. When I wrote home, I would sometimes put in drawings of camels and palm trees for Jill.

The site was now cleared, just left were the small diesel engine, and the narrow gauge rail track. I think a REME unit came to pick up the engine, I don't know if they also cleared the rest of the Nissen huts, as the food we cleared. Lieut Philips had his own lorry, and so, as we had the lorry and our essentials on board, and Sgt Madden with the driver, we were off again.

We arrived in Algiers, and Sgt Madden was told where to make for. (When we were on our own it was always Steve Madden and not Sgt Madden.) This was where we were to spend the night, Dusty and the others were already there. Dusty told us, tomorrow we would move on to Oran, where we would make for La Senia Air Base about four miles outside the city.

We got well along the way when Dusty's vehicle started to create trouble. There was a REME unit a few miles farther on, and Reg and the drivers of the two lorries managed to fix the vehicle up till we could pull in there. The sergeant in the office said it wouldn't be ready till next day, so Dusty travelled on in one of the lorries, and Reg, with Sgt Madden and myself, stayed behind. Next day Reg was informed the vehicle would need changing, but we managed to have a pretty good run and arrived at La Senia towards evening.

About half a dozen of our unit moved on to Casablanca to help out down there, Charlie was one of them, and now we were only a small party. I was told that this was a French air base, at present under the RAF. It had a long wide green stretch in the middle with an open saluting base at one end. The roadway was round the sides and two large blocks of two storey buildings for residential or sleeping quarters were on either side of the roadway. The airfield was on the other side of the roadway and buildings, and the entrance gates to the airfield were a bit farther along the road. There were French troops still occupying the building on the far side, but they were to move out. The RAF were occupying the building nearer the airfield.

We were then able to move from tents on the green and along with the RAF as they'd soon be moving, the Americans were taking over the airfield. We had a small building, which was only one storey but made into different rooms, and so we claimed that for Taffy's kitchen and a mess room, and two or three more rooms were vacant.

The road that came through the airfield gate entrance went along to the end of the airfield. After we left our sleeping quarters we used this road for a short way, when we came to a large shed, and here we were, this was our depot. It was a long shed, with a small door at this end, and a large door at the other end, which could be kept open when necessary. Towards the rear we came to the office, and into the rear was Dusty's office. Down the far end was a large refrigerator, which would be used for meat and other necessities so Taffy, our butcher (not Taffy, the cook) was going to be kept busy.

This was where we carried on till the end of the war. Italy had now surrendered, Mussolini had lost power, we heard that the tide was turning in the Far East, and we were waiting for the main invasion into France.

The next phase would be stores to come from the docks as there wasn't any base supply depot here now. A few days later we had to collect stores from the docks and gradually began to fill the shed up. We had two in the office now, that was Geoff and another, also a desk for the staff sergeant, and of course Dusty at the rear.

Myself, I'd been given a lock up in the centre of the shed. This would be used for special types of issues in the way of certain types of food, also rum, cigarettes, tobacco, sweets and chocolate, and air mail letters. This was my responsibility, the key to be kept in the office and the stock to be checked each evening.

Each morning we had a parade inside the shed before we started our duties, which was taken by the staff sergeant if Dusty was not there. There were still one or two units scattered around, and I think one or two RAF speciality units on assignments, which we had to keep in touch with.

We'd had a corporal come to us in a lorry to make arrangements for two or three different issues during the coming weeks. He came from a place called Oujda, and it was down in Morocco. He collected stores for Gibraltar Training Camp. We also had a squadron of the South African Air Force based over the far side of the airfield which had to rely on us.

Adjoining the gates as we went out to the depot was a small building for officers. This had four or five bedrooms together with toilets and washing facilities, and was occupied by Dusty and Lieut Philips, who preferred to look after himself rather than have a batman.

The RAF finally left, and the Americans started to move in. They made an inspection of all the sleeping areas. Before we were allowed to move over to the other side where the French had been they said it would have to be disinfected, the medicals said it needed cleaning. This side was quite all right. They had arranged the hospital which was taken over from the RAF.

And of course there was the chapel where we were told there would be three services on Sunday, Catholic, Anglican and I suppose Methodist or something like that. I don't know about Jewish. Nearby was a building for showers, and then a large building for meals, although we had the small place on its own where Taffy could see to our meals.

After the disinfecting had been done, we moved although we only occupied one room, as they were long rooms with a door and two windows at each end leading on to a balcony running along the front and rear of the building. There were stairs for the upper storey at both ends, also toilets and washing facilities. One room worked out to roughly eight beds on either side, giving plenty of room. We should now be able to look across to the Americans when they got established, and probably give them a wave.

We had received our mail, which was very welcome, except by Jack, who we called our barber boy. Poor old Jack received bad news. His wife had died, and he took the news badly. Everyone felt like rallying round, but it was Geordie his pal who stayed with him. Dusty sent for him. He was given a passport to travel to Algiers tomorrow to report there for a plane to England and his home, which was at St Neots, near Huntingdon. We all shook hands with him, and he had tears in his eyes.

Otherwise it was our own mail we'd got to study now. I had my usual from home, and also another parcel from Norfolk. The different things they'd sent me, they'd been really good. Of course I always answered their parcels and letters, the same as to home.

All was still well at home. They now had a lodger who worked up at Membury RAF airfield on specialist work. He was another Geordie, and he needed lodgings, it was Shady that brought him home. As our house, Upper Bockhampton Farm, at that time was in a bit of a lonely place, and there were no male persons at home, he was made quite welcome. He was called Larry.

We went through a Christmas, and had quite a lot of rain during the winter months, but otherwise it was medium temperature. Reg had now changed Dusty's vehicle, and often had to run him down into Oran, as he visited somebody there. I often went with them, me in the back, and so I saw quite a lot of Oran. Otherwise we spent all day at the depot. Taffy, the cook, came down to brew us some tea, and went back in the afternoon to prepare our evening meal.

Quite large American aircraft were now on the airfield. Our depot looked over towards the backs of the hangars and workshops, and we began to see their working force come along. We always walked along to the depot every morning, as it was quite a little way but a lot of the Americans, they didn't believe in walking.

It was surprising what they did. We saw a lot of them come along on a kind of truck like we used to make at home when we were boys but it was fixed up with an engine and a method of control. Some were made to carry two or three, and they gradually improved on them, just so they didn't walk. I didn't blame them.

For a time, we had our meals in with the Americans, but we didn't like their war time food, it was mashed stuff from tins, so we went back to our own, which was tasty; after all, we had our own butcher and cook. One evening, after we'd had our meal and were back upstairs in the billet, two or three Americans came over to us. They came all the way round to shake everybody's hand. They told us they'd flown over from England to this station, but didn't know there were any British here.

They'd never been to England before, they loved it. They'd been to London and different places just outside London, they liked London and the people they'd met. Some of them had met and left behind their future brides. They'd learnt to play darts, and had brought three dartboards with them, so they were waiting for us to go over to their room to challenge them. Next evening we went over.

They all flocked to us, the others that never came over yesterday, they shook hands and made a fuss of us. They brought out some beer and other drinks. Apart from a few games of darts, it turned out to be a right party, something we never expected.

They'd now started to run a bus service backwards and forwards to Oran during the evenings. It could be a bit dangerous after dark if you were walking, Arabs always sprang out from somewhere.

42. DAMAGED SHIP'S STORES CHECKED

We were kept pretty busy at the depot. There were still the one or two speciality units scattered about, also occasionally we got notified from the docks of a ship which needed something which we had to supply. They were mostly merchant ships although always under Government or Royal Navy control. They either came to us, or we delivered to the ship.

We now had some Italian prisoners to come to work for us at the depot. They were under the control of the French Army, and sent out to work for different units where needed. We had six come every day, and they turned out really good fellows, they got to know us really well. They would always call us 'Mr'. They would get brought in their lorry by their man in charge, who then collected them when they'd finished in the afternoon.

On one occasion, it was a British ship in the dock at Oran. It was in a convoy sailing to the Far East, but apparently had either hit a mine or something like that, and so had to be docked at Oran. Everything it was carrying had to be off loaded, for the ship to be repaired. What other stores it was carrying I didn't know, but it had a large consignment of different tinned foods.

This came under our notification. I was called into the office and given a large official sheet with the amount and types of foods the ship was carrying. I was to give the figure of each type of food that was standing on the dock and the amount of damaged tins which should be stacked separately. And so this meant putting on overalls, and going there with a couple of Italian prisoners and Nobby our lorry driver. When we got to the docks and I saw the consignment, I thought: "Phew! It's enough to sink a ship."

I looked about to see if there was anybody in the know when I heard a shout from one of the chaps who was looking over the rails of the ship lying alongside. He beckoned to me so I went up the gangplank to speak to him. He said the ship had been in dock a week, and he was responsible for the off loading but was waiting for me before it was covered over. So I went down and had a look round, I noticed tarpaulin sheets nearby ready to cover the stores.

There were quite a few stacks of different foods in cases and various vegetables in large tins. And so, the first day over after putting everything in order, with the help of the two Italian prisoners, we left everything ready for counting tomorrow. It was back to our lorry with Nobby who had been giving us a hand and back to the depot. Next day I got the two prisoners to walk over the tops of the cases and cans, to see if everything was packed properly together, and no openings in the middle. After that I started to take a count.

Both during the morning and about mid day the two chaps on the ship whistled us aboard for some tea. Also mid day Nobby and me went along to their cabin where we had a snack. The two prisoners had brought their drink, I don't know if anything else, although I did bring them a bit of chocolate down as they worked well, so they sat in the lorry for their rest break.

After completing my count I said we'd finish the job tomorrow, and so it was back to the depot. I went into the office and told them I should complete the form I had, and I should need another prisoner to complete the job tomorrow. I was ready for a wash or shower and a change of clothing as the sun was getting hotter each day. Although I oft times thought how lucky we were not to be with the invasion or in Italy.

Next day it was a good job I had an extra prisoner as Nobby had to go on to another job. So, with the three prisoners to help me I checked all my figures and then we attempted to sheet everything down to make it as secure as possible, as there were a lot of Arabs working on the docks, and they'd pinch anything. It was then Dusty came down to see what it was we were checking, as I told him I was just on the finish.

With that, after a good look around he jumped into his vehicle and was driven off. It needed the four of us to spread the tarpaulin sheets over everything and then get them roped and secured all around the sides. With that, after having to wait for Nobby to collect us, I went aboard ship to tell the chap that we'd finished the job.

The Americans at the air base had started to run their own radio programme. And so Geordie got his own radio set out, which he'd been given by the Consul's wife in Tunis, and tried it out on their wavelength, and yes, it worked. As he woke early to switch on, the sound that awoke all of us every morning was 'Oh what a beautiful mornin''.

We'd got a new intake in our billet, three Fleet Air Arm lads. Their plane had landed here to work with the American Air Force to give them practice in target shooting. It was only a small two seater plane, one for the pilot ('Pop' they called him) and the other for the observer or person responsible for manipulating the drogue which was pulled behind and was the target for practice with naval craft.

They got on well with us and, although they worked on the airfield, they knew to come to the depot for a mug of tea. George was the one who flew with 'Pop', and he came from Camberwell; little Jock was the engineer, and Henry, from Liverpool. I didn't know his qualifications.

I often used to go down to Oran with Reg during the evenings, as we got to know the people that Dusty visited. The man was English, we called him Pop, and his wife, I think she was Belgian, they were both getting on, and the daughter and son in law. Pop was a rather well built fellow, he was an ex guardsman, but that was before the war. I don't know how actually they came to be living in Oran but they were always pleased to see us.

Of course, we always tried to bring them something down to eat, on the quiet. They lived in a flat, as it was all flats out there in the towns. They also had a friend who used to call in for meals, she was Belgian and lived nearby. She worked in the French Government offices, as at that time Algeria came under the French. So this gave us somewhere to visit in the evenings.

When the war was nearly over, the son in law Henry told me I could have a very good job with the Oran Coal Company. I didn't know if that was where he worked, I didn't ask him but I gave it a miss. It was after the war and I was home and out of the Army, that I received the news from him that poor old Pop had died and was buried in Oran. I thought a lot of that. I couldn't send an answer as I didn't really know an address to send one to. But I appreciated his trouble in sending me the news.

We had one or two air raids at different times, but it was only hit and run, as I think the enemy had to spend all their time over France and Italy.

Taffy, our butcher, received various amounts of meat for the refrigerator which he had to cut up into different kinds of joints to be delivered, I think by aircraft, to different hospitals farther up in the beginning of the hills.

The Americans had cleared out a hangar, and built a platform at the end, and fitted a screen up for film shows. They told me that aircraft flew over nearly every day from the States to bring essentials and always a new film. And of course, now that had got going, that's where we spent a lot of evenings, always three or four of us, often with Reg if he was not driving Dusty anywhere, and always Geoff and Sgt Madden.

There had been a new intake of Americans. All young lads, I suppose straight from training. One evening we went to a film show, it was called *Brighton Rock*, a British film. As we were wearing our KDs, we were much the same as the Americans. A lot of these young lads were sitting behind us. When the show had finished and we were all making a move, we could hear them talking about the film and saying: "Those British people talk and dress like us and they've got cars and even look like us."

We thought little did they know there were some sitting in front of them. They didn't seem to know much about history. Another time, before the film show, they had some chairs on the platform for a question time, just to create some amusement. I think it was three a side. Anyway, they found enough volunteers to fill all the chairs, except one. The officer who was running the show then called down: "What about one of you British boys?" I was sitting next to Geoff, and he said right away, I'll go. With that there was a general clap.

The questions were really easy ones, and mostly concerning the United States. There were a few questions that were failed, although I seemed to know all the answers. Geoff passed all of his. Anyway, it made it a bit interesting. One thing I did notice, at all the shows it was all ranks, including officers, that sat together anywhere they wished.

We were still in contact with the South African Air Force who were in occupation on the far side of the air base. They still had to come to the depot for supplies but there was one good thing about them. They also received a certain amount of stores and foods from their own country, so a lot of the issues we reserved for them they just handed back; so that used to allow us something to take down to Mamma and Pop when we made our visits.

Just a short way past our depot the Americans had fixed up a petrol filling station and the chap who was in charge, his name was Spike. When we had our tea break during the mid mornings, he used to come along to join us and sit out in the hot sun, and drink a mug of tea with us. He used to enjoy that. He used to bring us bottles of Coca-Cola, all ice cold, as he said he was fed up with drinking that stuff. I don't know if they received an allowance.

We'd heard of the D Day landings, and now we were following each day's news. Sgt Madden told me that he'd become friendly with one of the Americans who, like him, was interested in photography. Of course, we weren't allowed to have a camera during the first part of the war, but now it was all right. The American wanted to give his old camera to Sgt Madden as he had had a new one sent from his home in the USA. He'd promised to get him some film.

I'd had some mail from home, also from Norfolk, although this time just a letter, as I'd told them to look after themselves more as we were not too bad over here. They told me from home that my cousin Lil's daughter Joyce was living back with them. She wanted to join the Women's Land Army but her Dad wouldn't give permission. Instead, she was working for my sister Win's brother in law Tom Bowsher along at his farm.

With another companion she drove the little horse and cart round the village delivering the milk. She had made lots of friends, and was very happy. She stayed till the end of the war, till she was seventeen.

We were still kept pretty busy. I got one or two long runs to do with the lorry. Although I took my turn. I did, on three occasions, travel south for about eighty or ninety miles to collect certain stores which I think were destined for hospitals. I went with Sgt Madden, with a couple of Italian prisoners. We eventually found the house, a lovely tropical type of house, a white or marble effect, and lovely and cool inside. It seemed as though there were a lot of vineyards about as I don't think there was any fruit. We got all the melons, oranges and dates where we were.

We met the owner, who I think was French Algerian, and could speak a bit of English. We had quite a few cases and small packages to put on the lorry. Sgt Madden had brought the paperwork which had to be checked against all the packages with signatures, and vice versa with the paperwork he had to bring back. There were a few names in French Sgt Madden couldn't understand, and so I helped him there, as these were wines that I knew from my hotel days.

We finished the loading and paperwork and with that the owner invited us in to an inner garden with a small table and chairs. He poured us all out a small drink from the bottle. He even sent the two Italians a drink as they were still with the lorry and had done a good job. After a lot of talk in broken English, it was "Merci, monsieur, bonsoir" and so to Oran.

During the summer time we tried to keep our room cool at nights with door and two large windows at each end open. The room itself was very high, so that helped to keep it cool. And of course during the summer we had to have our mosquito nets fixed over the bed. In the morning it was just along the balcony to the toilets or washing with a shower if needed, but the water wasn't that good. All those towns along the coast used treated sea water, we even shaved with it.

Towards the latter part of the summer was when the Sirocco blew.

That we didn't like. For one thing, it always seemed to be the hottest part of summer. That was why we kept the doors and windows open, but it was often when the wind started blowing, and then it was the sand blowing from the desert which seemed to blow through our sleeping room, through one door, and out the other. Unless anybody liked to get out of bed, perhaps nothing on, to close the windows and door. The first thing in the morning was to wash the sand from our eyes.

I always kept Dusty's uniforms in good order. It was getting towards the end of the year that he wanted them ready for packing, as he said he might be going on a course, and so I left him, as he said he would manage. Lieut Philips was always about.

One day before he left Dusty called me into his office. I thought: "What's wrong now?" He held a paper in his hand which he'd been reading. He said: "I was to remind you that quite a long time ago now, you were sent to the docks at Oran, to check a consignment of foods. The result of your check was found to be very satisfactory." I suppose this was passed from the Ministry of Food, through our HQ, then to Dusty, to pass on to me.

And so we went on, through Christmas. We did manage to have a good Christmas dinner, that Taffy cooked, with our new Captain, and the three naval boys. Sgt Madden took a snap of us, as he'd been lucky to get a film for his camera from his American friend. Both Reg and I helped Sgt Madden to develop his films, as we still had a couple of spare rooms in the building where we had our food.

And so we went through the winter months with the news of the war sounding good every day. We heard that Mussolini was being hounded by the Italians who were siding with the Allies. The war in Europe eventually came to an end in May that year, 1945.

188

One time, the South Africans took three or four of us out for a run in one of their trucks to a small town called Sidi-bel-Abbes. This was the HQ of the French Foreign Legion but we weren't allowed in the barracks. Otherwise, it proved an interesting day. We did see the Legionnaires about sometimes.

We had been given some good news, Sunday was to be an easy day. We could take the lorry along to a beach, providing two or three were left on duty. And so, the first Sunday, Taffy prepared some food for us to take, and said he'd have something ready for us to come back to. He preferred to sit down and read a book, and smoke his pipe. The Italian prisoners we took with us, as there were only four of them that came to the depot now, and they'd got used to us.

We went through Oran on to the coast road, and we came to a rather large bay, more of an inland bay. This I was told was where the French fleet was based until the Royal Navy attacked it, before it could be used by the Germans. This upset a lot of the people in the village here or who lived around this area. For a long time afterwards, when they saw any British troops passing, they would 'Boo' them. This place was called Mers-el-Kebir but we went farther along to Bou-Zadjar where we could run the truck to the beach.

This was where we settled every time we came during the rest of the summer. It was a bit rocky behind the beach which allowed us to get out of the sun's rays. We hardly ever saw a soul. It was nice to get into the water although one had to be careful of the underwater currents, otherwise it was always the same flow, as there are no tides in the Mediterranean. Anyway, with us poor swimmers it was all right if we didn't swim too far out. Two or three were good swimmers, especially Fontana, the best of the Italian prisoners. He was the one I always used to take on any special job, and he could speak a bit of English. He was a good underwater swimmer, and there were times when he would be swimming alongside us, and the next second he would dive down and it would be such a long time before he would show up, always quite a distance away, we always used to get scared.

The three Navy boys built us a small sailing craft which we used to put on the truck and take to the beach with us. We also had an Argentine Air Force lad billeted with us for a time. He used to come to the beach at times and he would search for places where he could find a diving point, he liked high diving.

We never saw much of our new Captain, it was mainly Lieut Philips who was in charge, and he was popular with the American officers. One day he took a few of us on to the airfield to see their latest bomber, which had landed from the USA the previous day. It was quite a large four engined machine, and quite a few of the American boys were having a look at it, but we couldn't get too near, as it had two armed guards on duty.

The small sailing craft built by the three Navy boys, at the beach at Bou-Zadjar. Vic is far left

Since the war in Europe finished, things seemed to be going a bit quieter. We had now reached the month of August. It was during one evening, we had finished our meal, and the regular routine was then to lie on the bed for a short while perhaps for a read or a chat, when suddenly such a lot of shouting erupted, with "Yippee!" and "Whoopee!" which made us all sit up wondering what the noise was about. It began to get louder, and Cpl Impey, whose bed was right by the door, jumped up to look over the balcony.

Then he shouted back: "It's full of the Americans running about the square, around the flag pole and saluting base." Then there was a pistol shot, then another, then it was full of shots being fired in the air, they seemed to be firing all over the place. We counted three shots which went through our open windows right into the ceiling. Cpl Impey advised us all to get under the beds or on to the floor until the over excitement had died down and we knew the reason.

It was a bit later on when we went down to find out. It was good news, the war with Japan was over. Of course it still kept noisy over on the American side, but after a lot of chatter we went back to our sleeping quarters, as it had got quite dark and a Sirocco was beginning to blow up. It was then our staff sergeant, and Sgt Madden, came in about the news. And so, amongst our little lot here with all our talking, it was thoughts of home, and a silent prayer.

Next day, the Americans held a short service and parade, and later on, it was announced that there was to be a military parade through Oran. It turned out to be a good day with crowds of people to see the parade. We had a busy morning, and had to deliver a lot of stores down in Oran, after that we stayed to watch. I don't know

191

where the troops in the parade came from, but they put on a good show. Sgt Madden took his camera.

We were into the month of October when a couple of our few number received their papers to move and get home, also two or three from the rest of our unit who were in Casablanca. It was now all excitement. Reg had received a leave pass to go home for three weeks, as being still in his twenties he had to wait for his discharge. Each one of us had started to get our things packed ready.

It was during November when I received my discharge papers and to return home to England in three days' time. Two others had theirs too, one was our staff sergeant, he was a nice chap, a good singer, and his home was in Tunbridge Wells in Kent. And so the important day came, everyone had to come to the station. Some had already left, some you would be leaving behind for their turn, yet we'd been living together like brothers for the past five years. You were just inclined to feel that little bit sad.

And now we had arrived at the station, to wait for I don't know how long, as this was not British railways, but the next best thing to take us to Algiers. After a long wait, the train crawled in. And so it was a matter of moving to get on the train to deposit our bags and everything, when I heard someone shouting. I looked, it was Charlie, who had been stationed at Casablanca.

He shook hands with me, had a big smile on his face, and I thought he was going to cuddle me. Another one was going home with him. So then it was saying goodbye to the few left on the station. Although their turn had got to come, you didn't like shaking hands, to say goodbye, we'd all been together for such a long time. As Sgt Madden was there, I said: "I'll see you in London, Steve."

There were just us few in the compartment earmarked for us, also a woman with a small girl about seven or eight. I think the woman was French. She seemed a bit nervous being on her own with us lot. Between us we managed to give them some chocolate, and as I was the only one who knew any French, I asked her if she was all right. I think she began to feel a bit more comfortable.

And so it was morning the time we arrived in Algiers, and then to the docks where the ship was waiting for us to board, as we were informed, for Napoli. There were quite a lot of other troops on the same journey as us, and that's when we seemed to lose touch with the others. Anyway, there was Charlie and me, so we never worried about the others. It was about mid day when we landed next day, and we were then off to a transit camp just outside the city.

After the third day we boarded the train and moved off. It seemed such a pity to see on the journey all the destruction that had to take place before any progress could be achieved in the war. In Rome, we had to change trains, we then arrived at Rimini, at the other side of Italy. This was from where we moved on to Milan, and we were nearly a week at Milan. We then entrained for our next move. I must state that all these had been pretty long and full trains with quite a lot of troops travelling home.

We finally stopped at a station, we were told to get out. I looked up to see the snow capped mountains in front of us. I said to Charlie, it must be the Alps. I could then see some fellows drinking fresh milk. We both went along to where the girls were selling the milk, and bought a carton each. It tasted so lovely and fresh. Charlie reminded me: "This is our first fresh milk for nearly three years."

*Part of a
card to
Vic from
ex-PoW
Fontana*

A merry Kristmas to You from yours
old prisoner of war working at the
59 D.I.D. Oran, La Senia.
   I remember You and alls your frends
Please write me something about
Mr. N.E. Madden (the seargent) and if
possibl give me his address.
   Thank You very much and all the
Best from me and my family

Yours very sincerely

Horico ...

We were told to put our packs properly labelled into a compound, then to go to a low building where food was being served. I noticed it was prisoners of war who were doing the serving, I think they were German, mostly elderly. There were British Army supervisors on duty. At one end of the room there was a platform with a small orchestra, all elderly German musicians, and they played really well. I thought, they should never have been called up into the army. I was inclined to feel a bit sorry for them, I thought of our Italian prisoners who worked for us, they seemed to be quite happy.

In the morning we arrived at Calais and we soon made our way to the docks. At Folkestone we disembarked, then went to find our train, and at Aldershot, buses were waiting for Woking, so that's where we finished up. So with that, I looked at Charlie, and said: "I'd better say cheerio, or goodbye, as this is where we'll get lost amongst this crowd. Give my regards to your wife and all your family. I'll try and come up to see you."

So we shook hands and went our own ways. I was in deep thought. It was just before Christmas when I entered the Army at Guildford, it was now just before Christmas that I was on my way home. And that was five years between, and a lot of things had happened.*

*Two of these things, according to Vic's army records, were that he was ranked as a corporal for pay during army release and he was awarded the Africa Star, 1st Army Clasp, a medal for service in North Africa between 10 June 1940 and 12 May 1943 inclusive. Asked about these omissions, Vic said in 2001 that his Captain, Dusty Miller, had wanted him to become a corporal, but he refused. He wanted to stay with the others, as a private. As for the Africa Star, he said everybody was awarded the medal, and he thought you had to go and collect it, and he didn't. Len Wohlgemuth did not collect his service medal either and his daughter-in-law Jill, Vic's niece, suggested that possibly a lot of men felt the same, perhaps just glad the war was over and wanting to start afresh, perhaps not wanting glory when their mates had been killed and thinking the medals were being dished out to everyone. – Editor

It was just like starting life afresh, and trying to pick up the pieces, especially as things were still in short supply and rationing was still in force. I got on well with Larry the lodger, he came down from the North to work on a job at Membury airfield. I think now, as he'd got used to the South, he wanted to bring his wife down here to live, perhaps a bit nearer to the coast.

My eldest sister Win had been working at the Royal Ordnance Depot at Didcot during the war, like a lot of the villagers, and was still carrying on. Also both Uncle Tommy and Shady worked there. And so my other sister Gert stayed at home to help our mother to run the house and to look after her daughter Jill, who now went to school. My mother, who was born in 1870, was in her later seventies, but she still thought she was a young woman.

Win's daughter Jean and her three little girls had gone back to London as her husband Bert was now out of the Army. They had been allocated one of the new prefabs being put up because of the housing shortage caused by the bomb damage. Other relations and friends who had visited Upper Bockhampton to avoid the bombing and air raids had also gone back to their own homes.

I was beginning to get used to civilian life again, I was getting used to Lambourn again, I used to call it my second home, but I must say, I missed London. I also missed the warm and hot weather. I must mention that we had celebrated a Christmas, which was a peaceful and perhaps a happier one this time. My brother Sid and his wife May came down from London, also May's sister Cis. Their older sister Kate lived in the village with her husband Freddie and little boy Jimmy, so of course they came round.

Auntie Kate and Uncle Percy were already down with us, so we had quite a houseful and as I sat at the piano, my mind went back to our Sunday evenings, years ago, and the time when Jack and Geordie pumped the pedals for me to play the 'Marseillaise' in Tunisia. I don't think I'd touched the piano much since those days.

It was a little while later when I decided to go to London for a short visit, and stay with Sid and May and Cis in the three bedroom flat where they lived at Clapham Common. Their flat, in a mansion block, was on the second floor, which was the top, and it was two flats on each landing. I soon found the flat, May was home to greet me, as my brother and Cis did not get home from their work until early evening, and May now only worked part time.

I would go out with May to do her shopping or anywhere else she needed to go. One day she suggested we go out for the day, and have a good look around, to my delight. And so the first thing was to jump on a bus and go to Sloane Square, from where we started our walk about. May was telling me that this area she knew very well as this was where she worked, at Beauchamp Place.

And so we finally got to Beauchamp Place, a rather quiet area, all types of small private buildings and houses. It was a private house, with a basement where she and another two young women worked, both were friends of May. One was Edie Morley, she lived near May, and I am still in touch with her. The other was Molly, and I forget her last name. It was all hats they made, which were mostly for well to do, and one or two titled, people.

The business was run by three women, Miss Fox, Miss Harrington whose married name was Mrs Allen, and Miss Harding. Miss Fox and Miss Harrington had worked together at Bond Street before they set up as partners at George Street (later St George Street), Hanover Square. They were bombed out of there in the war, then went to Grosvenor Street and moved to Beauchamp Place after the war. May worked for the business before Edie Morley joined them at St George Street. May said their favourite customer had been the Queen, who is now Queen Elizabeth the Queen Mother, as she told them they were the only people that could make the style of hat she likes to wear. They always used to speak of her as the Duchess of York, May said she would arrive in the showroom upstairs, and May and the other workers in the basement had instructions to stay there, and be quiet.

May told me the three women were all very nice and treated the three girls very well, inviting them to their homes occasionally and a couple of times taking them to lunch at the Savoy Hotel. That was when they started to feel first class. May told them her brother had been killed in the war, and Miss Fox in particular took an interest in his daughter Jill. She sent her presents, mostly from Harrods.

On one or two days I wanted to do my own visiting. On the first occasion, I got rather annoyed with myself. I went to visit Charlie Dear, my pal from the Army. I was on the way to the Elephant and Castle, where he lived, when I wanted to check his address. I stood there searching all my pockets to no avail and so I came to the conclusion I must have mislaid it, or lost it.

Another time I thought I would look in at the Waldorf Hotel to see if I still knew anybody there. I left it until the afternoon when I knew everything was quiet, I went as usual through the staff entrance at the rear where I asked to see M Manceau, who was responsible for the staff. He came to see me, and seemed surprised and pleased and took me down to the Grill Room where they used to sit when off duty.

There I met two or three others I knew, but otherwise I was told it was all new staff, mainly female, and so, they told me, that meant the Waldorf wasn't a first class hotel now. I had quite a little chat, as they wanted to know all my war time experiences and travels.

So after a cheerio, and wishing them all the best I made my exit, coming out through the large kitchen, which seemed quite empty and lonely and I then wondered, what had happened to the Italian boys I used to know. I knew a lot of them had been sent to Canada by the government at the start of the war. After I came away, I thought, after my five years in the open air, I could never work inside again to the extent I had at the Waldorf.

So, I walked all around the places I knew, the theatres close by, my favourite area which was Covent Garden and then into Charing Cross. It was getting towards evening time, and I thought I would call in for a drink before making my way to Sid and May's. I was just passing the Coliseum when I came to a pub I often used to go into. And then I did have a bit of a surprise, behind the bar was Marco, one of the Grill Room's Head Waiters before the war. He told me he had finished with the hotel life, and had taken over the pub.

I thought before I went back to Lambourn, I would find Reg's address, and meet his people and his wife. I soon found the house, in Tottenham, north London. The door was answered by a young person who stood and looked at me, then I mentioned my name. With that, she grabbed my arms and even gave me a kiss, of course it was Reg's wife. Reg's mother and father came out from the back room to see what all the fuss was about, and then it was all chatter.

I asked about Reg, and they told me they'd heard all about me in the letters he'd written home. And of course, they had to ask me all the questions, where we went, did we get hurt at all. And so, after such a lot of talking, I said I'd better make a move. I was thinking on my way to Clapham, what a nice person Reg's wife was, and I suppose she was living in with his people for the time being. Reg's father was home in the day time, as working for the national press, like Reg, he worked at night time.

And I now thought I should have to start to find myself a job. After some consideration I thought I would try for a job at Didcot depot, at least for the time being. And so, that's what I did, and got settled in, I was responsible for stores returned from different units. I did hear from Charlie Dear, and I wrote to him, and I heard from Reg, who told me he had been discharged.

As I was now getting used to work, and the days were beginning to get brighter I thought I would arrange for a long weekend at Sid and May's, and pay a visit to Reg. Everything seemed to turn out very well. Reg said he wanted to take me to see Steve Madden, our former sergeant. This wasn't such a great distance away, and after finding his home, it turned out to be such an enjoyable afternoon.

Before I left Reg's in the evening, he called me aside, and told me that his wife was expecting a baby, their first. All being well, would I like to be a godfather. Well, I could only say yes. It was getting towards the end of the summer when they wrote to tell me they now had a baby son. And so I spent a long weekend at Sid and May's and attended the christening on the Sunday at Reg's parish church.

I was now getting used to Lambourn. Larry the lodger had left, as his job at Membury finished. It was a short while after this that Shady brought another lodger to us. He was a tall young fellow, and he came to work in the racing stables. It was a stable training jumpers, as I thought he was too tall to ride for the flat racing. He told us he came from Buckfastleigh in Devon.

I always used to notice that he was very particular with his boots, that was ordinary boots for riding and knee boots. If muddy, he would wash them first and then if it was dry, hang them out in the wind, and treat them and finally polish them. He never told us much about his family, although we would never approach the question. After quite some time, he took his leave, and went back to Buckfastleigh.

Meanwhile, I had heard that Len Wohlgemuth was home and had moved with his family to a flat near the Kennington Oval, and George Oliver was back at home with his mother, as his brother Ted had got his own flat. Now I felt I could still keep in touch with all those that seemed to me to be part of the family, and so I began to feel a bit more satisfied. We heard news that Len and Rene had another son, born in September, Peter. They had a daughter during the war, Janice, but she had died at nine months old.

I travelled to work with my sister Win on transport supplied by the depot which started at Market Place, and went over the Downs. During the evenings, summer or winter, my sisters Gert and Win would often take our mother out for a walk, and call at the Lamb Inn for a drink, and a chat with others she knew, especially Auntie Nell, who was our mother's sister in law, and lived over nearby the Lamb in our Granny Taylor's old cottage. There she enjoyed her evening.

Once a week Win and Gert would go along to the Social Club just along the road, they held dances, or whist drives or anything with some interest or the other. During these times, especially winter, I would stay in, as Gert's daughter Jill would go to bed early to be ready for school in the morning and she knew there was somebody at home. I would probably be smoking my pipe or reading or listening to the wireless. Summer I would do a bit of gardening, which I now began to take a bit of interest in.

Friday nights Jill was allowed to stay up later, as she had no school the next day, and I used to play cards with her – usually Rummy – while we listened to the Light Programme, and joined in some of the songs. Two of our favourites were 'Uncle Tom Cobley', and 'The Song of the Flea'. Saturday evenings I went to the Lamb as well, perhaps to give a tune on the piano, whilst Jill stayed at Auntie Nell's with cousin Margaret (always known as 'Pud').

Sunday afternoons I liked to go out for a walk whilst the women rested after getting Sunday dinner. Jill usually came with me, and we would walk up Long Hedge or Thorn Hill to the woods, where she would pick primroses, or bluebells and other wild flowers to take home to Gert.

Like many other isolated houses and cottages there was no electricity laid on. We had to rely on oil lamps. Every week Mr Pontin would call along in his pony and trap selling oil. And with Mr Bodman with the coal, we did manage to keep really warm, although after New Year our winters seemed to get very sharp with plenty of snow. The water was inside in the back scullery in a sink with a pump, but after a while a tap was laid on. We had a copper which led off from a part of the kitchen.

We also had a fire and range in the kitchen, but after the war when things were beginning to pick up, as we had no gas in the house, we bought ourselves a Calor Gas stove. The sitting room had a door which went into a short passage which led out to the stairs, also another door which led out to a rather long hallway at the back of the house. This led down to the front room where we had the piano, and also to the side door. We didn't use the front room much, mainly at Christmas, and other times we had visitors.

There was also a window in the hallway which opened out to the back garden. It was more of a square garden than a long one. What we called the brook, or to give it its proper name, the River Lambourn, ran along the bottom. The River Lambourn rises in the Lambourn Woods just the other side of the village. The springs rise into what we call the fish pond and from there the river starts to run. We had a big apple tree with a swing, and also a small crab apple tree. We grew a lot of flowers and vegetables.

At the end of the garden was a shed and the toilet, which had two seats and was emptied twice a year by one of the villagers, known as Captain Little. Once my brother Sid's sister in law Cis was using the toilet, and she didn't realise that Captain Little was on the farmyard side, shovelling out the contents.

The farmyard ran alongside the garden. There were some barns and some stables, where two carthorses were kept, also some pigs and chickens. These belonged to Eddie Bracey, and were looked after by Jack Sheppard his farmhand. Opposite the front of the house was a meadow where the Bowshers kept their cows which Auntie Kate called the 'meadow ladies'. The cows used to be taken up to Beale's Farm to be milked, and we would often meet them on their way back if we went to the village. We would also often meet a string of racehorses.

Time moves on and it was now getting on towards the end of 1947. We had a wedding to look forward to. It was my cousin Betty, Auntie Nell and Uncle Tommy's daughter. She was marrying a young chap called 'Jock' who had been a soldier at the prisoner of war camp between Lambourn Woodlands St Mary and Baydon, some three miles away. He came from Glasgow, that's why we knew him as 'Jock', but his name was George Lang.

Betty and Jock Lang's wedding in December 1947: back (left to right), Betty's younger sister Margaret, Vic, groom and bride, Betty's father Uncle Tommy, Betty's older sister May, a friend of Betty's; front, Betty's brother Tom's daughter Pam (left), Jill

The wedding took place in December, and I'd been asked to be the best man. There were five bridesmaids, who included Jill. It turned out to be quite a good day, and everything went off very well, with quite a good few people at the church. It all looked very picturesque for a December day. Betty and Jock lived with Betty's sister May for a while, and later managed to obtain a caravan which was situated in Mill Lane, until such time when there would be a house available.

My mother was still very active. She still went out to do the family shopping, a bit different to her only sister, our Auntie Kate. She suffered with rheumatoid arthritis and was unable to walk. She could just move about with two sticks, but later had to use a wheelchair. She'd already attended quite a number of hospitals, but once it set in, at this stage there was no cure.

The main trouble now was that Uncle Percy, who was getting a bit older, still felt the effect of the gas attacks he received during the 1914-18 war, and so, had to be careful in moving her about too much. Whilst they were still living with us, it was not too bad, as downstairs she was comfortable, but I had to carry her upstairs to bed each night. In the mornings our mother and my sister Gert would manage to lift her down, stair by stair, if Percy wasn't there. The staircase being winding helped to make it more difficult.

It was just after the war when they went back to their new flat, still in Perivale, as their house there had been bombed whilst they were in Lambourn. Of course Percy was now at his retiring age, and was soon expecting to finish his job with the insurance company he'd worked with for a long time. He knew Auntie Kate was getting worse and so his intentions were to move back to Lambourn to be near the rest of the family.

He wanted to take me to his offices to meet some of his work friends and superiors when he retired. I arranged to take our mother up to stay for two or three days, and so was able to accompany him to the 'do' at the offices. It turned out quite a jolly affair with quite a lot of chat, and I was introduced to his superiors. We were given a couple of drinks, and after a lot more talking and a look around, it was back to the flat. He still had his car which he had used all the time during the war, when he could get the petrol.

My brother Sid and his wife May had mentioned to us that they now got on very well with their neighbours in the next door flat. They were three sisters, and they each went to work during the day. The eldest was named Eva, the next was Daisy, and the youngest was Vera. As George Oliver used to spend his spare time at our home, and we were now at Lambourn, he went to Sid and May's. That was where he met Vera. And now it was going to be a wedding.

As George and I had been together since our early schooldays I should be best man once again. Sid would give the bride away as they had lost both their parents, and May was to be matron of

Royal Ordnance Depot, Didcot, outside Shed B5. Win is in the second row, partly hidden by the soldier sitting in the front row third from right; Uncle Tommy is standing far right, wearing a cap

honour. The wedding took place in the church on Clapham Common, and quite a large crowd turned up. George's brother Ted made a lovely three tier wedding cake, as he was a patissiere at the Waldorf Hotel with me before the war. It turned out very well.

We were now looking forward to the summer. As things were beginning to quieten down a bit I'd been thinking about a holiday. Sid and May told us they would like to go to Brighton, with next door. As we could also join, and make a party, that was arranged, as was a booking at a double apartment with somebody we knew. Our mother, with Win, Gert and Jill, and myself, travelled by coach from Newbury to Brighton coach station, where we had arranged to meet the others, who travelled by coach from London.

It was enjoyable walking around amidst crowds of people, and it was always a pleasure in the afternoon to be on the beach in a deck chair probably with an ice cream. There were ten or twelve of us all sitting in a half circle. I don't think Jill liked the beach too much as it was a pebble beach, it was her first holiday at the seaside, and she was expecting sand.

It was during one afternoon when we thought about a cup of tea, being a glorious afternoon with a long sit down with a lot of chatter and laughter, one or two had a doze. We found quite a decent café large enough for our crowd and we made ourselves comfortable. It wasn't very long afterwards that I felt somebody pat me on the back. I looked round to see somebody in a white jacket. I stood up and he shook my hand. I then remembered, I said: "Solly."

It was a Jewish boy I knew before the war when I was working in the hotel. He was about my age, but he didn't stay there long. He joined his cousin with a fruit and vegetable stall in Berwick Street Market in London and I often walked around there to see him. He said this café in Brighton was run by his cousin, and he was working with him. And so I wished him all the best, and rejoined the others. Altogether, we had a very enjoyable holiday.

Auntie Kate and Uncle Percy had now arranged to move down to Lambourn. They'd bought a piece of land and a caravan, rather high up behind the railway station on a level with the school. This small piece of land was quite near a couple of bungalows so they were not isolated. One of the bungalows belonged to Bill Mould who we happened to know, so they soon made friends.

Also, as the bungalows were connected with electricity, Percy arranged for the caravan to be connected. As this was a new modern caravan, it would help to complete the job. One thing was that Auntie Kate felt she was still near the rest of us family, and also Percy felt the same for some of his family who were still living in Bristol, his home town.

In 1950 Jill passed her scholarship which meant she moved on to the Girls' Grammar School at Newbury. And so from September, she travelled on the train, twelve miles there and twelve miles back, leaving home before eight in the morning, and getting back at five o'clock. One boy and one girl from Lambourn passed that year, but she didn't have to travel on her own, as quite a few older children went to the girls' school or St Bartholomew's, the boys' school.

So now that Jill was away all day, that gave Gert, her mum, the chance to do a small job, to help herself along with her war widow's pension. She went to the infants' school, what we called the small school, to help Miss Ethel Jacobs, the Headmistress, to take the children to the big school at the top of the hill for their dinner. Of course she had to look after them during and after their meal, to see they managed to keep clean and tidy. And then, along with Miss Jacobs, she helped to bring them back down to the small school and her job was then finished. That was from Mondays to Fridays. And then it was a matter of going home as Mum was on her own cooking their dinner. They always got Jill's dinner for when she came home from school.

Into 1951 I read in the papers about March time, that Ivor Novello had died in his flat. I happened to know this flat, just a single entrance which seemed squeezed in between the Strand Theatre and the Waldorf Hotel. I had served him quite often when he came into the Grill Room, he stayed at the flat when he was appearing at his shows at the Theatre Royal, Drury Lane, and that was quite a few years. Otherwise he had a lovely house by the river near Maidenhead.

It was about this time when a little incident happened in Lambourn, in which Freddie Rodbourn and Kate, his wife, and son Jimmy were involved. Kate was the sister of my brother Sid's wife May, and she and Freddie and Jimmy were living in a small row of old proper stone cottages, I think about four or five, just the other side of Lambourn railway station. Leaving the Bockhampton Road a footpath led up through the gates to cross over the railway lines, and then up the hill to the cottages.

They lived in an end cottage with the usual ground floor, and a bedroom upstairs. As this row of cottages stood on their own, and at the top of the hill, it was open to all kinds of weather, and we had been having a lot of rough and high winds. It was when I got home in the evening I heard the news. The end wall of Freddie Rodbourn's house had fallen down.

Gert had gone up to see if they were all right. She could see the end of their house was wide open, with all rubble lying outside, and there was Kate, sitting in the armchair with a cup of tea, singing to herself, and Jimmy running around ready to go to school. Freddie had gone to the landlord to find out the situation. So Gert was satisfied nobody had been hurt. As a matter of fact, Kate seemed quite the opposite, singing away as though it was a normal day or she was on the beach. Gert thought it happened during the early morning, but they soon got up and hurried downstairs before the bedroom got down first. It was mainly the outside wall which had collapsed, but of course they couldn't stay on. They managed to share a house in Newbury Street with people they knew until later they had a council house in Bockhampton Road.

I read in the papers that the King and Queen were to open the new Festival Hall and exhibition which had been built on the Embankment. This was a large bomb site which occupied all the area between Hungerford railway bridge and Waterloo Bridge. Of course the main building was the Festival Hall which was a concert hall, and then there was the Dome of Discovery and a towering aluminium needle called the Skylon, besides amusements and an area for dancing.

Later we went up to Sid and May's, so we could go to the Festival of Britain on the Saturday. And so it turned out to be a real happy day. Plenty to see, crowds of happy people, and of course all alongside the river, which helped to make it so enjoyable. In the afternoon I went on to the dance floor which was all in the open. I danced with May, and Gert and Win, and Cis. We also went to the pleasure gardens at Battersea, which looked quite magical with the trees decorated with fairy lights.

During the summer we had a surprise visit from Len and Rene Wohlgemuth, and their three boys. Paul was now thirteen and very tall, Michael was a year younger, and Peter was five. They were able to come down because Len had won a brand new taxi from something the taxi men he was working with had organised amongst themselves. Otherwise they could not have managed the visit, having no transport of their own and not able to afford train fares for the five of them. It was good to see them again.

In 1952, and into February, the front pages of all the papers bore the headlines 'The King is Dead'. Although we, like everyone else, heard it on the radio. This also meant 'Long live the Queen', who happened to be Princess Elizabeth and who happened to be away on an official visit to Kenya.

We had a bit of good news a little later on. We were told that our house was to be connected up for electricity, so things were beginning to look up. I'd also noticed, looking over from our back garden across the brook to the large meadow on the other side, the building workers were dumping their machinery and other material, which, I presumed, was preparing for housebuilding, as, since the war finished, there'd been quite a lot of housebuilding going on.

And so we went through the rest of the year until December when the weather seemed to get bad. It was rather a heavy smog, fog and smoke combined – most people still had coal fires, and this was before smokeless fuel. It got so thick that people and traffic had a job to see where they were going. This was mainly in the towns. The news mentioned that thousands of people in London died from the effects of the smog, and thousands in other areas of the British Isles

George Oliver with his daughter Jennifer, who died in the 1952 smog. They are outside Marlborough Mansions, Bromells Road, Clapham, where they lived next door to Sid and May

209

suffered from respiratory disease. It was then we received the sad news from May and Sid that George and Vera Oliver's baby Jennifer had died apparently through the smog. She was only about two years old. We didn't get this in Lambourn, it was a type of humid weather, quite misty, but unhealthy.

And now we were in 1953, with very rough weather. It was towards the end of January and into February when we read of gale force winds and flooding around the coast. On the east coast over three hundred people were killed, and thousands were left homeless.

During March cousin Joyce married Arthur Rockhill. Joyce and Arthur both still lived in Wedgwood House, in London, where we lived before the war. It was a very nice wedding which was held at St Mary's Old Lambeth. Going back on to home ground it seemed to make all the difference. When the year was getting on, we received the sad news that Joyce's dad Syd had died. In time, Joyce and Arthur went to live in Orpington in Kent, into a house they bought, and where we still go to visit them.

Cousin Joyce and Arthur Rockhill's wedding (from left), Arthur's brothers and mother, groom and bride, Joyce's sister Pam, her mother Lil, her father Syd and brother Arthur

And so, everything was finally getting prepared for the coronation. That would create a lot of excitement. Eventually the day arrived, June 2nd, which turned out to be a proper royal occasion. The news mentioned that more than thirty thousand people camped out on the route to Westminster Abbey during the night. I can't remember we celebrated in any special way, but I expect we read about it in the paper next day, we took the *Daily Mirror* and the *News Chronicle*. A month later, Len and Rene had a fourth son, Martin.

About this time, Uncle Jim settled himself in Lambourn. Auntie Alice had died during the war years, and there was only his daughter Doris who he was living with in Kew. Her husband had died some time ago, and she was expecting to marry again. So he thought he would come back to where he was born. And so he stayed with us, and would go down to the Lamb each night, and have a drink, and I think a game of cards.

Win and Gert still often went to the Social Club along the road if there were any dances or social evenings on. I would go along if they needed me to play the piano. Also during the summer time there would often be a coach outing to the seaside or anywhere special. Always something on. I seemed to have given up dancing.

Uncle Jim

At times I would think back to before the war, when I was working with Bruce at the hotel, and on our off duty hours we would slip along to the Astoria Dance Salon for an afternoon or evening dance session. We always knew the same girls for dancing, and it was always the well known bands we heard and knew. I then think to the present day, and wonder where everything's gone to. Although the music stays within me, somehow it seems to be a different type of life. I suppose that's the changing years.

Another young fellow used to come home on one or two evenings. He used to go to the Social Club and he was friendly with Win and Gert. He worked in the stables, for Fulke Walwyn. He was Welsh and his home was in Llanychaer, three miles outside Fishguard in West Wales. He seemed to be quite a popular type of chap, and he got quite used to our family. Of course as we got to know him a bit more we always called him Taffy, but his name was Gwynfor James.

He told us that before the war he used to work up in the Lake District with one or two of the well known fox hunts, he used to see to the hounds. His father had a lot to do with horse dealing and they all had to ride horseback from when they were quite young. That was three brothers, and three sisters. They still lived in Wales, and spoke Welsh. His mother died soon after we knew him but his father was still alive.

He came to the Lambourn area before the war and went into the stables at Ashdown House. And he was there for quite a time, but he found it a bit isolated as it was nearly three miles to Lambourn, or a couple of miles to Ashbury which only had a pub and a shop. Of course, it was a little better if one had a cycle, but only two or three had cycles.

All this family news he liked to describe on winter evenings when he used to come down to visit us, as I think he also found it, as I should say, very 'comforting' to be able to talk to other people about his own young life.

212

As he told us, he went back to Wales at the beginning of the war, and went to work in the big naval depot two miles from Llanychaer, but settled right deep in the valley, it was called Trecwn.

After the war he came back to the Lambourn area but went to work for Fulke Walwyn's racing stables at Upper Lambourn. He told us he, with another fellow, used to lodge with a couple of people in what was called the Terrace, but they weren't the right type of people to get on with. One or two evenings their lodgers liked to go out for a drink and a chat, or perhaps somewhere else, but they weren't given a key, as the couple used to lock the door at 9 o'clock every evening and go to bed.

So if their lodgers weren't home by 9 o'clock, they were expected to stay out for the rest of the night. After learning all the ways and means they always managed to get through the window. But he'd left that place, and was now staying with George Pottinger and his wife in one of the new council houses in Northfields.

The council had started to build houses in the meadow at the back of our house. I had noticed there was now quite a row of houses, and we were told that cousin Betty and her husband Jock had been allocated a house. So that would be a change from their caravan, and it had come just at the right time as they had a baby son born. They named him Ian. The estate was to be named Woodbury.

I had now been told that the farmer who owned our house, that was Eddie Bracey, would be needing the house as his son was getting married shortly, so we'd got to think about things. We did our best to make a move, but there never seemed to be any possibility, and of course we'd had two or three notices to move. We finally had a notice to attend court. Meanwhile Uncle Jim had acquired an almshouse, and so Percy arranged to help him to move when it was ready for him.

And so the day arrived for me to attend court. I had to go to Hungerford, so Percy took me. As I belonged to a union, they'd arranged for their solicitor to attend on my behalf. Of course I had to attend as our mother was too old to go. When I acquired the house at the beginning of the war, I used Mum's name, as I didn't know how long I would be absent. The solicitor told me what to say, and after a lot of questions and answers it was arranged for us to stay on a few more weeks.

After that, I wrote a letter to the council to state our position. After a week or two we had a letter from Mr and Mrs Bracey to say that Major Dunn and his wife had suddenly left Deacon's Cottage, which was right opposite to where they lived in Newbury Street, and had left them the keys. And so they asked us if we would take it over.

We accepted. This cottage which I passed every day on my way to work was really two cottages (or even three) made into one. Three rooms at the front downstairs (a small living room, a large sitting room, a dining room), then kitchen at the rear with a scullery, and

Deacon's Cottage, Newbury Street. The photo was taken by Jill's penfriend, Danielle

larder, with a type of stable door in the kitchen which opened out to the back garden. Upstairs there were five bedrooms, and another in the attic, two bathrooms, and three indoor flush toilets. Also two stairways, one each end of the cottage. There were two electric stoves, and a Rayburn stove in the kitchen. There were also a few pieces of small furniture which had been left behind and of course we claimed them. We had a small piece of garden at the back which was lawn, and trained fruit trees, and a fish pond.

As we now found we had plenty of room, we asked Taffy if he would like to stay with us. He agreed, as he said he thought we were more like his home back in Wales. After a while, I was told that Eddie Bracey's son did not want to live at Bockhampton, and so it seemed the house was still going to stand empty after all our rushing and tearing about. Still, so far we hadn't done too bad. Uncle Jim had settled down all right in his almshouse. For the time being, he still called in for his meals, as he hadn't so far to walk now we were right in the middle of the village.

There are two lots of almshouses in Lambourn, the Ten Almshouses for tradesmen where Uncle Jim was, and the Five Almshouses for others, the ones in the Lane where Shady lived. He looked after himself, but we always took him his Sunday dinner up. I would sit with him for a while and have a chat. He always brightened up when he saw me walk through the door, he was always sitting by the fire smoking a cigarette.

One morning my sister Win and I went off to catch our bus at the Market Place. Whilst waiting for the bus to arrive somebody came along to tell us that Shady had died in his sleep. So Win said she would go back home to take the bad news. I thought it was no good me going back home, so I carried on to work. When I arrived home in the evening it was arranged for Uncle Jim, Shady's elder brother, to arrange for his funeral.

I knew Shady would never be able to keep any money for very long, and so it was left to Uncle Jim to pay. Although Shady always seemed to be the black sheep of the family, yet I felt a bit sorry for him. He never brought himself right up to standard. He let himself go, he was just comfortable as he was. But he was well liked and very popular when he was in the Army. I was sad when he died.

We were now getting quite used to living in Deacon's Cottage. Taffy seemed quite happy and comfortable living with us. He was now working for Freddie Templeman, the trainer, whose yard was just a short way along from where we were, at the corner of Station Road.

It was during the spring time, April 1954, that Uncle Jack died. Gert used to stay with him and his family when we visited Lambourn when we were young. Uncle Jack used to win quite a few prizes at the flower shows, he was a good gardener. His work was carpentry, and he also cut hair for some men in the village, out in the garden when it was fine.

Jill was getting on very well at school, and was busy interested in the French and German languages. Her penfriend came over from France, and stayed with us for a month in the summer of 1954. Jill used to take her out and about, and Gert took them to London a couple of times; her name was Danielle. She enjoyed herself with us. She lived with her parents and two sisters in a small flat just outside of Paris, and so it was very different to stay in a village in an old cottage, and she took lots of photos. Jill then went with Danielle to her home. They exchanged visits again two years later.

We had been on family holidays to the seaside at the Isle of Wight and Paignton in Devon, also Gert and Jill had visited Taffy's family in Wales. Every summer, my brother Sid, his wife May and May's sister Cis came down to visit us, and also my brother Lal with his wife Dolly from Liverpool, and every year we would go to stay in London with Sid and May. They would always book up a West End show for us. We saw some very good shows, one was 'Bless the Bride', and sometimes a variety show at the London Palladium.

It was also during the summer time, we heard from Sid and May that Sid's firm would be moving from Walthamstow in north London, and starting in the new town of Stevenage in Hertfordshire, about thirty miles from north London. The firm had allocated its workers new house accommodation if they were willing to go. Sid and May had accepted the offer, and they took May's sister Cis with them, so both she and May had to give their jobs up in London.

May decided she would stay at home, and enjoy the house and a garden at the back. Cis had always worked in the needlework business, most recently for Digby Morton, a top couturier, but she found herself a job at the Nivea factory in Welwyn Garden City, where quite a lot of business places were. They all seemed to settle down well. It was just after we heard the news of their move, that I heard from the council, to inform me that we'd been allocated a house in Woodbury.

May and Sid's new house at Stevenage (left)

This was a four bedroom house, semi detached, with bathroom and toilet upstairs, also a toilet downstairs, and garden back and front. The garden at the back was long enough to grow vegetables, and a few fruit trees and bushes.

And so I felt we could now make a fresh start. Although we were very comfortable in Deacon's Cottage, and quite happy, the trouble was we felt insecure, so now we could feel a bit more independent. I must say that this occupied our time for the rest of the year, what with arranging furniture about and trying to do a bit of gardening before the winter began to settle in.

Taffy now worked for the Milk Marketing Board, at a dairy in Newbury. We now had a regular bus service running to Newbury. He got on well at his job, and after a while he became a full blown Union official, a shop steward, he'd always been a strong Union follower, and attended Union meetings. And so this was something else to occupy his mind, besides his work, and I think this was where his main interest lay. He had always been interested in politics, and was a strong Labour supporter.

The back garden at No. 9, the Woodbury house allocated to Vic

I think it was during this summer that Auntie Kate and Percy moved. They had bought a piece of land at Crowle Corner at the top of the High Street, and had had a bungalow built. They seemed very comfortable. So much easier now, as the caravan was a bit awkward for her. Percy couldn't lift her about too much; and so if things became a bit awkward, he would always send for us. Otherwise they could rely on Mr and Mrs Hailstone, the blacksmith and his wife, who lived opposite, to come over any time to give them a help if needed.

It was during the month of November we heard the news that cousin Joyce had a baby daughter and her name was Jennifer. So we now had a Jennifer Rockhill in the family tree.

When we went into our new house in Woodbury, I noticed that from the front we were looking straight over to the back of our old house at Bockhampton, and then when I went into the back garden, the thought struck me: when I was young, and spent a lot of time in Lambourn with our Granny, and cousins Jim, Cis and Dot, our Uncle Harry, their father, used to run a butcher's shop. Cis, who was four years older than me, helped her dad to deliver meat ordered for the weekend by customers or racehorse owners who lived about.

And so he had a pony and a nice high two wheeled trap, and it was kept in a shed with all the harness. But the pony was kept in this field where I was now standing. When it was an open field, it seemed much larger than now with the houses here. It was early on Saturday mornings when I would go with Cis to this meadow, in what we called the Eastbury Road, to get the pony, and bring him back to get him harnessed up.

We soon came to the five barred gate, and then the fun began. Sometimes it would be quite easy to catch the pony, another time he would be busy feeding himself in the far distance and then suddenly look up to see us coming towards him, when he would get ready to start playing games. Being quite a large field it was easy for him to get well out of the way, but we always managed in the end. We would walk him back, and Cis would then harness him up to the trap and drive him up to the shop.

I would help to take the different orders out to Cis and she would check them into the vehicle, and I would jump up along with her and then drive off. This would often be a full morning job until we got back for dinner time. And so, suddenly bringing myself back to life, after going back all those number of years, I found myself still in the back garden, and realized I was now living back in Lambourn.

It was during 1957 that Uncle Jim, our mother's brother, died in May. He was eighty four. He always wore a distinctive waxed moustache. Mother told us that when he was young he had been captain of Lambourn Cricket Club, and had ridden a penny farthing bicycle. He had a butcher's shop in Lambourn, until he moved to Kew during the 1914-18 war. It was Cecil, his son, and daughter Doris who came down from London, and arranged his funeral. He was taken to Oxford Crematorium.

Jill left school in the summer, after she had taken her A level exams, and applied for a suitable job in the Civil Service. She was notified of the date she had to attend an interview, which would be held in an office in London in the Burlington Arcade, which is in Piccadilly. I suggested to Gert it would be better if I took Jill up on the day as I knew just where to make for. Gert agreed.

It was a nice day when we went up by train. I had made sure of the time of the interview, so we had no worry there. "From Paddington Station," I said, "we'll go on the bus to Piccadilly so that you can have a look at London, and I'll show you around."

We got to Piccadilly, and had a good look around, and we carried on walking, until we eventually reached Trafalgar Square, where we had some lunch, in the Lyons' Corner House. Whilst we were there, I told Jill the story, the story of the last time I came here. It was during the Battle of Britain just before I went into the Army.

I had spent all night in the Waldorf with two others, as we were working late duty when the air raid started and lasted through the night. We could not get home so we had to kip down on the floor which often happened. I tried to have a sleep, but it was a noisy night. In the early morning, I told the others I was going to wash and change and go out for breakfast, as our kitchens were still silent.

It had now quietened down outside so I made my way down the Strand to Lyons' Corner House, where Bruce, my commis at one time, and I often went if we were hungry. I sat at a single table on the ground floor. It was after a short quiet spell when the air raid siren started to sound again. Things were going on as normal where I was. There weren't many customers, and I was still waiting to order, when it started to get noisy. Bombs were beginning to drop when suddenly there was one big crash.

Some of the windows crashed in, all the lights went out, the candelabra crashed from the ceiling as I darted under the table. Bits of the ceiling were still falling down, I kept where I was for the time, I was feeling a bit shaken. I could hear people shouting, as the air raid wardens and police had entered the building looking for casualties. I managed to pull myself up, and shake a lot of the dust off me. As the air was still full of dust, I thought I would get outside. An air raid warden came over to ask if I was all right, as I had a bit of blood on my face. He took me over to where a medical team were working. They looked at it and cleaned it, as it was only something grazed my face from the ceiling. They told me there were a few casualties being attended to, so with that, I went out into the fresh air, after saying a prayer to myself.

This was the story I related to Jill while we were having our lunch. I think it was because I had returned to the very same place, but of course a different atmosphere, that I just had to say something. I never liked to mention these happenings in my memoirs, as it was the same in my army days, there were many happenings which I wish to forget.

And so, we made our way to Burlington Arcade. We went into the waiting room where there were two or three young people awaiting their interview. We didn't seem to have to wait too long before Jill had her interview. I think she then felt a little bit easier, and so we carried on having a look around. I suggested we had some tea, and then we made our way back to Paddington Station.

During that summer, we had two or three visits from Len Wohlgemuth's eldest son Paul. He was doing his National Service, and was stationed at RAF Compton Bassett, just the other side of Marlborough. On one visit, I took him round to see two or three people. We also went in to see Auntie Emily, as she liked to tell him all about her son Fred who had been in the RAF during the war and was sent out to Southern Rhodesia. Later, Paul was sent out to Iraq, and Jill agreed to write to him.

It was in December when she was told she had passed her Civil Service interview, and was to start work at the office of the Inland Revenue in Newbury. And so she was now on her own, and doing very well.

Our house at Woodbury looked out on to a roadway which led down from the main road at the Lambourn end right on the same spot where the five barred gate used to be which we went through to catch the pony, years ago. They were now building houses opposite our houses on the other side of the road. Their back gardens went down to the river right opposite Upper Bockhampton Farm.

Taffy had been helping a lot in the garden, and doing all the digging and sowing a lot of the seeds for vegetables, although I'd been seeing to the flowers. We'd had some nice rhubarb at the end of the garden. And this was what kept us occupied for most of our time.

About this time, we had a television set. The reception in Lambourn wasn't always good, but it did give us an enjoyable evening, especially during the winter months when we couldn't work in the garden much. It was able to take us to so many places here and about, while we still sat here in Lambourn. We could now see the sports meetings, and some of the race meetings. My brother Sid and May had told us that they had bought a television set. So we wouldn't miss anything each time we paid a visit.

Sometimes we would spend a few days with them. We travelled up to London, and then managed to go on the Green Line bus to Stevenage. They were quite used to it now, after finding it a bit different living in a house with a garden and not a flat. They found it hard work on the garden, as it was all clay soil there and it needed a lot of digging. Small garden in the front, that was grass with flower edging. The back was larger with lawn and flower edging. They had three bedrooms, with bathroom and toilet, kitchen, and rather large sitting room, and small type of spare room.

They didn't have very far to walk to catch the bus, or to find the few shops such as paper shop with all necessities and chemist and one or two others, otherwise it was a bus ride to get to the town centre. This was the place where all the shops were, also a market, buses to all different parts, and the main railway station. Although I think May missed the London shops. Many of Sid's friends who he worked with in London also moved to Stevenage.

One was Bill who lived in a house that nearly backed on to May and Sid's back garden but just a bit further along. I think Sid mainly travelled to work with Bill in his car, as their work place was in the industrial estate which joined the town centre. May had become friends with Bill's wife Nell, and with other neighbours, and Cis made friends at work. Not all the workers got used to it, some preferred to return to small flats in London. We rather enjoyed Stevenage.

I was still working for the Royal Ordnance Depot at Didcot, and I'd recently had a promotion. One thing, we'd got the bus to take us, so that did help a lot, especially in the winter time. Some winters when we'd had a lot of snow the blizzards always managed to pile the snow at the top of Syncombe Hill, which made it impossible for the buses to get through. It was not only our buses, three for Didcot, but the buses from Harwell Atomic Station, quite a few of them, and they were all lined up on the hill.

It was because we finished earlier at Didcot we were the first at the top and we used to catch the full blast of the blizzard. The Harwell buses farther down the hill would manage to back down and go another way, as some had to go to Hungerford and places in that area. As for us at the top of the hill, it was more often than not that the blizzard was still blowing, and it was just at this spot where it seemed to blow across as though through a channel. And that's where we had to leave the bus and make our own way.

It meant a short way through the driving wind, until we reached the trees, and from then on it was all quiet, just walk through the snow across the downs, and then downhill to Lambourn, and home, about two hours late. At least, we were always with a group, and not on our own. I often used to think of my time in Iceland, although it was a bit different then. For one thing it was much colder, but of course we were equipped with a different type of clothing and footwear. One year we had been allowed to leave off work a bit earlier as the police had warned of bad travelling conditions.

We'd even reached Wantage, when we were blocked by an accident which had just occurred. It was two lorries going in different ways when one skidded into the other which blocked the roadway. They were jammed into each other, and it was well over an hour before they were freed. Of course it was dark when we were travelling up Syncombe Hill, and when we got to the top there were two cars stuck in the snow, and so that meant waiting for the snowplough to come before we could move any further. So that meant walking.

It was a good three miles, and we made a start, a crowd of us walking along like a lot of pilgrims. Although it seemed a lot better in the valley, and it was now bright moonlight. We now had a nice family living opposite us. It was the father, who was unable to work for some reason, who was out with his young son, who was still at school, I suppose making their way to the fish shop, no doubt to get their supper: he saw me walking on the other side and shouted out: "What a lovely evening." The way I then felt, I could have thrown a snowball at him. I've often thought which was the better, a blizzard or the Sirocco.

We'd now heard that cousin Joyce and Arthur had a son born, this was another to the family tree. They said his name was Bernard. It was also about this time, May 1958, that we then received the sad news that our Win's daughter Jean had died suddenly. It was just the same with her dad. Jean was thirty eight, about the same age as her dad when he died. She had a son and four daughters, the youngest five years old. The eldest was Valerie who was eighteen, just a few months younger than Jill.

Soon after the war, they had been very lucky, as Bert had a half share in the winning ticket in the Irish sweepstakes, and so they opened a greengrocery business in Dulwich which they soon changed to a car hire firm. This was where Jean died, although I think they had leased the premises as a car repair business by then. Of course Win had to go to London to see what she could do.

In June 1959, we received news from Liverpool that my eldest brother Lal had died from cancer. He was only sixty, but of course this was the effect of having to mix with tobacco all these years. Our mother told me that when he left grammar school he went to Faulkner's tobacco factory which was situated in Blackfriars Road near the Borough, not very far away from our old home. He used to come home for lunch break every day. He was sixteen.

When he reached the age of eighteen he was called up, as the 1914-18 war had been going on for two years. Mother said that his wages were paid the whole time he was in the Army, and he'd been to France, and was one of the lucky ones to come back, and so, his job was waiting for him. He just carried on normally, got married, to Dolly, and had a son. It was 1939 when Faulkner's merged with Ogdens, and so that meant a move from London.

They settled down quite comfortably in Liverpool as at first it seemed strange, but he got on well at his new place of work and also with the other workers. My brother Sid and May, and myself went to Liverpool to attend the funeral, a cremation. We met quite a few members from the firm who all mentioned how popular Lal was.

We travelled up by train to Lime Street and it was Lal's son Peter and my cousin Cecil from Kew who were both waiting to meet us, as Cecil was a brother in law to Lal, as their wives were sisters. Peter was married, to Maureen, who we found was quite a nice girl, they got married in 1950 whilst he was doing his National Service. He worked in the pathology laboratory at a Liverpool hospital. During the summer after Lal died, Sid and May and myself arranged to go to Liverpool for a week to take Dolly for trips out.

At the beginning of 1960 Jill was transferred from the Newbury office to Wandsworth Tax Office in London. She settled into her new accommodation, and also into her new office, and seemed to be doing pretty well. Uncle Tommy, our mother's brother, and Betty's dad, died in Newbury Hospital. He hadn't been well for quite some time. Anyway, Auntie Nell had still got another daughter Margaret with her, so she wouldn't be on her own.

In April Jill and Len Wohlgemuth's son Paul became engaged and

Jill and Paul Wohlgemuth's wedding at St Mark's, Kennington Oval. This group on the church steps is almost entirely family members. Next to Jill's bridesmaid Glenda is Gert and behind her to the right is Vic

said they were getting married in October in London. I wasn't really surprised after Paul making a couple of visits. It created a bit of excitement in the next few months. We arranged to stay with cousin Lil for two or three nights at her flat in Wedgwood House, next door to our old flat.

The wedding was held at St Mark's at Kennington Oval, where Paul was a regular worshipper, and the reception at a hall close by. I gave Jill away, and of course the best man was Paul's brother Michael. Jill had only the one bridesmaid and that was her friend from Newbury Girls' School, Glenda. The wedding went off in pretty good time, and there was quite a large crowd which attended. It was all very enjoyable.

Michael met Win's granddaughter Valerie at the reception, and they became friendly, and married the next year. And so it was back home again after our short stay talking about people we knew, and had not seen for a long time.

It was mostly during the summer evenings, when I would have a walk round to my cousin Alice and her husband Phil for a chat. Also,

Cousin Alice and her husband Phil's home, Riverside Cottage

some years after her dad died her mother, our Auntie Emily, gave up the house, Millbrook in Mill Lane, and now lived with them. This was my aunt who used to teach the piano for many years. In the house I would find Alice and Aunt, have a few words, and then go outside, where I would find Phil sitting in the garden. He was a blacksmith, a fellow who loved the open air life. After they were married they used to do a lot of camping and he was a good swimmer, and would often swim in what is known as the fish pond in the Lambourn Woods, where the River Lambourn rises.

It was a very picturesque cottage which was their own, right alongside the river, Riverside Cottage, and he built a model lighthouse in the river. It was a very good garden, although not large. Apart from a small piece of lawn underneath the trees, the rest was vegetables, with two or three fruit bushes, and a couple of glasshouses, one which contained a whole grapevine.

Of course I knew him years ago, before he married my cousin, but not to know him well. He would always want to talk about the war, and my army experiences. A lot of things I would never wish to write or talk about, even the early days of the London bombing. They were not things that needed to be talked about, the sights I used to see were horrible. Nobody would want to know about such things. I saw a lot of people in pieces after the bombing. I never felt like telling anyone, and I didn't want to remember.

He would ask about everything, but I would just tell him something different, although just as interesting. He had a brother who was in the Royal Navy during the war, but Phil was in a reserved occupation. I think he would have much preferred to have been out with the forces.

I had the idea that he wasn't a fit man. I didn't like to ask or mention anything to him or Alice, but a while afterwards when I happened to call round Alice told me he had collapsed in the garden, and she ran to the doctor's house on the other side of the river, and he ordered the ambulance to take Phil to hospital. The same thing happened a couple of times after, and the last time he died in hospital.

It was just about this time, March 1961, that my cousin Pam, Lil's youngest daughter, was married at our old church of St Mary's Old Lambeth. Her husband to be was a young man named Frank Bate, who came from Birmingham. And so with all Frank's family and a few friends coming down from Birmingham, and all our family and friends at this end, it made a good crowd. The wedding turned out very well.

One of us from home would always make a visit up to Auntie Kate and Uncle Percy to see how they were getting on. Percy went out if he wanted to visit the shops. He didn't leave Auntie Kate on her own for very long, although she always had the telephone alongside her.

Percy's brother Frank and his wife had been to see them from Bristol. This was his second wife, as his first wife died a long time ago. She had a son from her first marriage as her husband had died, and Frank had two daughters. We knew them all quite well. We were told that her son wanted to marry Frank's eldest daughter Evelyn. His younger daughter married and then went to America.

They also got visits from my cousin Gwen and her husband Jim who lived at Feltham, near Heathrow. Auntie Kate and Percy had always been close to that side of the family as Gwen's father was Uncle Hinton, one of Auntie Kate's, and our mother's, brothers. Years ago when Auntie Kate was able to move about quite normally, she used to visit them quite a lot when they lived at Twickenham.

Auntie Kate and Percy told me that as they still held a piece of land next to their bungalow, a bit farther along Crowle Road, the doctors had approached them about buying the land to build a new surgery as Lambourn would be having three doctors from now on. Some time later I noticed a group of men busy talking and studying the area, and when I went into the bungalow they told me they had sold the land to the doctors. I thought this was a good move, as in the past the surgery was held in the previous doctor's spare room.

Also, just round the corner from them in Baydon Road, we now had a small Catholic church, with a priest's house alongside, the Church of the Sacred Heart. This was needed, with all the number of racing stables we have in Lambourn, and people coming to work here, quite a lot of Irish amongst them. I now began to see quite a few new houses being built in different places, one area was further along Baydon Road, which made me think that Lambourn would soon become a large village.

Now occasionally I would sit and ponder how a few years ago there were paraffin lamps, and horse driven vehicles, and the carrier used to fetch goods from Newbury; then our little old train that ran to Newbury and back. Even our houses now had bathrooms and gas ovens for cooking and electricity; more and more people had a car. I suddenly realized all the changes that had taken place, and appreciated all the benefits we seemed to derive from them.

I began to notice our mother getting quite feeble. She didn't have any real medical problems, but she was beginning to lose her strength. Between my sisters Win and Gert, and myself, we moved her bed downstairs so she could have constant attendance, and the doctor arranged for the nurse to attend her each day. Percy would often bring Auntie Kate to sit by the bedside, being her only sister.

As Win had now retired from work, it meant Win and Gert took turns in sleeping downstairs in an armchair during the week, and I would take a turn over the weekend. During the spring time of 1963 Mother died quite peacefully, just a month before her birthday. She would have been ninety three. It was a very nice funeral, with quite a lot of relatives and friends in attendance.

It was after the funeral I wrote to the person in charge of the housing department at Hungerford Rural District Council. I explained about the family who were still left, being myself the son, who was single, and my two sisters, who were both widowed, with Taffy, our lodger. I wished from now on to take the house over under my name, it still being the same surname as before, Cox. It wasn't very long before I received a reply, telling me to carry on. And so we felt a bit easier. It was only four of us now living at Woodbury.

We received some news from Jill to tell us that she had been transferred to Limehouse Tax Office, which was situated near St Paul's Cathedral, in an area called Little Britain. Since their marriage she and Paul had been living in a flat at Clapham Common. Later, in 1964, they moved to Bexleyheath in Kent, where they had purchased a house, and they have lived there ever since.

That year also Taffy received sad news from his home. It was his brother's son who was an amateur boxer. During a boxing tournament the previous evening, he was knocked to the floor and never recovered. It was mentioned in the national newspapers, but both Taffy and myself had gone to work before they were delivered and we knew nothing about it until we got home in the evening.

It seemed such a pity as he was only a young chap, twenty one years, with a wife and baby just recently born. His name was Lyndon, but we just called him Lyn. And so, Taffy arranged to go to Wales the next day to be with his brother and wife, and Lyn's twin sister. When the funeral was held, he said what a large crowd there was, with quite a lot of sporting people.

It was during 1965 we received news from my brother Sid and May that George had died. My pal George Oliver had collapsed and died on the racecourse at Epsom. I think they said that Vera, his wife, was with him. He loved his racing, he couldn't have died in a better place. He was fifty three. His brothers were Ernest and then Bill, who as far as I knew were still living, and then Tom, and Ted who also died suddenly. George was the youngest. For some reason I was unable to attend the funeral, but it was Sid and May who went.

One evening when I had arrived home from work, as usual I came through the rear part of the house and through the kitchen, Win told me that I had a visitor waiting in the front room. I went in and found him in conversation with Gert, to tell me it was Mr Gay Kindersley from East Garston, four or five miles away. And so I sat down and he told me he wanted to arrange a short entertainment at a dinner.

He'd already made contact with a popular concert singer who lived at Shefford, the next village to East Garston, who I knew. Also three lads who worked in the stables, who were very good singers. He wanted me to take on the piano accompaniment. Well, I thought why not. So I agreed to help him out, and he arranged a date for us to meet, and mentioned the name of one of the stable lads, Michael, who would come from Upper Lambourn to pick me up.

I said Michael happened to be a friend of mine, so he said it was Michael who told him where to contact me. So with that, he thanked me as I saw him out to his Land Rover and he drove off. And so it was now for a cup of tea, and to tell Win and Gert all about it.

First of all, we might just as well mention who Gay Kindersley is. He happens to be one of the Guinness brewery heirs. He also owned racehorses and himself was an amateur rider, the national hunt champion amateur in the 1959-60 season. He lived at Parsonage Farm, and that was where we were to meet. When Michael called to take me to East Garston in his small van, he told me it was through their head stable lad that Mr Kindersley found him as somebody had mentioned him being a good singer.

It wasn't very long before we arrived at Parsonage Farm. The gates opened into the drive, the drive ran through the estate right up to the front of the large house which stood a bit high up with white pillars at the main entrance. We walked to a side door alongside the open air swimming pool. After a knock, it was Gay Kindersley who opened the door with a "Welcome!"

We went into a medium size room at the back of the house where there were three others all talking. One was Bill Ormond, a concert singer. We were shown into a much larger room with a grand piano, and we all sat down. Gay Kindersley told us the dinner was being held in a few weeks' time. He would like the singers to arrange their songs with the pianist, and looked forward to a few rehearsals.

It was the next evening we started our rehearsals. I tried with Bill Ormond first with his type of songs, all the comical type, besides a few stories of his own, which were really funny. The other two lads sang in harmony, which wasn't too bad, and Michael, being Irish, sang Irish songs. I said to Gay Kindersley that after a few more rehearsals, it should reach up to your standard.

During the evening's workout, a friend of Gay Kindersley walked in and joined the party till we finished. I was then introduced to him, he was Don Butchers, Gay Kindersley's racehorse trainer. All the others knew him, and I found him to be a very nice fellow. Later, Michael told me the stables and yard were at the back of the house with their own entrance, and Gay Kindersley owned four or five horses. I learnt later Don Butchers looked after the business side.

It was during an evening that Gay Kindersley was not in, but Don Butchers was, that he gave us an idea of what it was all about. It was for the Mid Surrey Farmers' Draghounds, whose dinner was being held at the Felbridge Hotel near Lingfield. Don Butchers told us that Gay's father was Master of the Hounds, and Gay was one of the whips. Don told us he knew all the family. Gay's parents were divorced, his mother belonged to the Guinness family, his father was a big City man, and in touch with Royalty.

234

The next evening Gay Kindersley was there to welcome us, full of spirit and trying to sing a few songs that he'd learnt in Ireland, and he told us there'd be a crowd in a few minutes. Then a few trainers and jockeys walked in. First of all it was a lot of chatter and some music, then he wanted to take everyone out for a drink at the Swan at Great Shefford.

It was just like a convoy going out through the gates into the main road. Of course drinks were free and easy (no breath tests then), but for myself I enjoyed one drink, and had a very interesting talk. It was Willie Robinson, the jockey, who came over to speak to me. He was the jockey who won the 1964 Grand National the previous March. He was interested in the piano and music.

And so on our next visit to Parsonage Farm we were told the date of our entertainment would be in a fortnight on a Friday evening. The Friday evening came, Michael called for me, and then it was off to Parsonage Farm. Don Butchers was in charge, as he told us that Gay Kindersley was in bed with a throat infection, but he would be taking us as he knew where it was and everyone there. And so after quite a long way, we arrived at the hotel which stood on its own on the main highway.

Don took us in to be introduced and provided with drinks amongst all the crowd. Shortly afterwards everyone was told to take their places in the dining room, which was quite a large room with a platform at the end. We were shown to our own table which stood just by the platform.

It was a really good dinner and of course with a couple of speeches after, especially to say how sorry they were that Mr Kindersley was unable to attend. And so it was then they wanted to hear a few songs whilst they sat back to have a smoke. Bill arranged to go on first with a couple of his comic songs and a couple of his stories which created quite a lot of laughter and applause. Altogether it turned out very well, with the occasional call for Bill to give another story, or song, although the other lads got good applause, especially Michael with two songs.

And so it finally got into a lot of talking to a lot of different people until 12.30 am. We then walked round into the reception area, and we saw Don. He then brought over the two top people who were responsible for the evening's arrangements, and said how pleased they were with the entertainment, as everyone enjoyed it.

On our way going, and coming back, Don told us quite a few things that Gay Kindersley had told him. Some things made us laugh. Gay went to Eton and then did his National Service in which he nearly got thrown out, as he couldn't make a soldier of himself, although, as Don told us, he knew how to ride a horse. And although he'd been brought up with Society, he was just as happy with the rough and ready guy.

It was a few days later when I received quite a nice letter from Gay Kindersley. He stated how he wished to thank me for helping to turn the dinner party into a very joyful evening. Don Butchers had told him how everything went off well, as their previous dinners never had any musical entertainment. He also stated that he only wished he could have been there to have sung 'Slattery's Mounted Fut'. Lord Oaksey had told him it was the Queen Mother's favourite song.

Taffy, when he worked at local racing stables, with one of the two horses he looked after there

The depot at Didcot where I worked was to be transferred to Bicester with staff who wished to go. Some staff left to go to Harwell Atomic Station. The Lambourn and Hungerford staff would be transferred to Thatcham which was the Army's Southern Command supply depot near Newbury. The bus would pick us up at the top of Woodbury, so we wouldn't have to walk up to the Market Place.

Taffy was thinking about moving to Harwell, as there'd been such a lot of changes just lately at the milk depot. For some time, he had been thinking of getting a car. He had been learning to drive with a friend from the village who worked with him, so he was able to practise on the way to and from Newbury each day. He passed his test, and bought a Ford Anglia, so we thought the best thing was to find a garage. Some were still vacant at the end of Woodbury, so I applied for one which we obtained.

We had one or two nice rides round our local area, and then he took us to Fishguard to meet his youngest sister Margaret and family who he always stayed with. Gert had met all the family, but for Win and I it would be a first visit, and for all of us the first by car. His eldest sister Jenny and elder brother Jim, who was not married, and lived with Jenny, were in Llanelli, where Jenny had a shop in the covered market. Her husband had recently died. She had two sons and two daughters.

Both sons were teachers, the youngest in Guildford in Surrey, the eldest, who was married with one daughter, in Betws-y-Coed. He had been a pilot at the end of the war. Both daughters were married and lived in Llanelli. Taffy's other sister Dilys also lived near Fishguard. He'd always written to his family to tell them that since he came back to Lambourn he'd been lucky to find a happy and comfortable home, as it was at present. We made a start early on Friday afternoon. The journey took a lot longer, as the M4 was not completed yet. When we reached Carmarthen, Taffy thought we should make for Cardigan which proved to be a longer route but much better scenery.

It was getting dark, and of course we were beginning to feel tired, but from Cardigan we were on the last stretch of road until Fishguard, then to the village of Llanychaer about three miles further on. And so we'd arrived at our destination. The last house at the top of the hill. It was dark now. They could hear the car stop, and it was all rush to open the door, and let some light out.

Willie-John who was Margaret's husband was already helping us all out of the car, with a kiss and a cuddle and finding out who was who. And then it was over to the house to meet Margaret and the three children, that was Ann the eldest one, and the two boys Arwel and Aneurin. And so after everyone had met everyone else we had to sit down to eat and still carried on talking. Of course his family

Margaret, Willie-John, Arwel and Ann at Llanychaer

always called Taffy by his real name, Gwynfor. They were Welsh speaking, but kept to English whilst we were there.

After a good night Taffy thought he would show us round Fishguard, and after a good look around and a bite to eat, we visited his sister Dilys and her husband, where we spent a very enjoyable afternoon. We then called to see her daughter Raydene and Ray's husband Gareth, they had a lovely bungalow nearby. It was after tea Willie-John took us for a short walk down the hill following the small road to the right until we came to the small bridge over the swift flowing river which rises in the Gwaun Valley.

And so we thought we should have a walk back to have a little talk with Margaret. Both Willie and Margaret told us the history and stories connected with the Gwaun Valley. It has been noted in the guide issued to tourists that this is the valley where time has stood still. 'Hen Galan' the old New Year is still celebrated, and all the people and children visit each other's homes with music and songs. That is January 13th. It dates back to the old calendar used till 1752.

Willie said we'd go down the pub for a drink and it turned out to be a real enjoyable evening. The piano was being played and as the evening wore on, so the singing got more melodious. Of course, which was quite natural, the singing would be in the Welsh language, but if they realized there were visitors then they sang, and spoke, in the English language. Even our Win was singing well.

She knew the Welsh songs and hymns as when she was young she, with cousin Lil and Auntie Kate (who wasn't much older than Win) would go very often to Hyde Park Corner where all the Welsh and Irish singing took place during the evening. Tourists would stop and park their cars to join in. We finally made our way back but Willie stayed on. I don't know what time the pub closed, I think it stayed open all night. Little did I think that this was the beginning of quite a few holidays in Wales, and a friendship with the family that has continued to the present.

Some little while after we came back home Taffy's brother called. This brother I'd never met before. He only stayed for a short time. Taffy told me his name was Bryn and he was married with two daughters who were both married, and a son. His wife still lived in Anglesey where their home was.

Taffy told me that Bryn was different to the rest of the family, he gave himself up to drink at times. He wandered away from home but always managed to keep in touch, and was working in the Forest of Dean. The other brother I met when we went to Fishguard. His name was Dewi, it was his son who died in the boxing ring.

Taffy was now working at the Harwell Atomic Station, and I think he was better off there. I was a lot better off at Thatcham depot, I had also received an upgrading and had taken charge of all the adventure training equipment for the Southern Command.

I had to attend a couple of training lectures each week, as I must understand the condition and type of stores I should be issuing, such as skis, hill climbing gear, mountaineering gear and ropes, caving gear, canoeing gear and sleeping bags. So there was a certain amount of responsibility connected with the job, especially where the different types of rope were concerned. I had four staff to work under me.

Gert received a letter from Jill to say that she would soon be leaving her job at the Tax Office, as she must prepare her home for the start of her family which should be around Christmas time.

Things at home had been keeping us busy in many different ways, we didn't realize the amount of time that had passed so quickly. Gert went up to Jill's, and we received news from her to say that Jill had been presented with a son on December 22nd, her birthday. So that was a birthday present for her and our Christmas present. They named him John. May, being a twin of Jill's dad Charlie, and having no children of her own, always thought of Jill as half hers, and was as excited as if she had become a grandmother herself.

Of course the other grandparents were my friend Len Wohlgemuth and his wife Rene, but it was not the first time for them as their son Michael and his wife Valerie, Win's granddaughter, already had three children, Jonathan, Nicholas and Gillian. We also received news that cousin Lil's daughter Pam had received a baby daughter on Christmas Day, they had the name of Karen ready for her.

It was soon after Christmas that Win had to go into the Royal Berkshire Hospital in Reading. She had not been well for some time, she had cancer trouble. I wrote to Gert to tell her, and she hurriedly returned from Bexleyheath. Paul brought Jill down in the car so that Win could see the baby, when he was about a month old.

Only a short while after we received the news that Win had died. Her nephew Jim Bowsher was sitting by her bedside during the night when she died. He was a nephew on her husband Bert Bowsher's side, from along the farm. He was a fireman in the Reading Fire Station and had come off duty to sit by her bed. I thought a lot of that. Jim died a few years later in the same hospital. And now the family had got depleted to just three at Woodbury.

In the spring we had a visitor call, one of Taffy's brother Bryn's daughters, Diana. Her husband David was a flight engineer in the RAF, and she had met him in Anglesey when he was stationed there. He had been transferred to Fairford in Gloucestershire, and they were living with their young son at Stratton St Margaret in Swindon, so they were not far from us. She wanted to find us and give us their address so that we could go to see them.

She came over in their own car on her own, as David was on duty at the airfield. She said to Gert that it was a pity all the other relatives were such a long way apart. Taffy and I reached home before she left and Taffy promised to go over one evening.

We paid the first of several visits the following week when we met David. He seemed quite a nice type of fellow, I think he was from Manchester. They told us that the house they were in belonged to the RAF and they wanted to start their own house, probably in Highworth, not far away, where new houses were being built.

Auntie Kate and Percy had moved to my cousin Gwen's at Feltham, near Heathrow. Gwen offered to look after them in the summer of 1965 after being told on a visit to Lambourn they would otherwise have to go into separate homes. They sold their bungalow, and the money was used to build an extension to Gwen's house, so they would have their own bedroom and sitting room and toilet with washbasin, and of course Gwen would see to their food. This was the best thing they could do. We had had a run over to see them.

We also had quite a few trips in the car to Stevenage and we'd got to know the place and a lot of the people quite well. Occasionally, we used to like to go over to Hitchin, they had a good market there.

Gert had written to Taffy's eldest sister Jenny in Llanelli to ask if it was all right for her and Gwynfor (Taffy) to come down at Easter, also to bring me down. I told Gert to say that I could stand up in a corner somewhere. Good Friday soon came, and we arrived at Jenny's at tea time. There I met Jenny's and Gwynfor's eldest brother Jim and their lodger, Mr Jones. They just called him Jones.

A bit later on Jenny's daughters Peggy and Glynwen called round with their husbands, and so, it finished up in the front room where I was introduced to a nice piano, and we had a musical evening. Next day we went for a walk around Llanelli to see the shops and the covered market where Jenny had her open type shop selling fresh meat and dairy produce. Just a short distance away from the market stands the Town Hall which is surrounded by a small park and gardens. This was where Jim liked to sit on a seat during the day and find somebody to talk to.

Come Sunday, after lunch, Glynwen and her husband Denzel called round. Gwynfor had promised to take Jenny for a run out, so Denzel said they would join with us, so that was the more the merrier. Denzel was a very nice fellow, and a Trade Union delegate, and when Gwynfor tried to create an argument about Union matters, Denzel was the person who knew what he was talking about.

And now for our run out, Jenny wanted to go to Burry Port, not very far along, and Glynwen said after a look round, a bit farther to Pembrey. Burry Port was where a few people did a bit of fishing. There was a small dock below where we were standing, only wide enough to have a couple of craft side by side and there were a few wall ladders to climb down to the boats.

A bit farther along we saw Jenny talking to somebody who had climbed up out of a small boat that had just come in. They were showing her inside the basket they were carrying and took something out. It was somebody she knew who had been doing a bit of fishing, and they had given her a couple of mackerel. Taffy mentioned afterwards that everybody in Llanelli knew Jenny.

After a look around then it was off to Pembrey where into the woods we went with Glynwen, looking for different types of blossoms to paint. Next morning, Glynwen and Denzel walked in. As I had told her I was interested in paintings she thought she would bring round one of her first paintings to give us. It hangs on my wall to this day.

That was the year, 1970, when Taffy's sister Margaret's daughter Ann married an earlier lodger of Jenny's, Iori. He came from near Fishguard and was working in the bank in Llanelli. Jenny knew his father as he ran a chicken farm and took eggs to Jenny to sell.

And so it was now back to work sorting out adventure training gear. I had been told that my brother Sid was under the doctor, and it was quite likely for him to be moved to hospital. After a while, the doctor told May that he had improved a lot and that a few days' holiday would probably help a lot. I wrote to May to see if she would like to arrange a few days in the Isle of Wight and I would go with them to help. Gert and Taffy would go down to Fishguard.

Later on she wrote to tell me she had arranged a flat at Sandown. They would catch a coach from outside their row of shops which would take them to Portsmouth, where I could meet them to catch the ferry. Now the day had arrived and I got off to Newbury to catch the coach to Portsmouth. It was a good run down, and it took me right to the front near the railway station where the pier was.

I noticed Sid was bent over a bit, and was not walking too well. We arrived on the island and at Sandown we had a taxi to our flat. This was at the top of the two storey house but we preferred a lower one, as my brother couldn't climb the stairs. The owner checked on the house next door which also was his property and found he had a flat vacant on ground level. The next thing we did was to locate the Red Cross to hire a wheelchair to take Sid out, as he couldn't walk much. I hadn't realized he was as bad as he was.

We took him out in the chair, and his appetite was good, and so that was how we spent the week. The weather was good, but I think he was anxious to get home. The day we left, amongst all the crush it was the boarding and landing off the ferry that seemed a bit troublesome, but they now felt a bit easier. I had told May to hold him all the time while I carried all the cases. We reached where the coaches picked up. I was hoping to see them on to their coach and get comfortable with their heavy case as I felt a bit concerned for them, but unfortunately the Newbury coach came in first.

So it was a quick cheerio and off in no time. I felt a bit worried on the way home, although I thought May had informed their friend Bill to meet them with the car. On the way home my memory went back to the previous summer when May and Sid and myself spent a happy week's holiday on the Island, but in a different flat.

We got about quite a lot, and one of our best surprises was when we walked into a nice little café and it was my pal Len Wohlgemuth's sisters Alice and Girlie running it. It was then a kiss and a cuddle, much to the customers' enjoyment. But it was a bit different this year. I don't think we had the phone laid on, so I had

Vic (right) on an earlier holiday with May (left), Sid and Cis

to wait for a letter from May to hear they managed to get home all right, and Sid seemed to be a lot better.

When I got to work after my holiday I was called into the office to be told that a three ton lorry had been ordered to collect four canoes which were being specially made. I waited to collect the paperwork and noticed I had to go to Twickenham, alongside the river. And so, after I left my second in charge for the rest of the day, it was Roger the lorry driver who came up to tell me he was ready. After stopping for a cup of tea, we soon found ourselves at Twickenham.

After a hunt along the towpath I found the workshop with a small road alongside which the lorry could back down. I went into the workshop and found the boss. He was a youngish man, and he seemed quite pleasant. He knew what I'd come for and pointed to the four canoes all ready and waiting. There were three or four other men, all a bit older but busy working, and the boss started to show us round, which proved very interesting.

Some canoes had an air pocket inside each end and one or two had a different type of seat. Then Roger was wanted on the phone. He came back to tell me, when we had loaded the canoes we were to proceed to a depot which was in north London to pick up a consignment. He often had to go there so he knew where to make for. After the canoes were secured on the lorry, we sat up in the vehicle for our half hour to eat our lunch.

When we were looking round to find the workshop, we had to go down two or three different roads, and I could recollect our Dad and Mother often bringing Gert and me along one road to see Uncle Hinton and Auntie Rose and our cousins Bill who was then a young man and Gwen who was small. It was when we had to go through this road that I remembered the name, and I just thought how strange, after all these years, this was where we used to come.

So on we went. We went through Richmond and then later on,

along the side of Kew Gardens and right round to Kew Green where I noticed the house where Uncle Jim and Auntie Alice used to live. And so we carried on till we turned on to the North Circular Road and after quite a long way we reached our destination. We had to wait a long time until Roger could pick up everything which he had to bring back to the traffic department. Now we were on our way back with plenty of traffic, and we finally reached the depot to find it was closed.

The traffic office was still open with somebody on duty, otherwise the police were on duty and the gates locked. Roger handed in all the packages he had to collect. I then mentioned how was I to get home, a bus journey. Roger said to the traffic foreman he would take me in his car, as he lived just outside Newbury, and his wife was used to him being late.

The traffic foreman told Roger: "I'll see you're all right." And so we had to be let out through the gates and it didn't take long to reach Lambourn. I thanked Roger, and sorry for keeping his wife waiting. Only a young chap, but a very nice fellow.

We were into the New Year 1971. The news told us that we'd got to prepare for decimal currency. So now we should have to do a bit of studying. We were getting towards the end of March when May wrote to tell us that Sid had gone into hospital at Potters Bar. I wrote to May to tell her I should come to Stevenage and we could travel on the Green Line coach to Potters Bar. I'd made arrangements for myself as Taffy had been asked to work overtime for these few weekends so Gert had to stay behind to see to the food.

I went up the next Saturday and so went with May to the hospital. I think they were all types of huts in rows, all with different names. We found Sid sitting up in bed quite comfortable and pleased to see us. He said he seemed to feel quite well, and not in any pain. The doctor had been to see him, and they had a laugh. He said so far the food was good, so that's one good thing if you can eat it. And on

Sunday we set off again. Sid said they had male nurses, the one that came to the beds along their side was Burmese or somewhere along that way. Sid said he was only a young chap, but spoke good English. It was three or four weeks later that Gert and I with Taffy in the car went to Stevenage for the weekend. Sid said at times he didn't feel quite so well but it varied.

And so it went on like this until Sid died on May 2nd. He was sixty eight. The funeral was at Luton Crematorium, afterwards his ashes were interred in the same grave as our sister Win in Upper Lambourn cemetery. One thing about May, since she'd been in Stevenage, she'd made quite a few friends, and especially Bill and his wife Nell, the chap who'd worked with Sid, who would often call in to see how things were. Of course her sister Cis still lived with her. We would run up to see them as often as possible.

It was also during the spring that Taffy's sister Jenny wrote to say that her daughter Peggy's husband had died. He ran his own driving school, she didn't know if Peggy would keep the business on. Later she told us that Peggy had moved in with her, and could carry on the business from there.

We were discussing between ourselves at home that we should take May for a holiday while the summer was still here. We realized we had to move quickly to arrange for accommodation but we took a chance. We secured a reply from Weymouth in Dorset for a ground floor flat with all conveniences and with one large and two small bedrooms. This gave us six weeks to get ready.

It was now time to start. We made our way to Salisbury, Blandford, then into Dorchester, where we now turned off to Weymouth. We located our accommodation in the road just before we came on to the sea front. We found everything to our needs with Taffy and me in a small bedroom each and Gert and May sharing the large bedroom. The front garden was left open enabling visitors to park their cars. One car was already there when we arrived. It wasn't far for us to walk to the sea front and then around the town. Two or three days we would use the car for a run around the countryside to view Dorset, a lovely county. We liked to go into the town of Dorchester, it was a lovely old town, and they used to hold a lovely old market there. All around this area is known as the 'Thomas Hardy country'.

One day we had a run around the countryside, and then made our way down to the coast. We called at Bridport, a busy little place, and then moved on until we came to Charmouth, which more or less joins on to Lyme Regis. We wanted to call in to Charmouth, as Gert and I remembered that this was our Auntie Maud's home town.

After she first came to London, and then married into the family, our mother's youngest brother Sid, she used to like to tell us about her home, which she called the 'sailor's house'. I don't know why, but I remember she had a brother, his name was Bob, and he was in the Navy. When he was on leave, he always liked to come to London to visit her, and it was always followed by visiting us.

He used to like to come round especially on a Sunday when we had a musical evening, and he loved a sing song. I was then only about five or six years old. Of course he always wore his sailor's uniform, as in those days even when the Army or Navy were on leave, they still wore their uniforms. And so, looking around Charmouth, both Gert and I wondered if any of her family still lived there, but we wouldn't know now.

I would still sit down on the piano stool to run over a few notes or scales or perhaps a melody or two. I would still walk round to see cousin Alice some evenings. She told me she didn't play her piano now but when I tried the notes it gave a lovely tone and was in tune. I didn't know why she never touched it.

The years seem to pass quickly now as one seems to be getting a little bit older as we were already well into the new year, and it was just like starting all over again, and making plans for the summer. Taffy and myself had to make our holiday dates at work in good time.

We called at Jenny's at Llanelli, and took her up to see Cen, her eldest son, and his wife who live in Betws-y-Coed in North Wales, and stayed for a few days. And we then came back down to Fishguard and stayed the next week. We thought it would make a change for Jenny, as she told Taffy she hadn't seen Cen for a long time. Peggy looked after Jim and Jones and saw to their food.

On the way to Betws, Jenny said we must stop at Aberystwyth as she'd got to see somebody. We sat on a seat on the front, Jenny crossed over to the other side of the road, as this was like an esplanade with boarding houses or small hotels. She suddenly stopped and rang the bell, the door opened, and then a hug and a kiss and in she went. After some little while the door opened, and out came Jenny.

She told Gwynfor she'd been talking to cousins of theirs who now ran a boarding house during the holiday period. They would like us to stay the night. We had a light meal in the town and then it was back to the house where we were introduced to Jenny and Gwynfor's cousins who took us into their own private room which was nice and comfortable, and in which we spent the rest of the evening. They said how nice it was to see some relatives, as since they'd been up to Aberystwyth they seemed to have lost all contact with the rest of the family.

It was at Betws one day after the evening meal that Cen took Gwynfor and me for a walk out as he was telling us he was the captain of the retained fire brigade, and that's where we finished up, the fire station. He showed us all around, naming everything, and telling us about the different types of fire they had to attend. And then he pointed out the Land Rover and the mountain rescue gear in it. They had a mountain rescue party standing by, but I don't think he belonged to that. I knew a lot of the mountaineering gear, as I had the same back at work. Anyway that was all very interesting.

At Llanychaer it certainly made a change for Jenny to meet all the members of the family again. Of course this was where we had a lot of visiting to do, although we did manage to visit all of Jenny's favourite spots. It is in the late spring and summer when the cliffs in Pembrokeshire are covered with flowers of all kinds, and butterflies of many species, where in Britain elsewhere many are now extinct. Also bird life. It was many years following this that I continued to spend my holidays here, and I would always learn something new.

Monday morning, and it was off to work. My boss was pleased to see me back, and wanted to know where I'd been. He was taken aback when I mentioned Betws-y-Coed, and said we'd have a talk about this later on. It was late afternoon when I was clearing up a lot of my work to take into the office when he said: "If that's the finish, you may as well stay here and have a talk."

I did know that he'd lost his wife, and I thought he now lived on his own. He started to tell me about Betws-y-Coed and the times he went up there to see an old friend. His main trouble had always been that he didn't like driving on his own. As he knew I wasn't married he'd got the idea for me to accompany him, as it would be somebody that had to go to the same place.

I had to turn it down. As I told him, I travelled with my own people, and I knew he was apt to go on the drink. So he left it at that, and I hadn't told him that I didn't drive. Anyway he'd be retiring soon.

On our bus going to work there was quite a lot of talk about the Lambourn Carnival starting again at August Bank Holiday 1972. After so many years without a carnival, everyone was looking forward to it, this would be something to bring some life back to Lambourn. There was to be a fair, other entertainments and a procession. There were also raffle tickets which were being sold, so that meant buying a couple. I'd noticed some of the prizes on display in the Universal Stores' window in the High Street.

The top prize was a colour television, and second was a radio music centre. They were something worth winning. Sunday would be Carnival day, starting at 5 o'clock, and well before crowds of people were lining the route. Cars had come from all around the district, I'd never seen so many people in Lambourn. Taffy preferred to stay at home; being a Sunday afternoon he liked to listen to the hymn singing on Radio Wales.

After drinking our cup of tea, Gert and I made our way along until we came to the crowds, some had been waiting for over an hour but there was still room. We took our position right opposite the Lamb, so we could see the procession coming down Mill Lane. After what seemed a long wait, and talking to people standing alongside us, we could hear the band in the distance. It wasn't long before we saw them, quite a long procession, including two bands, which was worth coming out to see.

After it had gone by, I said we could walk up to the Market Place as after its tour, that was where it finished, and they would announce the prizewinners. That's where we found the crowd, packed shoulder to shoulder. The procession finally disbanded and the crowds eased off which gave us a bit more room to be able to hear the winning ticket holders. The first number came out. I looked at our number and then I heard our name. I couldn't believe it. We had won the colour television set.

Gert had been separated from me, and she couldn't understand why people kept congratulating her, being hard of hearing she didn't at first realize we'd won. It was a GEC model. So many people kept coming up to me to ask if I could sell them the set. Of course I had to disappoint them. That was why I bought a ticket, to win. Colour made viewing a lot more interesting.

We received some bad news: Auntie Kate had had a stroke and was in hospital, there was not much hope for her. Come Saturday we called over to cousin Gwen's and after lunch we made our way to the hospital, at Ashford. She looked comfortable, lying on her side but in a rather deep sleep. We stayed there for quite some time, when Gwen with Uncle Percy and her husband Jim came into the ward. We stayed to have another little talk to them.

It was nearly a week later when sad news arrived that she had died. Considering her suffering for quite a number of years, I think she'd managed quite a good age, eighty six. We attended the funeral in their parish church, she was then cremated, and her ashes were to be interred in Upper Lambourn cemetery. Percy had arranged for a plot to be prepared for Auntie Kate and also eventually himself. After a while Mr Rolfe, the Lambourn undertaker, came to inform us he now had the casket containing Auntie Kate's ashes so we attended a short service at the graveside.

It was surprising to find how the time seemed to pass so quickly and so many changes seemed to be taking over. I remembered when I and Gert were sent to Lambourn. I went to school, my teacher being Mr Wing, and to church on a Sunday, when the Vicar was then Rev Bagnall. He was the Rev in Lambourn for about thirty five years until the Rev Gotto took over, and since then there had been four vicars.

Quite a few friends we'd made since living in Woodbury, but now they seemed to be moving to Australia. They were all good people and we were sorry to see them go.

John was now three years old and growing quite sturdy. Jill said he'd been worrying her to come down to stay with his Nan, so in the spring she thought she would give it chance, and they left him with us for a week. He made himself quite at home and slept with his Nan which he seemed to enjoy.

When Taffy and me got home from work, he liked to show us how many holes he'd dug in the garden. Occasionally he would be talking to Frank Stacey whose garden backed on to ours and who liked to come out to do a bit of gardening after work. Frank told me John liked asking a lot of questions. One or two evenings, we took him out in the car, and of course he liked the colour television. It was the start of many visits. He always loved Lambourn and his Nan, and cried when he had to leave.

Things went along quite normally. It was gardening in the summer and of course making the most of the TV during the winter months.

In early summer we had a letter from Taffy's niece Diana, she now had another son. They'd moved from Highworth, and were living in Cirencester, and so Taffy suggested we have a run over to see them. We went along one evening. Diana was surprised to see us, as we hadn't let her know, but pleased. David was away. We felt a little awkward, as Diana was preparing a light supper for her and her sons, but she insisted on us staying, and so it finished up with all of us enjoying hot soup, and a light meal to follow, with a lot of talk.

Taffy mentioned about changing the car, as I think we had had a good run with it, and the next year he purchased a more modern one. Jill and Paul brought John down again. He'd grown up a bit, and now he went out to play.

We'd had a new family come to live just a short way down the road, but on the opposite side. They had four sons, two a bit older than John, one about his age and one younger. They liked playing near their house, but occasionally they would go just down the road near the bridge, and play by the river, although there was not much water. It would probably just go up to their knees if they went in but it was too cold, and a lot of weeds floating about, but it was clear water.

John was happy with a few mates when they came to play, otherwise he was happy in the garden. It was a run into Newbury on Saturday morning as Gert liked to do her shopping there, and Taffy wanted to give the car an extra polish during the afternoon.

One day, Taffy said he had a day's leave owing, so he might as well make use of it and we could go and find his brother Bryn at Clearwell, on the edge of the Forest of Dean. It would make a trip out, even if we couldn't find him, and so, I took a day's leave. Of course we had Gert and John with us. We went on the M4, then turned off to Chepstow, and on to Tintern Abbey, where we stopped for a picnic. There were quite a lot of visitors.

We had a look around the Abbey, but it is only the ruin there now. We all had an ice cream, and then we went on our way towards Monmouth and turned off when we saw the sign to Clearwell. There were only a few houses and buildings scattered about. I think I remember a pub.

We happened to see an elderly man in his shirtsleeves in and out of his small house. We called over to him and Taffy asked him if he knew anyone called Bryn. His face lit up, and he said: "He stays here, I'll go and find him." Bryn soon came along, and then the talking began. I don't know what the two small buildings along the side of the house contained or what they were used for, but the old chap seemed quite busy running in and out of them. It wasn't long before we noticed John running about and helping him.

It was all open ground we were looking at which stretched right up towards the trees along the top. I think I remember the old chap saying to John that behind the trees was an old castle, and the film people came here to help make the film of 'Robin Hood'. He made us a cup of tea, and gave John some peacock feathers before we started our move home.

Across the Severn we pulled into the motorway halt for something to eat and drink. It was then back into the car with John in the back with his Nan but standing looking over our shoulders to watch Taffy driving. After we'd arrived home he started to ask his Nan if she'd ask Taffy if he would let him drive the car as he now knew how to drive it.

Taffy and Vic in the back garden at home, August 1980

59. RETIREMENT

My birthday, September 2nd 1974, was the date of my retirement. Some of the higher grades liked to make a big do of it, but I just liked to carry on in the quiet way. I had quite a number of cards given me from around the depot, also a personal handshake from the Major and Colonel of the depot. Also the message from the Queen. And there I finished at the depot. Quite a few I'd known and worked with had already retired before me, so I don't think I left many behind who I can remember well.

Taffy also retired, about the end of the month. He said he now felt like an old age pensioner. We just carried on in an easy manner. It was at the end of the year when we received the news from cousin Gwen and her husband Jim that Uncle Percy had died. And so the family was still getting smaller.

We often got visitors. Jill and Paul with John, and May and Cis. During the summer time Gwen and Jim liked to have a run down to see us, Jim told us he liked coming to Lambourn. It was the same with my nephew Peter and his wife Maureen in Liverpool. They now liked to take their holiday somewhere in the South, book a cottage and do a lot of walking. Of course they liked to reserve one day when they drove over to visit us. This went on for about three years.

We had another visit from one of the Bowsher family from Canada, quite a young lady. Of course it was my eldest sister Win who she really came to visit, but we had to tell her Win had died. Win had been married to Bert Bowsher, and she always kept in touch with his relatives in Canada. The young lady said she was staying at Valley View in Lambourn. I can remember Uncle Ern Bowsher living there. He was the church organist. Another year we were visited by another of the Bowsher family from Canada. I think she was the daughter of the first visitor and she'd come to travel around England. We took her for a run around at different times.

The time had arrived in 1976 for Gert to go to stay at Jill's, as Jill would soon be preparing for the next to join the family tree. Gert would look after John, and do the cooking, and so that left me doing the cooking at home. Jill had a baby daughter born the same day as Gert's birthday, June 21st. This had also been the birthday of the baby's great grandmother Mrs Fitzgerald. And so John in his seventh year now had a baby sister Helen to help to look after.

We heard from Llanychaer that Taffy's niece Ann's husband Iori was to go away on a training course for a couple of weeks for the bank where he was working. He was the only employee in West Wales that was on this course. He had been told where to report, and the best method of travel. The college was either in Surrey or Hampshire. He was advised to travel by train to Reading and change on to a train to his final part of the journey, where transport would take them to the college.

Two or three days later, we received a letter from Iori to inform us that he was due to start at the college the Saturday coming. It was now Wednesday. He said he would like to come up on Friday if he might, to stay the night with us. He would come in the car. He said there was only one little favour, that was to leave the car with us, and Taffy take him to Reading in Taffy's car, to catch his train. This was how it worked out, and Taffy put his car in our garage. Gert was still up at Jill's. Anyway, we'd been managing all right.

Iori had been at college two weeks, and it was Friday we had to go to Reading to collect him. This was a job soon done. He thought he would stay the night, and go back in the morning. He had been working in the bank for quite a long time, and the one reason he had for attending the college was to make some advance. Also, there was his knowledge of the Welsh language which was essential for working in banks in Wales, especially West Wales. Taffy had told us that all the children in West Wales were taught both the English and Welsh languages. That year Taffy's sister Jenny died, also a short while after, his brother Jim.

It was the next year that we went up to Jill's, as cousin Joyce's eldest daughter Jennifer was being married. They lived not a great distance away from Jill and Paul, at Orpington. It was a very nice wedding, and it was strawberry time. After the wedding breakfast was over, Paul and John and I thought we would find out where the strawberry fields were, and bring some back. This we did, not very far away. We went in the car and picked quite a few, they were much enjoyed.

It was a bit later in the year when we received some bad news. My friend Len had died, Paul's dad. It was rather sudden, as he wasn't all that old, sixty six. I was two years older. He had had a heart attack. I remember going to the funeral and seeing his sisters Alice and Girlie, besides quite a few others I knew from our old days.

The next year Jill was expecting the next member of the family. Gert went up to stay, and then we had news in June that Jill had been presented with another baby girl. So that meant John would have to walk with one sister on each arm. Gert said they were going to name her Clare.

We now looked forward to the Lambourn Carnival each year. As a matter of fact it had been arranged for things to take place in the week leading up to it. It could be horse or pony trials, and another day or evening a sports event, always something each day.

Of course the usual Flower Show took place each year, which was now held in the Sports Centre, usually on a Saturday. I remember when I was very young and the Flower Show was held on the old cricket field along the Upper Lambourn road. That was known as the day of all days. I suppose it's Carnival that takes its place now.

We'd now moved on into the 1980s. And Taffy's sister Margaret and her husband Willie-John and their son Aneurin came and visited us for a change. We had always asked them. Aneurin drove them up in his car. They liked Lambourn.

Their two favourite places were the Universal Stores in the High Street and (apart from Margaret) the Lamb in the evening. They followed us into Swindon and Newbury, where they spent all day. They were just fascinated with the shops. Their daughter Ann and son Arwel had children, and so they were interested in buying things for the children. They couldn't buy all these things in Fishguard.

I noticed the year 1981 as this was when the London Marathon was first started with 7,747 runners entered. Now the number runs into many thousands, people in wheelchairs as well. It's become an annual event. I always like to watch it on TV, and see all the familiar places.

Two or three weeks later on we had rather a pleasant surprise. It was Taffy's nephew Cen and his wife from Betws-y-Coed. They brought sleeping bags indoors, as they wanted to stay for the night. Cen told us they'd come down to visit a friend of his, an ex pilot, who lived I think in Oxford. They wanted to visit us first, and so we were now busy making tea. After tea and something to eat, he wanted to take us to Windsor Castle. Taffy, Gert and myself were bundled into the rear seat. It was the latter part of April but a lovely sunny day.

Off we went, we certainly caught plenty of breeze. Not used to riding in an open top car, although later on it wasn't too bad. We soon found ourselves running into Windsor, and approaching the Castle, where Cen managed to park. We went into the parts that were open, and we certainly saw some lovely paintings and furniture, and then it was a look round the town, with the different shops and a stop for a cup of tea, and a walk alongside the river.

On our way home, we found that we were travelling slowly through

Kingsclere in Hampshire. Cen then told us that a person he knew told him there was a good fried fish and chip shop in the town. As it was beginning to get dark Cen stopped to ask where the shop was. The man told him it was just along the road, but closed that night. I said we'd got to go through Newbury, and we should pass a good shop there, just before you cross over the railway bridge into Bartholomew Street.

I think Cen was pleased with what he bought, really a good finish up to the day. They could now have a comfortable night (no sleeping bags) before their next port of call tomorrow. And so morning came, and it was not long before our guests were ready to go. It was a hurried goodbye and now a quiet sit down for us. With a cup of tea and a talk about yesterday.

It was during the year I heard that Auntie Emily, Alice's mother, had died. She had given me the only few piano lessons I ever had. She was ninety three. It was after a few more weeks when the talk was then all about the wedding of the century. That was the Prince of Wales and Lady Diana Spencer, which was to be held on July 29th. Flags and bunting were being assembled along the route of the procession. It was announced that a grand firework display would be held in Hyde Park on the previous evening.

Afterwards, the news reported that thousands attended the display and then made their way to St James's Park. The crowds just took the deck chairs to make themselves comfortable during the night, otherwise it meant sleeping on the grass. This meant an early rise to secure a place to watch the procession.

It was later on during the summer that Margaret and Willie-John came to stay for the weekend and brought Ann and Iori's two young daughters with them. They told us that Ann and Iori and family had moved from Fishguard as Iori had secured a bank manager's situation, which he'd been hoping for. Both Margaret and Willie-John mentioned how everyone seemed so pleased and happy that now Wales had a Princess of Wales. And so into the next year when a son was born to the Prince and Princess, the name of William, which seemed to create a lot more jollity. By then things seemed to be easing off throughout the country as the war with Argentina over the Falkland Islands had finished. This was called the Falklands war, and now I suppose it was up to Mrs Thatcher.

I had the news from my nephew Peter in Liverpool to tell me that his mother Dolly had died. After my brother Lal died she carried on in the same house on her own. She was over eighty years. In 1984, Cousin Lil who was more like an older sister died on Christmas Day. She was ninety one years. We always heard from Jill how the younger ones were getting on. John was starting secondary school, Helen was at the local primary school which was called Mayplace, and Clare would be following very soon.

Christmas 1981, in the living room (called the front room) at 9 Woodbury (from left), Gert, John, Jill, Clare, Vic, Paul, Helen

Taffy didn't seem to be making very much headway recently. He had quite a job to move along from his bedroom to the bathroom which was only a matter of a few steps. One evening we found him lying on the floor. He'd fallen out of the bed. It was a struggle to get him up and make him comfortable, then we rang for the doctor. It was a year ago when we had our last holiday, and since then he seemed to have been slowing up. We thought about getting rid of the car, and so finished with the garage.

The doctor thought Taffy had Parkinson's disease, but he would call again in a few days' time. Meanwhile, we found it very difficult to keep him in bed as he seemed to be so restless and would be on the floor in no time if we didn't stand a couple of chairs along the side of the bed to keep him in. The doctor gave him another test and felt he needed hospital treatment, for which he made arrangements.

As we waited for the ambulance, Taffy still seemed to have plenty of chat with the doctor who was Scotch. The doctor said: "As we're both foreigners we should be back in our own country," which created a laugh. One good thing was that he was taken to Sandleford Hospital, which belonged to Newbury Hospital, and was easy for us to make our visits by bus.

And so now it was just Gert and myself left to look after ourselves. Meanwhile, my sister in law May and her sister Cis had given up their house and moved into a residential home in another part of Stevenage. Cis was very frail, and May was getting rather forgetful, so it suited them. They both settled in quite comfortably, each with their own bedroom with washroom and toilet, and of course their meals in the dining room. Occasionally, we were able to visit them.

We often visited Taffy twice a week, once in mid week and then Saturday. This was a journey of twelve miles to Newbury, and then another bus to the Sandleford, but we soon got quite used to making our visits. Sundays we were unable to, as there was no bus service. As it was now good summer weather, when we went in to the day room we often found the large glass doors wide open and a lot of the patients sitting outside with chairs and tables.

And that's where we would find him. In the day room the men patients would sit on one side of the room, and the women on the other side, usually at tables with two or three others. There were four or five nurses on duty, and sometimes a male nurse, but not always, and of course the staff nurse, who was a really nice person.

One day when Gert was busy talking to Taffy, I heard somebody calling and I glanced round, it was one of the men patients calling to me. I went over to him, and he said: "Do you think you could give me a shave as the staff have been too busy today." So I told him to make himself comfortable and looked round for an electric shaver hanging on the wall, as there were about three on the men's side of the room. They were on long leads, I'd seen the nurses using them.

It then started the others off, they all wanted shaves. This often happened during my future visits, but I didn't mind being a help line in one way or the other. It was a couple of weeks later when Taffy's brother Dewi together with Margaret his sister and her husband Willie-John came up from Wales to see him.

During this year I thought I would book a holiday for Gert and myself for a break and so I booked for Eastbourne. We'd been used to the car, this time it was coach travel. It was at the Market Place we got picked up, my next door neighbour Pat Puffett took us up there in his car, and would bring us back. We had a good hotel with good food. We liked Eastbourne, altogether it was an enjoyable holiday.

Up till now, I had always enjoyed smoking a pipe. Even before my army days I started with cigarettes but couldn't get on with them. Whilst at Eastbourne pipe smoking affected my nose, and so, I gave smoking up. After a while as my nose still seemed to get clogged up, I went to see the doctor, who advised me to go to Newbury Hospital for an x ray, after which I needed an operation. After, I still felt a bit clogged on one side, but I then could breathe properly.

It was later, in November, when both Gert and I went to the wedding of cousin Bernard, Joyce's son, which was held at St Albans.

And so we kept up our visits to the hospital, and found Taffy gradually getting lower until he died just before Christmas 1987. His funeral was held on Christmas Eve which was a cremation, quite a large number of relatives came from Wales. It was a little later, after Christmas when Gert and I attended a short service in Upper Lambourn cemetery for his ashes to be buried.

Later on, Gert heard from Margaret inviting us down for the week. Gareth, her niece Raydene's husband, would come to fetch us, and her son Aneurin, with Margaret, would bring us back. This was something I didn't expect, now Taffy was no longer with us. We met a lot of people we'd got to know over the years. Also this time not travelling about in the car, it was a lot more walking. We really enjoyed our holiday, we'd spent so many holidays there, that it was just like another home. After a good journey home, the first thing Margaret asked, if we could take her up the cemetery to see Gwynfor's grave. She told us she was his favourite sister.

And so both Gert and me carried on in an easy manner, when I saw a holiday list from Barnes' coaches hanging in the window of the newsagent's. I obtained a copy, and so we made a study of it and thought we would choose a holiday in Scarborough from the end of May into the beginning of June. And so we booked.

As before, the coach picked us up in Market Place, and brought us back there. And Pat next door took us to the Market Place and would bring us back, and so that's how a holiday should be. Saturday we made our return home after a glorious week in Yorkshire, also visiting York, Whitby, Flamborough Head and Bridlington. We finished the year off with Paul and Jill and the children at Christmas time. The children now all growing up.

And so into the New Year, and spring, and then we received news that our sister in law May at Stevenage had been taken into hospital. She was eighty. And it was only a short while later she died. Jimmy Rodbourn, her nephew, and his wife Yvonne were going from Lambourn to the funeral, and they made the offer to drive us. It turned out to be a really wet and dismal day.

We were intending to call at the Home to join the funeral procession, as then it would go to the Luton crematorium. The going wasn't very good. We were on the main North Road, but we were blocked in with miles of traffic, just moving along slowly and the rain pouring down. I looked at my watch, and found we were well behind time, the funeral procession would have left the Home.

I told Jimmy to make for Luton. This we did for quite some way, until the car broke down. Jimmy got out to look at the engine, as he said he knew the trouble, but being out for just a few minutes he got wet through. I then got out to help him, and after both getting wet through we managed to start the car, and finished our journey to the crematorium to find the service had finished, and everyone was waiting outside for us to arrive. And so, it was a lot of talking and explaining and a look at all the flowers.

Our people then made our way to St Albans where Joyce and Arthur Rockhill's eldest daughter Jennifer lives, and had arranged a meal for us. This was a most welcomed break. We arrived home later in the evening. After a full change of clothing and a dry down as I'd felt wet all the day long, we sat in the warm. Gert and myself talked about this day's events. I said: "It's going to take me a long time before I ever finish thinking of this day."

266

I often walked round to Riverside Cottage to see how cousin Alice was keeping. She was beginning to look much older. It was about this time I came to know Mr and Mrs Stanley, Helen and Walter. They lived in a cottage in what we called Blind Lane which runs alongside George Bodman's coal yard.

It always seemed to happen that each morning when we were walking up to do some shopping, they would be coming out from the lane, I suppose to do the same. This was when we would do a lot of talking, and finally got to know each other a bit more. Helen was from Scotland, but I don't think she was in Scotland for any length of time as her speech was more English. Walter was English, and they were older than us. She told me that he always accompanied her if they were out walking, as he was blind in one eye.

I was told by elderly people who remembered Helen before the war that they lived in Upper Lambourn. She worked for Lady Elkins. Lady Elkins lived in her own house, and Helen and Walter lived in the cottage adjoining. When war broke out Lady Elkins moved to Scotland taking Helen and Walt with them. After the war, they all came back to Upper Lambourn.

Helen and Walter had I think four sons, and one daughter. The daughter was married with a family, and lived at Thatcham. She often called to see them as she drove over in her Land Rover. I think a couple of the sons were in the Navy.

They lived for quite a while in Blind Lane until they eventually obtained sheltered housing just off the High Street. During the summer time they always liked their little walk, and it would be quite often during their afternoon stroll, they would call in to see us. Often during the morning if we went shopping we would call in to see them and have a talk, and often the warden would be there. They were very interesting in all their talk and different stories. I think the most interesting thing they told us about was when they went on a tour of the Holy Land to visit Helen's brother. During the war, when he was in the Army, he met a Jewish girl in North Africa who was escaping from the Germans. He kept in touch with her until after the war, when he married her and went with her to Israel.

It was early in the year when the holiday programmes were issued and so, between Gert and I, I booked for a week's holiday to Newquay in Cornwall. I then found out that Helen had booked there for the same week. This was a larger hotel than we had in Scarborough, there was another coach party staying so it made a larger crowd for breakfast and evening meal. The other people were from the North, but we soon got to know them.

The first job had to be to start looking around Newquay, although I remember coming here with my brother Sid and his wife May, we stayed then at a private apartment. One evening Gert and I were sitting in the lounge, and Helen and Walt joined us. We started chatting, and so it went from one topic to another. Helen was telling us about when they came back to Upper Lambourn after the war.

Walt had to go to Ashdown House to see about logs, as they were in need of more wood beside their ration of coal. I didn't think to ask if she still worked for Lady Elkins. Walt chimed in to say he had gone on a bike. He had said he would probably be there all day so Helen made him bacon sandwiches to take.

Logs and lumps of wood were scattered all over the place and had to be gathered by hand and carried to where the truck was loaded. It was a lot of hard work, but he did have a man come over to help him. They carried on till they'd made a good pile, also plenty of brushwood for kindling.

They had quite a few stops for a talk and afterwards for something to eat. The man who was helping him sat alongside and started on two halves of cold chicken. Walt said: "I watched him as he ate his cold chicken, and he'd already finished them before I'd eaten half my sandwiches. I'd never seen anybody finish up cold chicken like he did. After a bit more talking, I then asked him what his name was. He said, 'I've only got one name and that's Shady'."

I let him finish his story about getting the wood home and then I told him Shady was my uncle. With that he burst out laughing, which made other people look around. Altogether, it turned out to be a very good week, with visits to Truro, Falmouth and Padstow, although I think we enjoyed Scarborough and Yorkshire the most.

It was during the following week when we had a letter from Jill asking us to go up and visit them in a week or two's time, as Clare was performing in a concert by Bexley Music School, and it was taking place in the Royal Festival Hall on June 22nd. And so this was something else we had to look forward to.

We went with Jill and Paul. Paul's Mum and his younger brother Martin came as well. This was my first visit to the Festival Hall, it is a beautiful place inside and out, although I must admit I still prefer the atmosphere of the Royal Albert Hall. We had an interval. Being a lovely sunny day we went out to look over the river, this I enjoyed all the more.

The railway bridge running into Charing Cross Station was just on our left, and then the Embankment on the other side where the trams used to run along to Westminster or Blackfriars. The Shell-Mex building was quite opposite, where once the Hotel Cecil was, next door was the Savoy Hotel. Along the front lay the Embankment Gardens in which during the summer evenings the band always played.

For those few minutes my mind had gone right back to when I was a lot younger. Of course all the way through the show we had to take a lot of interest in Clare playing her trumpet but altogether it was very enjoyable. As a matter of fact it was an enjoyable day as I felt at the time I was looking all around, and over the river, I'd come back home.

Jill and Paul's son John had intentions of joining the RAF when he left school, but failed one of the tests, so he went into an engineering apprenticeship with the MoD (Ministry of Defence). It was in the spring of 1990 when we had a letter from Jill to tell us that he had to go to Didcot RAOC (Royal Army Ordnance Corps) centre, next to the old Royal Ordnance Depot, for four weeks, and so he preferred to stay with us and travel to Didcot every day, he now had his own car.

We got his own bedroom ready. I worked out the route for him which was quite straightforward, and so he was all ready for the morning. Gert made him a good breakfast, we were thinking about him during the day, and looking forward to him coming home in the evening. He

At the wedding of Arthur Reading's eldest daughter Susan in August 1991 (from left), Vic, Joyce, Gert, Pam

arrived home about 5.30, when he was ready for something to eat. We then had to ask him how he'd got on. He said: "Nothing to do." He was the only one to be called in and being the first day, it was a matter of hanging about. This lasted for a few days when he said he had a few odd jobs to do in the camp. His main trouble now, was to get the car started in the mornings. Pat Puffett, our next door neighbour, was out with him each morning, helping him.

It was when Pat came in to have a cup of tea that he told me John needed a fresh battery. So I gave him the money to get it fixed up when he was in Didcot, which he did. Now things were going right. He told Gert and me that he had met his instructor and so he now drove an army vehicle with his instructor to visit ranges, such as Salisbury Plain and Bovington. He carried his pyjamas and toilet necessities as sometimes he would be away for more than a day. Once or twice he travelled up to Otterburn in Northumberland to visit different ranges.

And so he finished his four weeks. During this time it had given us a bit of interest to know all the places he'd been to. The next summer we had a letter from Jill asking us to go up for a few days, as Clare was appearing in another concert, this time at the Barbican. As Jill and Paul would be taking Clare a bit earlier, we should be travelling with Paul's mum Rene and his younger brother Martin in their car.

I must say, travelling through Blackwall Tunnel and the East End of London gave me great interest. When I was younger and living and working in London, for visiting or any other reasons I went through parts of south or south east London, west and north, but I knew little of the East End. We passed through Limehouse into Commercial Road, and I noticed we were entering the City. And so, we managed to locate the Barbican.

We had to go upstairs to find our seats. The show turned out to be very good, the musical numbers and performance were quite an improvement on the show at the Festival Hall. And so, as Jill and Paul were waiting for Clare, we just carried on back, past St Paul's Cathedral. I had noticed a lot of new building in the City after the war damage.

Back home, we had a letter from Jill to say John would be down again for two weeks as he had to attend the Royal Military College at Shrivenham, about nine miles from Lambourn. He would stay at the college during the week, but wanted to spend the weekend with us. And then it was back to a quiet life, until Christmas.

The piano was getting a bit old, and I could never seem to contact a piano tuner. I thought that my cousin Joyce always wanted our old piano, so I would write to her to ask if she'd like it, she might be able to find a piano tuner round her way. And so I sent it to them.

Towards the end of May 1992 Cis died. Paul came down to collect us to attend the funeral, at Luton Crematorium. She never really recovered from her sister May's death, three years before. Later, Cis's ashes were forwarded to our undertaker for burial at Upper Lambourn cemetery, in the same grave as my sister Win, my brother Sid and his wife May. Also, my cousin Winnie, Betty's elder sister, had died, and her ashes were awaiting burial in the next grave, their family grave. And so it would be the one service.

I still had a walk round to Riverside Cottage to see cousin Alice. I noticed everything seemed to be in a bit of a jumble there. Her niece Nova, Harry's daughter, often came down from Long Ditton in Surrey to see how she was. I think she was now relying on her.

A bit later on, we had a letter from Taffy's sister Margaret in Wales. She would like Gert and me to come down for a week in August. Her niece Raydene's husband Gareth would come to fetch us, and she and her son Aneurin would bring us back. And so I rang through to them and made all the arrangements. Margaret's husband Willie-John, and Raydene's mother Dilys, Margaret's sister, both had died since our last visit. And so, after a happy week it was back home. We didn't know it then, but that was to be our last holiday in Wales.

Towards the end of the year, there was quite a lot of talk about both the Prince of Wales and the Duke of York, whose marriages had broken up. Of course it was news that had travelled all over the world. And now, it was in the Queen's Christmas speech as she mentioned the effects on the Royal Family. Of course, it had been our main subject to talk about during the last couple of months.

I now realized that the majority of our relatives and friends had died. We still had Jill and Paul and the family come down to see us, or we visited them, otherwise sometimes others in the family would come for a day, but not as many as in the old days. Also, we had the piano that always kept the family alive, and the family had now gone apart from Gert and myself, I suppose the piano had gone with them. It was now the television we had to rely on.

Still, it helped us through the winter. Especially if the weather held good for any racing to watch. It was getting towards the end of March 1993 when we began to read about the horses toning up for the Grand National. It was now the day, which made me wonder, it was April 1st, April Fool's Day. Come the afternoon and Gert and myself were sitting watching, and then the starter was getting up on to his stand, and so, all eyes were on the start of the race.

Unfortunately, it was the majority of people at the racecourse who were unable to see what happened, but of course it was the millions watching television who saw the starter pull the lever for the tapes to rise. They just spluttered around the horses' and jockeys' necks. After things began to settle down a bit, the starter attempted to use the starter flag. Even this didn't work properly.

And so the starter told the remaining jockeys: "No race," although some did make a start and carried on. The 'winner' who was then told the race was abandoned, covered his eyes. It all seemed such a pity. Still, there would be all the other principal race meetings to watch during the summer, with a cup of tea, as the racegoers drank their beer or whatever it might be.

Jill and Paul asked us to spend a week with them during September, which we looked forward to. Jill told us that she was taking us to Canterbury on one day. This was one place I'd wanted to visit from when I started school and I learnt about the Archbishop of Canterbury's London home, which was called Lambeth Palace, and also about the early history of Canterbury Cathedral.

We joined the crowd at Bexleyheath waiting for the coach and we were soon off and on our way, taking in every inch of the countryside. When I was a lot younger I always used to hear about the Garden of England, Kent. Even when I was at school, I knew quite a few of the boys who, at this time of the year, would go hop picking in Kent together with their families. Our family didn't go, but my friends the Wohlgemuths did.

The families would go to the same farmer each year. I used to see them on two or three mornings taking all their cooking utensils and whatnots on a barrow or pram along to London Bridge Station where they would catch the train for Kent. Farmers provided huts or shelter of a kind, they provided and cooked their own food. Of course the farmer paid them, although it used to make a holiday for them. Their last night before coming home was a proper camp fire and singing which I think went on half way through the night.

Now we were approaching Canterbury, and it wasn't long before we'd arrived at the bus stop. I could see the cathedral towers, shooting up behind the old houses. There were quite a lot of people also entering the cathedral as was the same in all the other cathedrals I've visited. I suppose we must have all been pilgrims. Even the Pope was a pilgrim when he visited Canterbury. When I was at school studying history and religion, I was taught the main reason for pilgrims visiting Canterbury Cathedral was to attend the

274

shrine of Saint Thomas a Becket, who was murdered in the cathedral. As we were walking round, it was all of great interest to me. Although I didn't see the shrine which was in a chapel on its own. I was told when I enquired that in the days of the 1500s when the dissolution of the monasteries occurred the shrine was destroyed and all that is left are fragments kept together.

After we came out, we came upon quite a long line of people waiting to enter a show of the *Canterbury Tales*. I'd often heard about the *Canterbury Tales*, a poem written 600 years ago by Geoffrey Chaucer in which he described the tales, the antics, and all the different goings on with pilgrims on their journey to visit the shrine of Thomas a Becket. It was said, the pilgrims came from all over the country, and other countries, and stayed in London for a few days.

And so it was in London where Geoffrey Chaucer started his tales, and the pilgrims set off from the Tabard Inn in Southwark, and this was the first scene in the show. We were in semi darkness and formed into small groups and moved into small rooms where we were shown the different stories. I suppose, it was by filming but everything was shown in the true colours of the medieval times with proper sounds and talking and even smells. As we watched each scene, we felt we were with the people we were watching.

It was then we walked around outside, I found Canterbury very interesting. I did notice that while we were waiting for our coach there were also three or four continental coaches waiting for their passengers. I suppose they would travel over on the ferry from Dover or Folkestone which were not a great way from Canterbury to their destination over the other side.

During the week we went to Dartford market, which was a good market. Another day we went along to Crayford to the Air Training Corps quarters for the annual inspection of the local squadron. John was in his twenties, and was a Warrant Officer, both Helen and Clare were cadets. They all looked quite smart in their uniforms.

After arriving home on the Saturday, I said to Gert that we should soon be into October, and so we must start saving for Christmas. Sunday proved a quiet day for us as we missed the young folk, but it's what we get used to. It was during the night, after being sound asleep, there was a sudden 'BOMP' which woke me up with alarm.

I jumped out of bed, never troubled about my dressing gown, I had to get out of the bedroom, when I saw Gert's bedroom door was open and the light on. But I could hear her calling softly at the bottom of the stairs. I said a prayer and rushed down as I could see she was trying to lift herself up. I asked her if she was in any pain, as she was still calling for Jill. She said she was all right.

And so I gently moved her, to try and lift her, as she seemed to be getting herself up. She still kept asking for Jill, I then told her we were now back home. I managed to get her upstairs and into bed and made her comfortable, and then told her I would ring for the doctor, as I now noticed a cut on her forehead. I looked at my watch, and the time was 3.30 am.

It didn't seem very long before I had to go down to open the door to the doctor. It was Dr Powell and his wife who was also a doctor and was a daughter of Dr Osmond, one of the other village doctors, and Mrs Osmond. I did tell the doctor I was a bit worried in getting Gert up to bed. The doctor stripped the bedclothes back to test her, and found everything in order, and looked at her forehead. He bathed it, and said she was all right, but they would call tomorrow.

With that I thanked them both and showed them downstairs. I then went upstairs, to find Gert getting back into bed after using the commode along the side of her bed. I made her comfortable, as she was looking tired. I fetched a blanket to cover round myself and sat in the small armchair alongside her bed and just left the small light on. I didn't seem to sleep for the rest of the night.

I was glad to see the daylight, and to get up and wash. I cleared and straightened everything up, made some tea which went down like a birthday present. I then went back upstairs and found Gert was awake so brought her a cup of tea. She seemed a lot better.

I thought I would wait until after the doctor had been before ringing up to Jill and giving her the news. I rang up to cousin Bet along the road as, no doubt Jock had gone to work, she'd come running down. Bet agreed with me, when I told her, that I thought the reason for Gert not causing any injuries to herself was because her mind was far away and she was wandering. We had noticed for some time that Gert was not quite herself, and was getting rather confused. After this accident, she got worse.

The doctor found her OK physically, but to stay in bed and rest for the day. During the day I kept thinking about something to guard the stairs. I then realized that we had an older type baby cot in the shed, it was wooden and had been taken apart. I got busy, and so was able to fix a gate over the top of the stairs, with fixtures in both ends to lift the gate in for the night or out for the day. That made me feel easy when I went to bed.

Jill came down for two or three days, and Gert seemed to get a bit better, but she couldn't any longer carry on with a lot of the tasks she used to do, and from then on I had to do most of the household jobs. In January John came down to take me to Swindon and Jill came with him, as it meant her staying with Gert while I went. I wanted to buy a washing machine as we only had a gas copper, but to bring it home right away.

John had come down in his Land Rover. I was surprised he knew more of Swindon than the people who lived there, it was West Swindon we went to, where I'd never been. I purchased an automatic machine, with all the necessities to fix it in, and at the works entrance the storemen loaded it on to the Land Rover. After reaching home it was a bit of a struggle to lift the machine on to the ground, but it was finally in its position underneath the sink in the kitchen where John connected it to the water pipes ready for use.

A couple of weeks later I had to go into hospital. For quite a few weeks I'd been attending the eye specialist Mr Choudhuri at Newbury Hospital, but he had now arranged for me to go into the Royal Berkshire Hospital at Reading. And so Jill would be down, to be with Gert. I had arranged for a hospital car to take me.

I was in a ward of four beds, and next morning, it wasn't very long before the porter came in with the trolley and I was lifted on and away and into the operating theatre. I was put on the operating table and then given an injection, which soon put me to sleep. I woke up on my bed and found I had a shade over my eye. The next day I was allowed home and I had my eyeshade in case I needed it.

I rang through for Jack Castle, I always knew him when we were young, and he was one of Lambourn's volunteer drivers. And so we reached home, to find both Gert and Jill glad to see me, and that workmen had been in to start on the new heating. The council had decided to put central heating in all the houses on our estate, and the workmen had started on our house. Jill had asked them to do our house last, but they couldn't or wouldn't, and I had to be careful to keep my eye covered and to stay out of their way if I could.

It was drawing near to Easter, when I was due back in hospital for the other eye. I booked my hospital car in good time, as there were not many drivers that did the long runs to places like Reading or Oxford because of the town traffic. Also, some drivers were going away over the Easter holiday. Jill and Paul came down for the Easter week.

278

I was in the same ward. They bypassed my lunch, as I was travelling on the trolley that afternoon. And so it was now into the operating theatre where there were three doctors waiting, all young men. I was put on to the operating table, and the doctor who was looking down at me asked me if I needed a general anaesthetic. I said: "Not this time, Doctor," as I had made up my mind to take note of what happened if I could.

One doctor did give me a jab, a local anaesthetic, I didn't notice any pain. They covered my eyes and my face although I just managed to see the doctor as he was bending over me. I felt him starting to work on my eye. All the while he was talking to me, telling me he was going away to the Lake District for Easter to do hill climbing.

Anyway he was working for quite a little while, when I heard him mention: "All finished." And so they started to clear my face of the cover I had to wear, which had made me feel uneasy all the time. One of my operations was for glaucoma, and one for a cataract.

It was the man who started the volunteer drivers who came to collect me. His name was Mr Bailey. I think he had come from the RAF and had, with his wife, come to live in Lambourn. It was then he started to develop the volunteer cars, mainly for those people who had to visit the surgery, and the hospital from the surgery. He was quite talkative on the way home, even with one or two songs.

Time went on until June, when Jill came down for the week covering her mum's 82nd birthday, June 21st. And soon after, it was our week's holiday to the Isle of Wight, and Jill and Paul were also bringing Paul's mum Rene. They picked us up, and then we went to Southampton, where we boarded the ferry. Jill had booked a bungalow at Ventnor. Jill and Paul's two girls, Helen and Clare, were also coming down, but they were travelling by coach as it was too many for the car and they were to sleep at a boarding house.

The first night I dreamt of when I was younger, and I spent holidays on the Island. George Oliver and myself came for a couple of years, and another pal who worked with me at the Waldorf Hotel. I think about five holidays we spent there and also we went in a big family party soon after the war. I was there two years before the war, I had to take a late holiday, and as I was on my own I booked for a holiday camp. This was a place called Wootton on the way from Ryde to Cowes.

This was their last week of the season, and although there weren't that many there it was enough to make the final week a real happy week. The owner and his wife had their own motor launch and took us along Southampton Water to see the liners. When we went out the crowd of us went together, even when we went to the theatre at Shanklin to see the entertainer Tommy Trinder. We were afterwards introduced to him and he came back to the camp with us.

And so, altogether we had a jolly good week at Ventnor. And so it was now back home, we carried on as usual. Gert managed to do a bit of cooking, but was getting more muddled. Otherwise she just preferred to sit down and she liked her afternoon sleep. One day I thought I would give the living room a good clean over and a polish after dinner. Gert began to wake up from her sleep when I usually made our afternoon cup of tea. After which I put the furniture back into position.

As I went to do something else, my foot got caught, I fell forward rather heavily towards the fireside armchair and my head hit the arm. Although it was soft, it was the bump that made my head swim. Gert got quite worried. She wanted to lift me up but of course couldn't so she came round and sat in the chair to ask if I was all right. I was beginning to feel my senses returning and as I began to regain my strength, I started to move. I really felt sorry for Gert, as she was looking very worried.

After walking about a bit and finding that everything seemed to be normal I said: "We'll both have a cup of tea and sit down and rest."

During the evening I rang to Jill just to mention my fall, as I was thinking about her mum still worrying, and Jill and Paul came down for a few days. Things went on for a while after they had gone back, when I now had to help Gert to bed, and she would often wake me up during the night as well, and so I rang to Jill, telling her what I thought about some home help. She thoroughly agreed and so I arranged for a help to call in every evening at 9 o'clock to take Gert up to wash and put her to bed.

Another help would come to do a bit of cleaning and shopping, as I didn't like to leave Gert on her own whilst I went to the village which was a mile walk. And I was nearly eighty six, getting arthritic, and had a four bedroom house and a long garden to look after. Annette was the regular one in the evenings except for her night off or sometimes two nights. She was quite a nice person. Gert's face used to light up when she came in and Annette would give her a hug. I used to hear them laughing and talking upstairs and afterwards she would come down to have a short chat.

She told me she came from Orkney where her mother and family were still living. She was married with two grown up sons and her husband mostly worked abroad. Her home now was at Headley, on the other side of Newbury. Her hobby was keeping three dogs which she entered in all the shows. And so, her talk could be very interesting. She then had to go on to Bedwyn on the outskirts of Savernake Forest, where she stayed overnight to attend to a young paraplegic.

This went on for quite a little while until close on Christmas Gert seemed to have a bit of trouble so I called the doctor, who said there was nothing serious but she needed to go into hospital. She was taken into St Margaret's Hospital at Stratton St Margaret; cousin Betty and Jock used to take me in to see her. Jill and Paul and family arranged to come down for Christmas, and in the big room, festively decorated, that led off the ward, we helped to make up the crowd of visitors and spent Christmas afternoon at the hospital.

After Jill and Paul had gone home, I visited the hospital when Jock could take me. Once or twice Dr Osmond's wife took me, as of course she remembered Gert for the times when they took Meals on Wheels round together. After they'd delivered the dinners, Gert would finish by washing and cleaning the metal dishes at home, and then Taffy would drive her over to Hungerford to take them back.

It was early in February when they told me Gert was ready to come home, but I had to have a home help to stay each night as I couldn't leave her on her own. She missed Annette. A bit later on I heard from the Social Services that an arrangement had been made for Gert to go to the Grange, a kind of a rest home out at Blunsdon, about three miles the other side of Swindon.

Two young women came to take Gert in the car and would collect her after two weeks. I asked the young woman who had already been out to see me, to tell me where I could find the place, and I was told to leave it for two or three days as the idea was to give me a break. After a couple of days I had somebody to take me in the car as the place was right out in the country and no public transport.

I went along the side of the building, but there were rails all the way round, and the small gateway was locked. And so I went into the main building to ask for a key, I think they were nurses or they just wore white coats. One said to lock the gate after I got in and hand the key in through the side window. I suppose the home was locked to stop people wandering off and getting lost as later an attendant told me their main trouble was they'd lost their reason.

I found my way into the only place where the door was wide open and I saw men and women sitting about in quite a large room. There were a good many of them, most smartly dressed, the men wearing collars and ties and waistcoats. There were three women who I think were in charge and two rather young men, who I suppose tended the men. I asked one of the women if Mrs Fitzgerald was here and she said: "I expect you'll find her if you look around."

I said to the person who had brought me that this was the place. I then did happen to see Gert, busy talking to another elderly lady and she was pleased to see me, although it was hard to sit down as all the chairs seemed to be in use. After a while I thought I'd better make a move. I could see Gert was fairly comfortable, and I should be calling up again shortly. My next visit I saw her sitting in a corner looking out of the window. She saw me and waved her hand.

It was at this time, March 1996, that Paul's mum Rene died, and so they were a bit busy arranging the funeral and everything. When they came down, we went to the Grange. We saw Gert sitting on her own in a corner of the room and she soon cheered up when she saw us, otherwise she didn't seem very happy. We did a bit of talking, and reminded her she would be going home on Monday.

I had to contact the home helps again, and so that's how we went on for quite a few weeks. Jill couldn't come down for a couple of months, as she had been in hospital for an operation. Now Gert had a job to walk, then she got a bit awkward, although I used to do my best to help her, so I asked the doctor to call. He thought if she went to hospital they might help her with the walking at the same time as giving me a rest. I had this rotten head cold coming on.

The doctor rang through to tell me the ambulance would call tomorrow morning, and so I rang Jill to tell her. I told Gert also, but she looked a bit dreamy, she didn't know where she was going or what she was doing. During the day my head cold seemed to get worse, at times I seemed to be going round in circles and my eyes were running all the time.

And so, next morning, the ambulance took Gert to Sandleford Hospital in Newbury, where Taffy had been. I stripped the bed off and collected other things that would need washing, had something to eat and just took it easy for the afternoon, although it soon went. And so I gathered all the washing together ready for the machine. As for tidying up, and putting things straight, that would have to be left for another day, as I was now going to have a cup of tea, and give my eyes a rest.

Jill rang to tell me that Helen would be coming down to help out as she couldn't come herself. During the evening in walked Helen. She had come by train and then bus from Newbury. She mentioned that my eyes and nose were running and said: "Leave everything to me," and so I just went and flopped into bed. I think it was past 12 o'clock when I woke and had to go to the toilet, I could still hear the washing machine going. I thought: "Good gracious! She won't have any time to go to bed."

Anyway I did wake up feeling a little bit better in the morning. My eyes felt much easier. Helen went back to London that day as she had arranged to go to a concert with her boyfriend Jack in the evening, but she would be coming back the next day. And so the next day while Helen got on with the work, I went up to Sandleford and found Gert in the day room along with all the other patients sitting in an easy chair, and dressed the same as most of the others.

She was pleased to see me, but otherwise she wasn't very talkative although most of the others were the same. I told her that Helen had come down to do a bit of work, and she said: "Poor little soul," I suppose still thinking of her as a child. I asked the nurse where Gert's ward was. I must say it had all been altered since we used to go there to visit Taff. There weren't quite so many beds, and they were just on one side of the ward. On the other side were the windows, and a table and chairs in front of each window.

I reached home and found Helen had cleaned all the rooms

downstairs and all the bedrooms upstairs, all the windows, and now she was finishing off the ironing. Next time I looked for Gert in the day room but I couldn't see her at all. I looked into the nurses' room which was adjoining, and one of the nurses took me to her ward. She was sitting on a chair with a small table in front of her and alongside the first window, but just looking down to the bottom of the ward.

There were two other patients lying on their beds, sleeping. She didn't hear me. I walked over to her, and got another chair and put my arm round her. She had tears in her eyes. After a few moments she seemed a little better and I had to do a little talking as she didn't do much. I did bring her some jellies in to chew. I asked her if I should go out to get anything else she wanted, but I don't think she was interested. And so after spending most of the afternoon there, I said I must go to see how your little granddaughter is getting on which brought the tears again to her eyes.

I realized I had to hurry for the bus. If I missed it, I should have to walk down to the bus station at Newbury, quite a walk, to catch the Lambourn bus, which had happened before. When I came out of the gate at the front, the bus was there opposite. The driver was looking over my way so I put my hands up, to say wait for me as I had to wait to cross the road. So I was lucky this time.

Helen went back in the morning. And so, as I was now on my own, I thought I would go to the hospital three or four times a week. I couldn't go on Sundays, there being no bus service, unless anyone went in by car. I would often find Gert asleep, so perhaps I would just go out for a short walk round and come back and find her awake.

It was towards the end of September that Jill rang to tell me that her mum had been moved to the Argyles nursing home, which lies at the rear of Newbury Hospital. I knew where to make for, and it's only walking distance from the bus station. I could see Gert sitting up in bed, although she was sleeping. I noticed it was a double room, with a curtain spread half way across. I could see an elderly lady sitting up in bed on the other side of the curtain. She was looking at me so I went and spoke to her, trusting she could hear and understand me. She had quite a few family photos on her table, and I thought I would take some in for Gert to stand on the side table to give her something or somebody to look at.

Gert was awake now. I bent over and kissed her and told her where she was. I sat and talked for the best part of the afternoon. And so I kept up this up nearly every day except on a Sunday unless there was anyone to take me in. Jill and Paul came down two or three times with the younger ones, also my cousin Gwen from Feltham.

Meanwhile I noticed that Gert seemed to be getting weaker each time I visited her. Most times I would find her asleep, but I felt I must stay there to keep her company. It was towards the end of November when Jill rang me in the morning to tell me that she had just been informed by the nursing home that her mum had died.

Jill and Paul came down to make funeral arrangements and at the same time to help me move home. During the last few weeks, I could see that Gert was gradually going downhill and she wouldn't be coming home. I thought I wouldn't want to stay in this four bedroom house on my own. I had applied for a bungalow for the elderly, as I thought I could qualify for that. I was told a bungalow was vacant, and if I was interested I had to accept right away and leave the house within the week.

And so there was now a rush on. Paul took the carpets up, to take round to their new home in Close End and get them laid down. John would move what furniture I should need, he had the use of a company van. He had bought a house near where he worked in Croydon, and he would take some of our furniture which was in good condition and I'd not need. It was hard work sorting out a family's things, especially arranging the funeral at the same time, but cousin Betty and Jock helped out. I was in my new home by the day of the funeral. Everything seemed to have worked out quite suddenly. I thought about it many times later on.

When we arrived outside the church, there were quite a number of people waiting for us. These were relatives or friends who would follow us in. I first noticed Taffy's niece Raydene and her husband Gareth, from Fishguard, they'd travelled nearly two hundred miles that morning. After the service it was then to the crematorium, just the other side of Swindon, and another short service was held.

And so it was then back to the Community Centre, the Lambourn Centre, right opposite my new home where some village friends had arranged various foods and drink to help with all the talking which helped us to finish the day.

It was now near Christmas and it made a pleasant change as John asked us to his house, me, Jill and Paul, Helen and Clare. Altogether it was quite a good house. The bedroom I felt very comfortable in, and I slept in one of the beds from Woodbury. It was a very good size garden, although it was mainly lawn. On Boxing Day we were joined by Paul's brother Peter and his wife, who is French, and two sons, her mother who had come over from Brittany, also Paul's youngest brother Martin, so it made quite a crowd. And so I had a very enjoyable Christmas.

Jill and Paul took me back home to Lambourn. And so, it wasn't very long before we were told that Gert's ashes were ready for burial. Jill and Paul came down with Clare. It was quite a nice little service. It took place in the grounds of the church, right alongside the tower.

And so, after everyone had gone home, and I was in my new home, alone, it was when I would sit quietly, and start to think things over. Gert and myself were the two youngest of our family which I think was very large, and after me there seemed to be that gap between Gert and myself and the next eldest.

Anyway, as I now got used to my new home, I gradually forgot all about the history, I just carried on in my own way, following the day's routine. I would probably go out to do some shopping in the morning, which wasn't very far, and after making myself a little bit useful doing a few jobs indoors, then it was the radio or television. My cousin Betty and her husband Jock would always call round once or twice during the week for a cup of tea and a talk. And so, that's how I got used to life living on my own.

Christmas and Easter and Bank Holiday time Jill and Paul would always come down to take me back up to Bexleyheath and of course during the stay, it would enable me to make a visit over to see cousin Joyce and her husband Arthur at Orpington.

Jill and Vic on a visit to Len's sister Girlie – Anne Parsons née Wohlgemuth

At first I had to get used to solid fuel heating again, but since then I have had gas central heating put in. I also had to learn to use an electric cooker, and hadn't any room for a washing machine, but I have coped.

It has been over three years since Gert died and I came here to live. And now it's the year 2000. It was last September when I celebrated my ninetieth birthday, Jill and Paul had made arrangements for my celebration to take place in the Community Centre just opposite my bungalow. Apart from a few friends that came it was mainly relatives and their families, I was told there were nearly ninety of us. Several were in their eighties, some only a few months old, many relatives had come from quite a fair distance away.

My cousin Harry's daughter Nova had made a cake in the shape of a book which was appropriate, as for some time I had been spending my afternoons writing my memoirs. Family photos and two long family trees were stuck up on the wall, and were found to be very interesting. And so it turned out to be quite a happy Sunday afternoon. It was next day, after breakfast, when I just sat down and tried to remember who everyone was, which I think I gradually managed to work out.

And so, it's now I carry on from day to day just doing the usual each day jobs. My leg troubles me with arthritis which doesn't allow me to do much walking, and I have had one or two falls, so I don't go out on my own. Cousin Betty is now my only relative in the village, and she brings in some of my shopping including my pension. I also have a home help named Mary who lives just down the end of the road. She comes in twice a week. She will also bring me anything from the shops as she lives quite near them and I just have to ring the phone which makes it quite handy.

Betty likes to call in one full afternoon a week for a cup of tea, otherwise she'll often call in during the mornings for a coffee on the way home from her shopping. Often she'll have her friend Pat with her. Of course she feels more on her own now it's two years since Jock died. It's also very often she calls in on a Saturday about mid day after coming from the hairdresser and we have a coffee together. Sometimes I have other visitors. Jill rings every Sunday, and sometimes I have letters or phone calls from friends and relatives, but mostly I still rely on the radio and TV for company.

And so it happened yesterday when I had switched on to watch the Trooping of the Colour which I've watched whenever I could since I was old enough to go and see it. It was at that moment that Betty walked in and when she saw what I was looking at she just sat down. She had forgotten about it. She told me how she often went to London for the day to see the Trooping of the Colour or other royal occasions, especially when her sister Margaret was living.

It was the Queen Mother she wanted to see, as she always liked to study her hats. I said: "Watch carefully as her coach has just left Buckingham Palace," and at that moment the TV picture showed her carriage going round Victoria Memorial into the Mall, where we got a good view of her and the hat she was wearing. I told Betty that when my book came out, she would read about my sister in law May, who mentioned about making the Queen Mother's hats.

I don't spend too much time watching TV during the day unless it happens to be something special or interesting, it's the evening time mostly. Of course there are quite a few shows that I look forward to watching, especially the news, but I mostly prefer listening to music. During the weekdays I like to look at the evening Swindon paper, or a book or magazine, although my eyes are now beginning to feel a bit worn or tired.

And so, comes Sunday. Now, living on my own, I like to treat it as Sunday, as different. I wake and get up at the same time and bathe. After breakfast, I just clear things up, and during the morning time there's very often a church or chapel service on the TV which I like to watch, and of course it's always dinner to prepare afterwards.

And so afternoon I might read a bit, or put a record on until I make a cup of tea after which the news comes on the TV followed by the 'Songs of Praise'. I switch off, then make myself comfortable alongside the radio to sit and listen to some music.

My usual Sunday evening programmes are from 7 o'clock when Richard Baker comes on. I've always enjoyed Richard Baker, even when I've seen him on TV. When he's running his show on the radio he likes to talk all about the record he's going to play, who wrote the music, which makes it all really interesting. Very often he tells you about his home when he was young and his mother started to teach him the piano. I think he said it was in south east London where he lived with his family.

Another name I enjoyed listening to was Hugh Scully, he used to take over from Richard Baker when he was on summer holiday. He could always put on an interesting programme, and between some of the records he mentioned some very interesting stories, all connected with the musical world. I have to mention one story. It was when he was young, and he went to work in two or three places. This place he mentioned was Boosey and Hawkes' shop situated just off Piccadilly, and it's connected with most parts of musical instruments or things connected with the musical trade.

And so he worked in this store and was interested in the different musicians that came into the shop. When I was younger I was taking violin lessons from my Uncle Percy, as mentioned earlier in my story. Perhaps the violin strings would break or the bridge or other little things would need renewing. This was when Percy would ask me to go to Boosey's to buy any of the essentials and then show me how to fix them on.

It is also from 9 o'clock to 10 that Alan Keith comes on the air to give his programme, which gives me a very pleasant hour. It was about two years ago and I was waiting for Alan Keith to announce himself with his rather deep voice, and then suddenly a voice came out:

"This is Richard Baker wishing Alan Keith a very happy ninetieth birthday." I didn't realize that Alan Keith was ninety years old and he is still carrying on.

I still enjoy my Sunday musical evening and now it would be 10 o'clock. Alan Keith's voice comes through: "I wish you well, and a very good night to you all," and then his signature tune 'Danny Boy'. And with that, as I am myself now beginning to feel tired, I think of the song from some years ago – 'Let's put out the lights and go to sleep'.

Vic at his 90th birthday party in the Lambourn Centre, with cards pinned on the wall, the cake in the shape of a book on the table beside him, and some presents. Photo by Ian Lang

BILL OF BULWELL by Bill Cross. As a child, Bill watched returned soldiers from the First World War live in poverty. He saw miners turned away from the pits after seeking work. He vowed he would never become a soldier or a miner. But he became both. This Nottingham man's life story is now in its Second Edition. Available through bookstores, libraries or direct from the Publisher (£9.50 post free UK). ISBN 0 9516960 1 7

Alice
from Tooting (1879 -1977)
by Alice Mullen (1879 -1977)
Including recollections of her daughter Bertha Mullen (1910-)

Few working class women of Alice's generation wrote their life story. We share her endurance, her beliefs, frail health, ambition to improve in her work, her parents' marriage break-up, two World Wars, being a mother and a stepmother, and a content old age living with her daughter in Chard.

'Ordinary' Lives ②

Edited by Anne Bott

ALICE FROM TOOTING by Alice Mullen (1879-1977), including recollections of her daughter Bertha Mullen (1910-). Not many working class women of her time wrote their life story, but Alice did. It was discovered after her death. This book is "biography, local history, social history and a lot more," says the *Journal of Kent History*. It is a book "you cannot put down," says *Local History* magazine. Available through bookstores, libraries or direct from the Publisher (£8.95 post free UK). ISBN 0 9516960 4 1

Flo Child Migrant from Liverpool
by Flo Hickson

Placed in Barnardo's aged almost 5; sent two years later in 1928 (without her brother and sister) as a child migrant to the Fairbridge farm school in W. Australia: by mid-teens, Flo's fate was live-in domestic work...

Flo is a battler and made a life. But, revisiting Fairbridge in her 60's, brought her to a crisis point and she faced coming to terms with her harsh childhood, loss of family and country. Her life story, told with awesome honesty, illuminates the complexity of abuse and its survival.

'Ordinary' Lives **3**

Edited by Anne Bott

FLO: CHILD MIGRANT FROM LIVERPOOL by Flo Hickson has been welcomed both in the UK and Australia. It is the life story of a girl 'migrant' forced to leave her siblings and relatives, and to be sent to Australia, to suit the policies of Governments in order to populate the Colonies with 'good white stock'. Available through bookstores, libraries or direct from the Publisher (£9.95 post free UK. Post free Air Mail Australia, sterling equivalent of Aust $32.00). ISBN 0 9516960 3 3

Geoff: 44 years a railwayman
by L.Geoffrey Raynor

Nottingham Victoria Station North Signal Box 1939

Geoff: Rufford Signal Box

Born in Carlton, Nottingham, Geoff joined the LNER as a Messenger Boy at the city's Victoria Station in 1939. He progressed to Train Register Lad, Signalman, Controller and finally Senior Accident Clerk at Doncaster. His life as a railwayman is described in detail in the context of his Nottingham childhood and marriage to Janet, who faced cancer. Later came retirement in Lawford, Essex. Geoff was in the first group of POW relatives allowed to visit Thanbyuzayat Cemetery (Burma) where his brother is buried.

'Ordinary' Lives **4**

Edited by Anne Bott

GEOFF: 44 YEARS A RAILWAYMAN by L. Geoffrey Raynor includes railway detail not often available, for example his work in the Signalling and Accident Section, Doncaster. His railway life, starting as a Messenger Lad at Nottingham Victoria Station, is set in the context of his childhood, later domestic life and retirement. Like all books in this Series, Geoff's is much more than a collection of episodic recollections: it is an autobiography. Available through bookstores, libraries or direct from the Publisher (£9.95 plus £1.50 p & p UK). ISBN 0 9516960 6 8